Old Favorites, New Fun

Physical Education Activities for Children

DR. DAVID OATMAN, EdD
Missouri State University

Human Kinetics

Library of Congress Cataloging-in-Publication Data

Oatman, David, 1953-
  Old favorites, new fun : physical education activities for children / David Oatman.
      p. cm.
  Includes bibliographical references.
  ISBN-13: 978-0-7360-6282-4 (softcover)
  ISBN-10: 0-7360-6282-3 (softcover)
  1. Physical education and training--Study and teaching (Elementary) I. Title.
  GV363.O15 2007
  613.7'042--dc22

                          2006026772

ISBN-10: 0-7360-6282-3
ISBN-13: 978-0-7360-6282-4

Speed Stacks is a registered trademark of Speed Stacks, Inc.

The Web addresses cited in this text were current as of October 2006, unless otherwise noted.

Acquisitions Editor: Bonnie Pettifor; **Developmental Editor:** Ray Vallese; **Assistant Editor:** Derek Campbell; **Copyeditor:** Alisha Jeddeloh; **Proofreader:** Red Inc.; **Permission Manager:** Dalene Reeder; **Graphic Designer:** Fred Starbird; **Graphic Artist:** Denise Lowry; **Photo Manager:** Laura Fitch; **Cover Designer:** Keith Blomberg; **Photographer (cover):** Brenda Williams; **Photographer (interior):** © Human Kinetics, unless otherwise noted. The photo on page 75 is © Image Source. The photo on page 262 is courtesy of David Oatman; **Art Manager:** Kelly Hendren; **Illustrator:** Mic Greenberg; **Printer:** Versa Press

Printed in the United States of America   10 9 8 7 6 5 4 3 2 1

Human Kinetics
Web site: www.HumanKinetics.com

United States: Human Kinetics, P.O. Box 5076, Champaign, IL 61825-5076
800-747-4457
e-mail: humank@hkusa.com

Canada: Human Kinetics, 475 Devonshire Road Unit 100, Windsor, ON N8Y 2L5
800-465-7301 (in Canada only)
e-mail: orders@hkcanada.com

Europe: Human Kinetics, 107 Bradford Road, Stanningley, Leeds LS28 6AT, United Kingdom
+44 (0) 113 255 5665
e-mail: hk@hkeurope.com

Australia: Human Kinetics, 57A Price Avenue, Lower Mitcham, South Australia 5062
08 8372 0999
e-mail: liaw@hkaustralia.com

New Zealand: Human Kinetics, Division of Sports Distributors NZ Ltd.
P.O. Box 300 226 Albany, North Shore City, Auckland
0064 9 448 1207
e-mail: info@humankinetics.co.nz

TEACHERS

by Clark Mollenhoff

Teachers, you are the molders of their dreams.
The gods who build or crush their young beliefs of right and wrong.
You are the spark that sets aflame the poet's hand
or lights the flame in some great singer's song.
You are the gods of the young—the very young.
You are the guardian of a million dreams.
Your every smile or frown can heal or pierce a heart.
Yours are one hundred lives, one thousand lives.
Yours the pride of loving them, the sorrow too.
Your patient work, your touch, make you the gods of hope
That fills their souls with dreams,
and make those dreams come true.

Courtesy of Mrs. Jane S. Mollenhoff.

Contents

Acknowledgments

Iwould like to thank several people who contributed their skills and knowledge in order to make this book a success.

First, thanks to **Lynn, Jamie, Chris, and Joy,** who tested and approved many of the activities addressed in this book, especially to Lynn for "Roll the Bod."

Thanks to the following students and professional educators for their contributions:

- **Students in my PED 431 classes,** particularly Emily Baker, Chenille Bayless, David Calloway, Duane Cox, Tricia Dochtermann, Kayla England, Christy Goans, Phillip Hodge, Josh Lashley, Brad Lotz, Craig Moody, Teresa Moots, Christian Nord, Todd Sanker, Nick Sharp, and Robert Woody

- **Students in my PED 341** Elementary Physical Education for the Elementary Teacher methods classes for refining and modifying these activities to make them suitable for elementary children

- **Mary Ann Bihr**, 1991 MOAHPERD Middle and Secondary School Physical Education Teacher of the Year, Oakland Middle School, Columbia, Missouri

- **Dr. Tommy Burnett and Dr. Keith Ernce,** heads of the department of health, physical education, and recreation at Missouri State University, for their encouragement and support in the development and completion of this project

- **Kathy Ermler,** associate professor, Emporia State University, Emporia, Kansas

- **John Hichwa,** 1993 NASPE National Elementary Physical Education Teacher of the Year, John Read Middle School, Redding, Connecticut

- **Wendy Lampe**, 1993 MOAHPERD Elementary Physical Education Teacher of the Year, East Moreland Elementary School, Joplin, Missouri

- **Joella Mehrhof**, associate professor, Emporia State University, Emporia, Kansas

- **Margie Miller,** St. Joseph, Missouri, public schools

- **Dr. Jim Phillips**, former assistant professor, Montana State University, Bozeman, Montana

- **Nancy Raso Eklund,** 1996 NASPE National Elementary Physical Education Teacher of the Year, School District 2, Green River, Wyoming

- **Larry Satchwell,** 1995 NASPE National Elementary Physical Education Teacher of the Year, Shiloh Elementary School, Lithonia, Georgia

- **John L. Smith**, 1989 NASPE National Elementary Physical Education Teacher of the Year, Ho-Ho-Kus Public School, Ho-Ho-Kus, New Jersey

- **John Thompson**, 1991 NASPE National Elementary Physical Education Teacher of the Year, Nampa Elementary School, Nampa, Idaho

- **Sue Tillary,** 1994 NASPE National Middle School Physical Education Teacher of the Year, Rockwood Valley Middle School, St. Louis, Missouri

- **Debbie Vigil,** 1994 NASPE National Elementary Physical Education Teacher of the Year, Antelope, California

- **Vicki Worrell,** 1993 NASPE National Elementary Physical Education Teacher of the Year, Tanglewood Elementary School, Derby, Kansas

Activity Finder

(continued)

Activity	Theme	Level	Page number
Chin to Chin	Team building (chapter 10)	III	204
Chuting Baskets	Parachute (chapter 12)	I, II, and III	263
Circle Chair Sit	Team building (chapter 10)	III	204
Circle Sit	Team building (chapter 10)	III	205
Circle Tag	Cardiovascular (chapter 2)	I	28
Circle Trust	Team building (chapter 10)	III	206
Circuit Stretching	Flexibility (chapter 3)	I and II	51
Circular Dribble	Parachute (chapter 12)	III	263
Circus Rounds	Eye–hand coordination (chapter 5)	I	96
Cleaning House	Eye–hand coordination (chapter 5)	I and II	97
Climbing the Mountain	Parachute (chapter 12)	II and III	264
Clock Stations	Muscular strength and endurance (chapter 7)	I, II, and III	142
Clothespin Tag	Cardiovascular (chapter 2)	II and III	28
Cold Stretch	Flexibility (chapter 3)	II and III	52
Color Fish to the Rescue	Body and space awareness (chapter 8)	I	166
Color Tag	Cardiovascular (chapter 2)	I, II, and III	29
Colors	Academic (chapter 11)	I	245
Cone Craze	Locomotor (chapter 1)	I and II	3
Cones and Dice	Locomotor (chapter 1)	I	4
Cooperative Fitness	Muscular strength and endurance (chapter 7)	III	143
Corner Wiffle Ball	Eye–hand coordination (chapter 5)	II and III	97
Counterbalances	Balance (chapter 4)	I, II, and III	76
Crab Soccer	Muscular strength and endurance (chapter 7)	III	144
Crab Tag	Muscular strength and endurance (chapter 7)	I, II, and III	145
Crab Walk	Flexibility (chapter 3)	II and III	52
Crazy Colors	Cardiovascular (chapter 2)	I and II	30
Cross the Beam	Team building (chapter 10)	II and III	206
Dance Mix	Rhythmic and dance (chapter 9)	I and II	179
Dance Tag	Rhythmic and dance (chapter 9)	I, II, and III	179
Daytona 500	Muscular strength and endurance (chapter 7)	I, II, and III	145
Deck Tennis	Eye–hand coordination (chapter 5)	III	98
Detective Valentine	Team building (chapter 10)	II and III	207
Dice Stations	Cardiovascular (chapter 2)	I and II	31
Dice Stretching Stations	Flexibility (chapter 3)	I and II	53

(continued)

Activity	Theme	Level	Page number
Gone Fishing	Parachute (chapter 12)	II and III	265
Group Warm-Up	Muscular strength and endurance (chapter 7)	I, II, and III	148
Guard the Trash Can	Eye–foot coordination (chapter 6)	II and III	126
Hacky Sack	Eye–foot coordination (chapter 6)	II and III	127
Hamster Dance	Rhythmic and dance (chapter 9)	I and II	180
Hand Squeeze	Team building (chapter 10)	II and III	211
Hands Up, Hands Down	Eye–hand coordination (chapter 5)	II and III	101
Hokey Pokey	Body and space awareness (chapter 8)	I	167
Hoop Coop	Body and space awareness (chapter 8)	I and II	168
Hoop Fitness	Body and space awareness (chapter 8)	I, II, and III	168
Hoop Mania	Muscular strength and endurance (chapter 7)	I and II	148
Hoop Travel	Flexibility (chapter 3)	II and III	57
Hoop Twister	Team building (chapter 10)	I	211
Hopping Patterns	Eye–foot coordination (chapter 6)	II and III	128
Hopscotch	Balance (chapter 4)	I, II, and III	76
Horseshoe Hoopla	Eye–hand coordination (chapter 5)	II and III	102
Hot Chocolate River	Team building (chapter 10)	II and III	212
Hot Potato	Eye–hand coordination (chapter 5)	I, II, and III	103
Hot Potato Tag	Eye–hand coordination (chapter 5)	I and II	103
Hula-Hoop Hug	Balance (chapter 4)	II and III	77
Human Bowling	Team building (chapter 10)	I and II	213
Human Chain	Flexibility (chapter 3)	II and III	58
Human Checkers	Academic (chapter 11)	II and III	249
Human Foosball	Eye–foot coordination (chapter 6)	III	128
Human Pretzel	Team building (chapter 10)	III	213
Human Pyramid	Team building (chapter 10)	III	214
Hunters and Gatherers	Team building (chapter 10)	I	215
Improvisation	Rhythmic and dance (chapter 9)	I	181
Introduction to the Parachute	Parachute (chapter 12)	I and II	260
Invent a Game	Team building (chapter 10)	II and III	215
Island Hopping	Academic (chapter 11)	II and III	249
Isometric Tag	Muscular strength and endurance (chapter 7)	I	149
Jingle Bell Parachute	Parachute (chapter 12)	II and III	265
Jogging Chicken Dance	Locomotor (chapter 1)	II	8

(continued)

Activity	Theme	Level	Page number
Men in Black Dance	Rhythmic and dance (chapter 9)	II and III	185
Merry-Go-Round	Team building (chapter 10)	II and III	217
Molecule Mania	Academic (chapter 11)	I and II	254
Monster Walk	Team building (chapter 10)	III	217
Mousetrap	Cardiovascular (chapter 2)	I	37
Move to the Beat	Rhythmic and dance (chapter 9)	I	186
Move to the Music	Body and space awareness (chapter 8)	I	169
Mulberry Hide and Seek	Body and space awareness (chapter 8)	I	170
Mummy Wrap	Team building (chapter 10)	II and III	218
Muscle Stretch	Flexibility (chapter 3)	II and III	60
Musical Hoops	Body and space awareness (chapter 8)	I	171
Musical Push-Ups	Muscular strength and endurance (chapter 7)	III	150
Name Toss	Team building (chapter 10)	I, II, and III	219
Nervous Wreck	Eye–hand coordination (chapter 5)	I and II	105
Number Chase	Parachute (chapter 12)	I, II, and III	268
Obstacle Course	Cardiovascular (chapter 2)	I, II, and III	37
The Old Brass Wagon	Rhythmic and dance (chapter 9)	I	187
Opposite Relay	Academic (chapter 11)	I and II	255
Over the Shoulder	Eye–hand coordination (chapter 5)	II and III	106
Over–Under Relay	Eye–hand coordination (chapter 5)	II and III	107
Over–Under Relay Rally	Team building (chapter 10)	I, II, and III	219
Paddleball and Jacks	Eye–hand coordination (chapter 5)	II and III	107
Palm Push	Balance (chapter 4)	II and III	78
Parachute Aerobics	Parachute (chapter 12)	II and III	269
Parachute Ball	Parachute (chapter 12)	II and III	269
Parachute Fitness	Parachute (chapter 12)	II and III	270
Parachute Pull-Down	Parachute (chapter 12)	I, II, and III	271
Parachute Turtle	Parachute (chapter 12)	I	272
Parachute Volleyball	Parachute (chapter 12)	III	272
Partner Hop Race	Team building (chapter 10)	III	220
Partner Hop Stretch	Flexibility (chapter 3)	III	61
Partner Hopping	Balance (chapter 4)	II and III	79
Partner Row	Locomotor (chapter 1)	II and III	14
Partner Spinning	Team building (chapter 10)	II and III	221

(continued)

Activity	Theme	Level	Page number
Rolling Raft	Team building (chapter 10)	III	228
Ropes Course	Team building (chapter 10)	II and III	228
Ruler of the Squares	Eye–hand coordination (chapter 5)	II and III	109
Rules of the Road	Body and space awareness (chapter 8)	I	172
Run the Gauntlet	Cardiovascular (chapter 2)	I and II	42
Santa Claus Is Coming to Town	Rhythmic and dance (chapter 9)	I and II	189
Scaling the Wall	Team building (chapter 10)	II and III	229
Scavenger Hunt	Muscular strength and endurance (chapter 7)	II and III	154
Scooter Obstacle Course	Locomotor (chapter 1)	I and II	18
Scooter Relays	Muscular strength and endurance (chapter 7)	I, II, and III	155
Scooter Sink	Eye–hand coordination (chapter 5)	II and III	110
Seven Jumps	Rhythmic and dance (chapter 9)	I and II	190
Shadow Dancing	Rhythmic and dance (chapter 9)	I, II, and III	191
Shadow Stretching	Flexibility (chapter 3)	II and III	63
Shadow Tag	Cardiovascular (chapter 2)	II and III	43
Shakers	Rhythmic and dance (chapter 9)	I	192
Shape Walking	Body and space awareness (chapter 8)	I and II	173
Sharks and Minnows	Cardiovascular (chapter 2)	I	43
Shepherds and Sheep	Team building (chapter 10)	III	230
Shoe Relay	Eye–hand coordination (chapter 5)	III	111
Shoes Together	Team building (chapter 10)	III	231
Shut Your Eyes	Body and space awareness (chapter 8)	I	174
Simon Says "Move"	Rhythmic and dance (chapter 9)	I and II	192
Simon Says "Stretch"	Flexibility (chapter 3)	I and II	63
Sit and Reach	Flexibility (chapter 3)	III	64
Sit Down	Parachute (chapter 12)	III	273
Smiley	Team building (chapter 10)	II and III	232
The Snake	Balance (chapter 4)	I	80
Snake Shake	Parachute (chapter 12)	II and III	274
Snap	Rhythmic and dance (chapter 9)	I, II, and III	193
Soap Bubbles	Locomotor (chapter 1)	I	19
Soccer Basics	Eye–foot coordination (chapter 6)	II	132
Soccer Slalom	Eye–foot coordination (chapter 6)	I and II	133
Soccer Square	Eye–foot coordination (chapter 6)	III	134

(continued)

Activity	Theme	Level	Page number
Turkey Tag	Cardiovascular (chapter 2)	I and II	47
Twists and Spins	Body and space awareness (chapter 8)	I and II	175
Ultimate Frisbee (Modified)	Cardiovascular (chapter 2)	III	48
Under the Bridges	Team building (chapter 10)	I and II	235
Valentines for the Heart	Flexibility (chapter 3)	I, II, and III	65
Veggie Values	Flexibility (chapter 3)	I	66
Vocrab	Academic (chapter 11)	II	257
Wall Sit	Muscular strength and endurance (chapter 7)	III	157
The Wave	Parachute (chapter 12)	I, II, and III	275
What Am I?	Team building (chapter 10)	I	236
What Do You See?	Locomotor (chapter 1)	I	22
Woodland Animals	Academic (chapter 11)	I	258
Workout Tag	Muscular strength and endurance (chapter 7)	I, II, and III	157
World Search	Academic (chapter 11)	II and III	258
Z-Ball Bounce	Eye–hand coordination (chapter 5)	II and III	118

Introduction

As a professional physical educator for 30 years, I've taught physical education at the elementary, junior high/middle school, high school, and university levels. Through these experiences, I've tried to focus on a major theme: creating a positive attitude of lifelong appreciation for physical activity. At the beginning of my career, the vast majority of students in my classes enjoyed being physically active. However, as time passed, a major change occurred. Currently, I teach at the university level, and I've noticed that many students in general education and professional education classes seem to show little interest in physical activity of any kind.

As a result of this lack of interest, our society has experienced some tremendous growth—but not necessarily in a positive fashion! According to Howell Wechsler and colleagues in the December 2004 edition of *The Journal of the National Association of*

State Boards of Education, children in the United States are getting heavier and heavier. These are the results (pp. 4-5):

- "The percentage of children who are overweight has more than doubled over the past 25 years. The rate among adolescents has more than tripled over the same time frame."
- "Ten years ago, type 2 diabetes was almost unknown among young people, but today, in some communities, it now accounts for nearly 50 percent of new cases of diabetes among children or adolescents. In addition, the Centers for Disease Control and Prevention is estimating that more than one in three children born in 2000 will eventually suffer from diabetes."
- "Children and adolescents who are overweight are more likely to become overweight or obese adults."
- "Obesity in adults is associated with increased risks of premature death, heart disease, type 2 diabetes, stroke, several types of cancer, osteoarthritis and many other health problems."
- "In 2000, the total cost of obesity (including medical costs and the value of wages lost by employees unable to work because of illness, disability or premature death) in the United States was approximately $117 billion."

Clearly, as physical educators, we need to redirect our focus to begin to curb this epidemic. Have we lost sight of what should be our primary goal—to share with people how physical activity can be fun? Physical activity doesn't have to be laborious. It can be enjoyable, and a planned physical activity program can lead to a healthier and longer life. In our classes, are we creating an atmosphere that encourages students to pursue physical activity in their leisure time now and later as adults?

I've long been an advocate of ensuring that physical education classes at any level are positive learning experiences that produce feelings of effectiveness and success. I sincerely believe that *Old Favorites, New Fun: Physical Education Activities for Children* offers a foundation of thematic activities that help promote positive feelings toward physical activity. The book was developed primarily for four types of readers:

- Physical educators who teach elementary classes in public or private schools
- Supervisors who teach elementary school children at day camps or summer camps
- Physical educators who teach professional elementary or middle school methods courses at the university level
- Elementary teachers and other individuals who supervise playground activities at public and private schools

By no means is *Old Favorites, New Fun* a complete collection of activities for elementary school children. My intent in developing this book was to offer an effective and practical assortment of games and activities that teachers and supervisors could use as a foundation in the continuing development of an activities notebook. As the title suggests, the book offers many well-known, favorite games that have been updated and enhanced to make them more useful and enjoyable, along with many all-new activities that can add to a teacher's core curriculum.

CHAPTER THEMES

The games and activities have been divided into 12 themes, one per chapter. Simply find a theme and peruse the many activities based on that theme. Each chapter includes games to improve and maintain one or more fitness or motor-development parameters in elementary school children.

The activities are grouped by theme simply to provide a useful level of organization. Naturally, some activities involve multiple aspects of fitness and overlap with other themes. Furthermore, many state curriculum guides address many of the same themes. For example, in my home state of Missouri, the physical education curriculum core competency guidelines (published by the Department of Elementary and Secondary Education in Jefferson City) specifically state the need for the following:

- Aquatics
- Body and spatial awareness
- Developmental games and activities
- Fundamental movement skills
- Gymnastics
- Rhythms and dance
- Sport and lifetime activity skills
- Personal fitness and healthy lifestyle

The activities in this book directly address five of those components.

- Body and spatial awareness
- Developmental games and activities
- Fundamental movement skills
- Gymnastics
- Rhythms and dance

Teachers and supervisors must keep in mind the varying levels of children's development and choose activities appropriate for their level. See "Activity Structure" on page xxi for more details.

Chapter 1: Locomotor Activities

Locomotor activities move the body from one place to another or project the body upward. The ability to move from one location to another in a variety of manners is the foundation of all movement. Being able to complete the activities in this theme allows children to master more advanced movement skills. Many of these activities focus on, but are not limited to, level I or grades K to 1.

Chapter 2: Cardiovascular Activities

These activities emphasize the development and maintenance of cardiovascular endurance. Virtually all of the activities in this chapter involve high levels of activity. Many of the activities move very fast, so teachers must be sure to supervise each game with safety in mind.

Chapter 3: Flexibility Activities

Flexibility is generally defined as the range of motion of a given joint or body part. Many physical activities demand a range of motion, but sometimes students cannot do the activity due to a lack of flexibility. These activities focus on improving flexibility and practicing flexibility during movement.

Chapter 4: Balance Activities

According to physical education researcher Robert Pangrazi, "Balance demands that different parts of the body support the weight or receive the weight" (2004, p. 301) while doing a variety of activities. This chapter's activities are based that premise.

Chapter 5: Eye–Hand Coordination Activities

This chapter consists of an immense volume of eye–hand coordination activities for children of all abilities. Being able to successfully complete eye–hand coordination activities not only allows students to be more successful in sporting activities, it also has a direct correlation to improved handwriting and reading skills.

Chapter 6: Eye–Foot Coordination Activities

Coordinating the feet with the eyes is sometimes quite difficult, especially for younger, less mature children. This chapter focuses on activities that assist in the development of this important motor-development parameter.

Chapter 7: Muscular Strength and Endurance Activities

Two parameters of physical fitness are muscular strength and endurance. The activities in this chapter focus on developing certain levels of strength or carrying on activities for longer periods of time.

Chapter 8: Body and Space Awareness Activities

As with locomotor activities, the majority of these activities focus on, but are not limited to, level I children. This theme involves where the body can move, specifically addressing general and personal space, direction of movement, level of movement and pathways, and planes of movement.

Chapter 9: Rhythmic and Dance Activities

Hundreds of activities are rhythmic in nature, and this chapter offers a variety of different types. Rhythmic activities frequently involve but do not require music. Seated activities emphasize rhythmic eye–hand coordination, while others are highly active with plenty of rhythmic movement and activity.

Chapter 10: Team-Building Activities

This chapter combines various components of gymnastics, tumbling skills, and combative activities along with cooperative, trusting, and group initiative activities. Most of these activities emphasize cooperation with a partner (or sometimes an opponent) to complete a task at hand. Some activities are competitive, but they don't stress winning or losing. Noncompetitive games, group problem-solving initiatives, and ropes courses are the foundation for many of these activities.

Chapter 11: Academic Activities

The movement activities in this chapter relate to what are commonly referred to as the three Rs—reading, 'riting, and 'rithmetic. Each activity focuses on one or more of the fitness or motor-development parameters addressed earlier in the book. In these activities, students use their knowledge of another academic area (such as science, math, or drama) to successfully complete the task at hand.

Chapter 12: Parachute Activities

Parachute activities have a positive effect on a number of fitness and motor-development parameters. Through these activities, children improve upper-body strength, cooperation skills, eye–hand coordination, and cardiovascular development. Parachutes are available in a variety of sizes to accommodate different classes. They're simple but unusual pieces of equipment that add excitement to any class. Many of these activities are highly active in nature and should be supervised with safety in mind.

ACTIVITY STRUCTURE

Within each chapter, the activities follow a general structure designed to make it easy for teachers to get the details they need.

Name

The name of each activity appears at the beginning of its section. In addition, all activities in the book are listed alphabetically in the Activity Finder on pages vi-xvi.

Level

Each activity has one or more developmental levels:

- Level I corresponds to students who are 5 to 6 years old (K to grade 1)
- Level II corresponds to students who are 7 to 8 years old (grades 2 and 3)
- Level III corresponds to students who are 9 to 11 years old (grades 4 and 5, or 4 to 6)

However, each class is different, and some students might need activities of a lower or higher level. Use the level designations as broad guidelines only. Instructors are responsible for choosing activities that are appropriate for the skill level of their group.

Area

Most of the activities can take place in any open space that is large enough for the students, such as a school gymnasium. If an activity can be conducted in another location, such as outdoors or in a multipurpose room, those options will be listed as well. However, the areas given in this section are just suggestions. Teachers are free to choose appropriate locations for each activity based on class size, safety, and available facilities.

Equipment

Most activities require teachers to provide pieces of equipment. In some cases, this section specifies an exact quantity (such as "36 small cones"), and in other cases, it offers only general guidelines (such as "blindfolds for half the class"). Regardless, it's assumed that teachers will provide enough equipment to keep all students active.

If music is part of an activity, this section also gives general or specific recommendations about what to play. However, any technological details (such as using CD players, cassette players, digital music, and so on) are left to the teachers. Whatever the method, a remote control will let teachers start, stop, and select music easily from a distance.

The appendix describes special equipment—items not commonly available in most elementary schools—used in some of the activities, including earth balls, lummi sticks, and Speed Stacks stacking cups. It also provides contact information for companies that offer the equipment. These vendors aren't the only ones available; they're simply sources I've used in the past.

Objectives

This section explains what could or should be achieved during the activity. These objectives are usually broad in nature and written in plain language, not the jargon of behavioral "objectivese." The basic objectives of an activity relate to the theme of the chapter, but some activities have additional objectives that go beyond the overall theme.

Setup and Description

This section explains how to prepare for and conduct the activity. Of course, teachers have the final say and should make adjustments where appropriate for best results. Activities that require extra caution are marked with a Safety icon; see page xxv for more details.

Modifications

This final section of an activity suggests one or more ways to modify it to meet the needs of a particular class, environment, or individual. Often, these involve tips for making the activity more or less challenging, conducting it in a different location, or modifying it for students with disabilities. Regardless, all professional educators and supervisors should modify the games and activities in this book as necessary to ensure that they are appropriate and safe for their students.

SUCCESSFUL AND SAFE CLASSES

Conducting fitness and development activities involves more than simply blowing a whistle and letting students run around. Physical education classes shouldn't be chaotic or dangerous. Teachers must consider issues such as dividing students into groups, starting the activities fairly, ensuring the safety of participants, maintaining appropriate levels of competition, providing enough equipment, and modifying activities as needed for particular classes or students.

Creative Methods for Dividing Groups

Think back to the physical education classes you attended as a child. Most of us can remember watching the teacher choose two students to be the captains, and then waiting as those captains picked their teams from the rest of the kids. Were you usually recruited right away? Were you ever the last child selected? Physical education teachers don't intend to hurt students with their actions, but this outdated method of choosing teams does just that. The same few kids always seem to get picked last. This process is harmful in a number of ways:

- It isolates individuals and alienates them from the rest of the class.
- It can destroy a child's self-confidence and cause emotional bruises.
- It emphasizes competition and winning rather than enjoyment and skill development.

Teachers and supervisors must implement less threatening, more creative methods of group division that respect the dignity of each child and promote positive experiences in physical education. In fact, unique group division can become a fun, challenging, and motivational aspect of your class. The concept itself keeps your creative juices flowing as you build a repertoire of original ways to assemble teams, small groups, or partners for activities. In addition, you can use the same methods when selecting students to help distribute or collect equipment or as an orderly means of class dismissal.

With creative group division, make your directions clear and simple. For example, if you want to split the group into two teams, give them two choices: "Close your eyes and do either the backstroke or the crawl stroke. Then open your eyes and find someone who is doing the same motion." Typically, because it's easier to spot someone doing the same motion, it's better to ask students to find a partner who is performing the same activity rather than someone who is performing the opposite.

Try to keep groups relatively small. One of the critical goals is to keep the children as active as possible for as long as possible. Too many students in a group results in too much standing around.

Of course, creative group division isn't foolproof. Groups won't always be equal, and an odd number of students will leave someone without a partner. However, these problems are easily fixed. To balance lopsided groups, just ask students to move from one group to another. To include a student left out of partner selection, turn an existing pair into a trio.

Be creative when it comes to dividing students into groups or teams. Don't be afraid to try a new technique (see "Ten Creative Tips for Dividing Groups"). Some of your methods might crash and burn, but in the process, you'll build an assortment of innovative, effective methods that you can modify as needed.

Ten Creative Tips for Dividing Groups

These tips are just some of the many possible ways to divide students into groups in a fair (and entertaining) manner. Use your imagination to come up with other creative methods!

1. Think of your given name. Now think of the first vowel (a, e, i, o, u, y) in your name. All those with a, u, or y, go to this side of the room, while all those with e, i, or o, go to the other side of the room.

2. All of you who like plain M&Ms go to this side of the room, and all of you who like peanut M&Ms go to that side of the room.

3. If your birthday is in January, February, March, or April, go to this side of the room. Birthdays in May, June, July, or August go to that side of the room, and birthdays in September, October, November, or December go over to that side of the room. (Call out only three months at a time in order to divide students into four groups.)

4. Close your eyes and either make an X or an O with your arms outstretched. Find someone who is doing the same thing.

5. Everyone close your eyes and cross your arms. If your right arm is over your left, you're on this team. If your left arm is over your right, you're on the other team.

6. Think of the seven digits in your home phone number. Add the digits together. Is the sum an odd or even number? Find a partner who also has an odd or even number as you do.

7. Count the number of eyelets in the right side of your right shoe. Find someone with the same number of eyelets.

8. Find a partner who has the same color of eyes that you do.

9. The different colored hoops scattered around the room are fruit loops. Hop, run, skip, or gallop around the room. When I say "Fruit loops," get inside or place a body part inside a hoop. Everyone who is in the same color of hoop is in a group.

10. If you had orange juice with your breakfast this morning, you're in this group. If you didn't, you're in that group.

Creative Methods for Starting Play

Starting an activity frequently creates confusion and arguments among players. Children often have strong opinions about who should go first, second, and so on; after all, the first move in a game often gives one player or team an advantage. It's up to the teacher to eliminate potential problems by offering creative methods to ensure a smooth start to any activity. Basing the decision on luck or chance helps make the process fair.

As with the methods for dividing students into groups, the variety of ways to begin a game is limited only by your imagination.

Flipping a Coin

This is one of the most popular ways to begin a game. A player, official, or another person makes a fist and places a coin on the thumbnail. The person flips the coin with a sharp flick of the thumb. It will spin in the air and the person can catch it or allow it to hit the ground. If the coin is caught it should be caught with one hand and slapped on the back of the free hand. Before the coin is revealed, students choose heads or tails. The student who guesses correctly has the privilege of going first or passing to the other team. If the coin is to hit the ground, students should choose heads or tails while the coin is in the air.

Hiding a Coin

One player holds a coin in one hand and hides her hands behind the back. She can change the hand that contains the coin or keep it in the same hand. She then brings the two clenched fists out in front and her opponent must guess which hand is holding the coin. If the opponent guesses correctly, he has the first move. If not, the first move belongs to the person who hid the coin.

Drawing Straws

One player holds as many straws, sticks, or matches as there are players in the game. One of the items should be shorter than the others, but all items should appear to be the same length when held in the hand. Players take turns drawing one item from the hand and the player who picks the shortest item begins play.

Picking Up Straws

Scatter numerous straws, sticks, or matches on a table. Players take turns picking up one at a time. The player who is left with the last straw begins the game.

Rolling Dice

An easy way to decide who is to go first is to roll dice. Each player rolls the dice and the player with the highest roll begins the game. You may even be able to purchase or make giant dice to make the spins more dramatic.

Stacking Hands

Two students take a broomstick or baseball bat in their hands. Starting at the bottom each person wraps one hand around the broomstick. The two players continue placing one fist on top of the other. The sides of the fists must touch. This process continues until there is just enough room at the top for one full fist. The player whose fist is on top begins the game.

Slapping Hands

One player extends his hand palm side down and the other player extends her hand palm side up. The fingers of the players are touching. The player with the palm side up tries to hit her opponent's hand before he can pull his hand away. If she misses, they change positions. The player who manages to strike the opponent's hand first begins the game. Each player gets one try at a time.

Counting Fingers

Two opponents stand with one hand clenched in a fist behind their back. One player calls odds and the other player calls evens. Both players together say "Once, twice, three, shoot" and reveal either one or two fingers in front of them. Players can also reveal up to five fingers or keep a closed fist for the number zero. The sum of the combined fingers will be either an odd or an even number. The person who called the correct answer begins the game.

Playing Rock, Paper, Scissors

Two students hide one hand behind their back and make it into a rock (clenched fist), a pair of scissors (two fingers spread apart), or a piece of paper (open palm). Players count "One, two, three" and bring their hand around front to reveal their choices.

- Rock breaks scissors (but loses to paper).
- Scissors cut paper (but lose to rock).
- Paper covers rock (but loses to scissors).

Showing Courtesy

As a sign of courtesy, one player may simply say to another, "You start the game."

Safety

By the nature of physical activity, students run the risk of injury. Depending upon the teaching philosophy or from the lack of active supervision of the instructor or supervisor, this risk of injury could increase or decrease. Throughout this book, Safety Notes (marked with the icon shown at left) denote activities that are inherently dangerous, meaning that the risk of physical injury could increase if teachers fail to give proper instructions, issue warnings, and maintain supervision. When conducting any activity that has a Safety Note, it is critical that you follow these rules:

- Clearly and accurately explain the rules or procedures to all students.
- Warn students of potential concerns specific to that activity.
- Provide any safety equipment (such as mats or spotters) deemed necessary.
- Supervise the activity effectively with safety in mind.

The Value of Competition

Although most of the activities in this book are cooperative in nature, some are more competitive. Competition is inherent to life; we compete for grades, jobs, positions, loved ones, professional advancement, and so on. However, there's also a difference between good competition and bad competition.

In physical education, good competition means that everyone plays hard but fair, with no elimination of players and no emphasis on who wins or loses. If an activity eliminates players, allow them to complete a small task—such as some kind of physical activity—and then quickly rejoin the game. It is the teacher's responsibility to set the tone for good competition.

In my opinion, bad competition has no place in physical education classes. This kind of competition focuses on winning at all costs, creating physically dangerous environments, consistently hurting students' feelings, and requiring that players sit on the sidelines and do nothing after being eliminated. If one of our goals as physical educators is to nurture enjoyment for lifelong learning through physical activity, how can we achieve that by allowing students to be injured, eliminated, and embarrassed?

Equipment and Court Distinctions

Each activity in this book includes an Equipment section listing any items necessary for conducting the activity. Ideally, teachers will provide enough equipment for the whole class to ensure a high ratio of staying on task. Students who must wait a long time for their turn aren't receiving the intended benefits of physical education and might become discipline problems. For example, a sport stacking activity would be more effective if all students have their own set of stacking cups. However, this might not always be possible due to budget constraints, equipment concerns, or class size. In general, you should provide enough pieces of equipment as you deem appropriate for the success of your class.

Some of the activities include less common pieces of equipment. These are described in the appendix, along with company contact information or ordering details in case you wish to learn more about or purchase the items.

In a large number of activities, the students begin at or move to various locations in the play area. Whether you're in a large gym, in a smaller multipurpose room, or outside on a field, you might need to use colored tape, cones, or some other means of marking boundaries or lines (see figure).

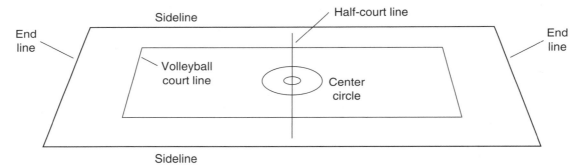

Modifications

Some people believe that sport is sacred and that we shouldn't tinker with the established rules of classic sports, games, and activities. However, to run a quality physical education program, sometimes modifications are necessary to allow an activity to meet the demands of a particular class, environment, or individual. Teachers can modify activities for any number of reasons, including the following:

- Keeping students more involved throughout the entire class period
- Conducting the activity in a smaller multipurpose room rather than a gym
- Reducing competition by making the activity more cooperative in nature
- Moving the class outside and adapting the activity to the new environment
- Allowing students with disabilities to participate in meaningful ways

As with other elements discussed in this introduction, the great variety of possible modifications is restricted only by the imagination. You are encouraged to modify the activities and games in this book to better serve the needs of your students.

Finally, it should go without saying that no sport, game, or activity should ever be modified in such a way that puts the participants in danger. Modifications should make an activity more effective and more enjoyable for students, not more hazardous.

INTERNATIONAL STANDARDS

This table shows you how *Old Favorites, New Fun* meets national standards for several different countries. Sample activities or sections of the book that meet these standards are listed.

National Standards Comparison

Country	Standards	How *Old Favorites, New Fun* addresses these standards
Australia (Victoria)[a]	Movement and physical activity—Perform motor skills and movement patterns with proficiency	Level I and II activities address the fundamental movement patterns of children. Example: Guard the Trash Can (chapter 6).
	Movement and physical activity—Identify the benefits of physical activity	Clear objectives identify the purpose and benefits of activities, such as working together, increasing strength, cardiovascular activity, flexibility, and so on. Examples: Clothespin Tag (chapter 2), Centipede (chapter 7).
	Health of individuals and populations—Describing what it means to be healthy	Activities based on muscular strength and endurance, flexibility, academics, and cardiovascular health require students to address specific physical fitness parameters and explain how their bodies are affected during the activity. Examples: Hoop Travel (chapter 3), Exercise Bands (chapter 7).
Australia (Queensland)[b]	Developing concepts and skills for physical activity—Enhancing physical performance in games, sports, and other physical activities through monitoring and evaluating movement sequences and applying basic movement concepts	Children develop and enhance physical performance in most or all activities. Individual juggling, team juggling, and other activities stress the importance of movement sequences. Examples: Split-Second Jumps (chapter 10), Snake Shake (chapter 12).
Australia (New South Wales)[c]	Promote physical activity every day	All activities were developed specifically to encourage children to participate in daily physical activity by making it enjoyable. Examples: Locomotor Tag (chapter 1), Car and Driver (chapter 8).
	Factors influencing personal health choices	The introduction discusses the impact of good and poor health choices on children and adults in society. Example: Introduction.
	The adoption of an active lifestyle	Activities throughout the book address the enjoyment and encouragement of physical activity on a daily basis. Examples: Obstacle Course (chapter 2), Hamster Dance (chapter 9).
	Fundamental movement patterns and coordinated actions of the body	Level I and II activities address the fundamental movement patterns of children and their effects upon future activities, academics, and sports. Examples: Frog Pond (chapter 1), Balance Beam Relay (chapter 4).

(continued)

Country	Standards	How *Old Favorites, New Fun* addresses these standards
Western Australia[d]	Knowledge and understanding of health and physical activity concepts to lead active, healthy lifestyles	In activities based on cardiovascular, flexibility, muscular strength and endurance, and academic themes, students understand the value of specific physical fitness parameters and explain how their bodies are affected during the activity. Examples: Streets and Alleys (chapter 2), Air Play With Feathers (chapter 11).
	Skills for physical activity	Activities throughout the book introduce fundamental movement skills, patterns, and progressions for students to develop and master. Examples: Juggling Partners (chapter 5), Foot Bowling (chapter 6).
	Interpersonal skills	Activities require students to cooperate in pairs or groups to accomplish specific tasks, to promote safety for themselves and others, and to develop positive social behaviors. Examples: Over–Under Relay (chapter 5), Field of Obstacles (chapter 10).
Canada[e]	In Canada, each province regulates its own physical education curriculum program for its schools. However, the overall learning outcome across all provinces is to develop the skills, knowledge, and attitudes necessary to lead active, healthy lifestyles. The Canadian Association for Health, Physical Education, Recreation and Dance (CAHPERD) supports and promotes this overall learning objective.	The many themed activities develop fundamental movement skills, progressions, and sequences along with knowledge of the parameters of physical fitness, and they encourage students to pursue active lifestyles. Examples: Juggling Scarves (chapter 5), The Wave (chapter 12).
Hong Kong[f] (Key Stages 1, 2, 3, and 4)	Motor and sports skills development	Level I and II activities address the fundamental patterns, progressions, and sequences of movement in children. Level III activities enhance and develop these fundamentals into sports skills, games, and activities. Example: Shut Your Eyes (chapter 8).
	Health and fitness development	Activities throughout the book address a variety of fitness themes and require students to maintain developmentally appropriate levels of physical activity. Examples: Cooperative Fitness (chapter 7), Find Your Partner (chapter 10).
	Knowledge of movement	In activities based on cardiovascular, flexibility, muscular strength and endurance, and academic themes, students understand the value of specific physical fitness parameters and explain how their bodies are affected during the activity. Examples: Exercise Band Exploration (chapter 3), Body Part Match-Up (chapter 11).

Country	Standards	How *Old Favorites, New Fun* addresses these standards
United Kingdom[g] (Key Stages 1 and 2)	Acquiring and developing skills	Level I and II activities address the fundamental patterns, progressions, and sequences of movement in children. Level III activities enhance and develop these fundamentals into sports skills, games, and activities. Examples: Frogs and Ladybugs (chapter 1), Soap Bubbles (chapter 1).
	Selecting and applying skills, tactics, and compositional ideas	Activities throughout the book introduce fundamental movement skills, patterns, and progressions for students to develop and master. Examples: Four-Corner Cartoon Traveling (chapter 1), Hoop Coop (chapter 8).
	Evaluating and improving performance	Activities throughout the book introduce fundamental movement skills, patterns, and progressions for students to develop and master, which will lead to more success in sport activities. Examples: Balance Beam Barrage (chapter 4), Lummi Stick Partner Tap (chapter 9).
	Knowledge and understanding of fitness and health	In activities based on cardiovascular, flexibility, muscular strength and endurance, and academic themes, students understand the value of specific physical fitness parameters and explain how their bodies are affected during the activity. Examples: Flexibility Stations (chapter 3), Jump Rope Exploration (chapter 6).
United States[h]	Demonstrates competency in motor skills and movement patterns needed to perform a variety of physical activities	Level I and II activities address the fundamental patterns, progressions, and sequences of movement in children. Level III activities enhance and develop these fundamentals into sports skills, games, and activities. Examples: Balance Beam (chapter 4), Introduction to the Parachute (chapter 12).
	Demonstrates understanding of movement concepts, principles, strategies, and tactics as they apply to the learning and performance of physical activities	Level I and II activities address the fundamental patterns, progressions, and sequences of movement in children. Level III activities enhance and develop these fundamentals into sports skills, games, and activities. Examples: Aerobic Circle (chapter 2), Academic Blob (chapter 11).
	Participates regularly in physical activity	The book's overall goal is to encourage children to enjoy regular physical activity. Using the activities consistently and correctly will allow children to participate in regular physical activity in their physical education classroom. Examples: Balloon Stomp (chapter 6), Scavenger Hunt (chapter 7).
	Achieves and maintains a health-enhancing level of physical fitness	In activities based on cardiovascular, flexibility, muscular strength and endurance, and academic themes, students understand the value of specific physical fitness parameters and explain how their bodies are affected during the activity. Examples: Muscle Stretch (chapter 3), Counterbalances (chapter 4).
	Exhibits responsible personal and social behavior that respects self and others in physical activity settings	Activities require students to cooperate to accomplish goals, to promote safety for themselves and others, and to develop positive social behaviors. Examples: Pipeline (chapter 10), Popcorn (chapter 12).

(continued)

National Standards Comparison   *(continued)*

Country	Standards	How *Old Favorites, New Fun* addresses these standards
United States[h] *(continued)*	Values physical activity for health, enjoyment, challenge, self-expression, and/or social interaction	All activities were developed specifically to encourage children to participate in daily physical activity by making it enjoyable. Examples: Tinikling (chapter 9), Lemonade (chapter 11).

[a]Adapted, by permission, from the Victorian Curriculum Assessment Authority, 2004. www.vcaa.vic.edu.au. The above material is an extract from material produced by the Victorian Curriculum and Assessment Authority, Australia. Students and teachers should consult the Victorian Essential Learning Standards website http://vels.vcaa.vic.edu.au for more information. This material is copyright and cannot be reproduced in any form without the written permission of the VCAA.

[b]By permission of the Queensland Studies Authority.

[c]PHPE K-6 Syllabus © Board of Studies NSW for and on behalf of the Crown in right of the State of New South Wales, 1999.

[d]Adapted, by permission, from the Curriculum Council of Western Australia, *Curriculum framework: Health and physical education learning outcomes headings* (Western Australia: Curriculum Council of Western Australia), 116.

[e]www.cahperd.ca

[f]By permission of the Education and Manpower Bureau, Government of the Hong Kong Special Administrative Region.

[g]By permission of the National Curriculum, United Kingdom. Reproduced under the terms of the Click-Use License.

[h]Reprinted from *Moving into the Future: National Standards for Physical Education,* 2nd Edition (2004) reprinted with permission from the National Association for Sport and Physical Education (NASPE), 1900 Association Drive, Reston, VA 20191-1599.

Chapter 1

Locomotor Activities

Locomotor activities move the body from one place to another or project the body upward. The ability to move from one location to another in a variety of ways forms the foundation of all movement. Being able to efficiently complete the activities in this chapter allows students to master more advanced movement skills; thus, many of these activities focus on level I.

The key to appropriate activity selection is choosing activities based on the abilities of the students in the class. The levels listed for the activities in this chapter are merely recommendations; you must use discretion in choosing activities according to your students' abilities. In general, level I activities are appropriate for kindergarten and grade 1; level II activities are appropriate for grades 2 through 3; and level III activities are appropriate for grades 4, 5, and 6.

Alligators in the River

Level

I and II

Area

Large playing space such as a gymnasium

Equipment

Hula hoop for every three students; peppy music that encourages movement

Objectives

Students will learn and refine a variety of locomotor skills.

Setup and Description

Scatter hula hoops, or islands, around the floor. The rest of the floor is the river. Choose two or three students to be the alligators. Play the music and have the students perform a certain locomotor skill. When the music stops, say "Alligators in the river!" The students then travel to an island to get away from the alligators. Only three students are allowed in one hoop at a time. After a few rounds, remove one or two hoops so that a few students do not make it to the islands and are tagged by the alligators. These students are not eliminated, however; they still get to play in the next round.

SAFETY NOTE

There is a real possibility for collisions in this game. Supervise carefully and prevent pushing or shoving.

Modifications

Try this game in different settings with other animals.

Balloon Motion

Level
I and II

Area
Large playing space such as a gymnasium

Equipment
Balloon for each student

Objectives
Students will move around in their own personal space without bumping into anyone while keeping their balloon in the air.

Setup and Description
Students each hold a balloon. At your signal, the students walk around the class and try to keep their balloon up in the air in their personal space by hitting it with their hands. They also try to keep their balloon from touching others' balloons or hitting the ground. If their balloon touches another person's balloon or hits the ground or if one student runs into another, they must yell "Pop!" and sit down, holding their balloon until you tell them that it is okay to try again. If appropriate, the popped students could simply do 10 sit-ups, push-ups, jumping jacks, or another exercise and then return to the game.

Modifications
This is a great activity for children with disabilities. For example, a student may be pushed in a wheelchair while tapping a balloon in the air. Address actions for children with other disabilities as needed.

Cone Craze

Level
I and II

Area
This activity can be played in a gym, multipurpose room, or outside

Equipment
8 to 10 cones per team

Objectives
Students will use eye–hand coordination and different locomotor skills to try to win the activity for their team.

Setup and Description
Break the class into two to four teams using creative division methods. Each team lines up single file. Set 8 to 10 cones in a straight line in front of each line so that the cones are all lying down for one line and all sitting up for the next line.

The first person goes through the line of cones and either sets the cones back up or knocks all the cones down. When the first person finishes and returns to the line, the next person does the reverse (knocking down the cones or standing them back up). Students can only use their hands to knock down or set up cones; they cannot use their feet.

Modifications

Use different locomotor skills such as walking, jumping, skipping, galloping, or hopping.

Cones and Dice

Level
I

Area
Large playing space such as a gymnasium

Equipment
20 to 30 traffic cones, poly spots, or play mats; large die

Objectives
Students will travel in locomotor movements throughout the gym.

Setup and Description

This is a fundamental movement activity that is noncompetitive. Scatter cones or poly spots or play mats throughout the area and assign one locomotor skill to each number on the die based on the skill levels of the students. Start with everyone standing in the center of the play space.

Roll the die. Students must then travel to and touch the correct number of cones using the correct locomotor skill. For example, if you assigned walking to the number 3, students walk to and then touch three different cones. Remind students that they should not touch or run into other students. When students finish, they should return to the center of the room, and when everyone has returned, roll the die again. You could also assign a student to roll the die. Pick students who do a nice job performing the locomotor skill, not just the students who finish first.

Modifications

●● Make this game more challenging by adding the number on the die with another number that the teacher selects. For example, if the die reads walk 3, add 4 to the number, so students walk 7.

●● If you cannot find a die big enough for the class to see, you can use a deck of cards. Take the face cards out so that students can only see numbers. You will need to have 10 locomotor movements in mind.

Four-Corner Cartoon Traveling

Level
I

Area
Large playing space such as a gymnasium

Equipment

4 posters of common cartoon characters; 4 cards with pictures of the same characters on them; exciting music that encourages movement

Objectives

Students will further their knowledge of locomotor skills by traveling throughout the play space.

Setup and Description

Before the lesson, hang the posters on the walls, one at each corner of the gym. Show the students how each corner of the gym has a picture of a cartoon character. When the music begins, they will move around the general space using the locomotor movement that you call out (e.g., skip, jog, gallop). When the music stops, they are to move (without pushing, shoving, or bumping into others) to one of the four corners and wait there until you pick one of the four cards from your hand (hold the cards up with the characters facing away from you as you choose). The students in the corner of that character card get to pick the next movement that the students will perform.

Observe the students' ability to correctly travel using the called movement. If they are having difficulty, stop the music, give students a cue to help them, and have them begin traveling again rather than picking a new movement. Be sure to correct any wrong movements.

Modifications

The cards and posters don't have to show cartoon characters. For example, they could show animals that the students may be learning about in science, states in the United States, countries around the world, or musical notes. Talk to the children's classroom teachers to find out what subjects they are studying; cooperative teaching and reinforcement of classroom teaching will likely be appreciated.

Four-Corner Locomotion

Level
I and II

Area
Large playing space with a flat surface such as a gymnasium

Equipment

Note cards with locomotor activities written on them (have enough cards to meet the needs of the class)

Objectives

Students will demonstrate that they can perform locomotor skills and will understand the importance of those skills as they relate to various sports skills.

Setup and Description

This is a nice warm-up activity. Place the note cards in the four corners of the gym. Using creative division methods, split the students into four groups. Each group should go to a corner of the gym. On the floor in each corner will be the note cards with a skill to be performed such as skipping, hopping, jogging, walking, and so on. Each of the students in the corner will look at one card and perform that skill to the next corner. When students get to the next corner, they look at another card, read the movement, and perform that skill to the next location, and so on. Change up the skills so boredom does not occur.

Modifications

- • Have students try to perfect the movements and not simply move through the task without effort.
- • Some of the skills may require extra attention. Work with the students slowly until they understand how to perform the movements correctly.

Frog Pond

Level
I

Area
Large playing space such as a gymnasium

Equipment

Anything that resembles a frog's lily pad (i.e., jump ropes, hula hoops, poly spots)—use 2 or 3 fewer lily pads than there are students

Objectives

Students will practice locomotor movements such as skipping, galloping, hopping, jumping, and so on.

Setup and Description

Scatter lily pads throughout the space. Set out enough lily pads so that there will always be a few children who will not have one. The students walk around the space, using all the open areas and not following others. When you call out the words "Ribbit rabbit," students find an open lily pad. In finding a lily pad, children should not push or shove each other.

The students who did not find a lily pad huddle together, choose the next locomotor movement, and recite the following for everyone to hear: "Little frog, little frog, please (locomotor movement) off my lily pad." The activity then begins again. When you call out "Ribbit rabbit!" again, everyone, even the children who were huddled together from the last time, tries to find an empty lily pad.

Modifications

- • You can use the concept of musical chairs by adding music to the lesson instead of calling out "Ribbit rabbit!"
- • This activity can be tailored to any setting. The activity can be used to finish math problems, work on spelling words, or whatever challenges the classroom teacher can come up with. For example, change the words to "Little frog, little frog, what's the answer to 10 + 17?" If the student is right, she skips (hops, runs, crawls) around the space.

Frogs and Ladybugs

Level

I

Area

Large playing space such as a gymnasium

Equipment

12 frog-shaped beanbags; 12 ladybug-shaped beanbags; 24 plastic cones; music that encourages movement

Objectives

Students will practice locomotor movements such as skipping, galloping, hopping, jumping, and so on while using their imagination.

Setup and Description

Scatter cones across the space and place a frog or ladybug beanbag under each cone. Divide the class into two groups using creative division methods. Students in one group are frogs and the others are ladybugs. When the music plays, all students move around the gym. Frogs look under the cones for ladybug beanbags and ladybugs look for frog beanbags. The object of the game is to get the beanbags of the other group out from under the cones and placed beside the cones before the music stops. There should be no fighting over the beanbags.

If ladybugs see one of their beanbags next to a cone, they may place the cone back over it, and if frogs see one of their beanbags next to a cone, they may do the same. Once a student places a frog or ladybug outside or under a cone they must run to a different cone—only one person may be at one cone at a time. There is no guarding of cones.

When the music stops, all students must stop and sit down in the center of the room or another specified section of the room. Ask a student who is sitting quietly if she is a frog or ladybug. If she is a frog, ask her to go around and place the cones back over all frogs. Have a student who is a ladybug do the same with ladybugs. Repeat the activity.

Modifications

- Instead of running from cone to cone, students can do other locomotor movements or move on different levels.
- If frog and ladybug beanbags aren't available, use beanbags in two different colors for the frogs and ladybugs.

Jogging Chicken Dance

Level

II

Area

This activity can be played in a gym, multipurpose room, or outside

Equipment

"Chicken Dance" song by Werner Thomas

Objectives

Students will perform a light cardiovascular activity while using active listening to pick up audible cues.

Setup and Description

Students spread out around the perimeter of the gym. During the chicken dance refrain, the students stop and execute the dance, and during the instrumental "verse," students jog around the perimeter of the gym. The chicken dance is performed by placing the hands in the arm pits, flapping the "wings," and walking around the space while lifting the knees high.

Students have found this to be a motivating way to do the chicken dance and still get a little cardiovascular challenge. It is also a great way to keep older students interested in the dance without feeling like they are doing a silly activity.

Modifications

- • Instead of jogging, the students perform a locomotor skill such as skipping, hopping, galloping, and so on.

- • Children with certain disabilities can participate in this activity. They may not be able to jog, but they can walk and then do the chicken dance.

Jump Rope Contest

Level
I, II, and III

Area
Large playing space such as a gymnasium

Equipment
As many short and long jump ropes as needed for the class size (ideally, one short rope per student and one long rope for every three students)

Objectives
Students will create a jump rope routine to perform for their classmates.

Setup and Description
Students create a jump rope routine. Some routines may use single jump ropes while others may use multiple people or routines that require longer jump ropes. Everyone must be involved; no one can sit out. First graders will compete with the other first graders and so on. Every class will practice their routine for two weeks and then they will present it to the other physical education classes.

Modifications
Present the routines to a PTA meeting or to the entire school at an assembly. This activity could also lead into Jump Rope for Heart fund-raising activities.

Locomotion Commotion

Level
II and III

Area
Large playing space such as a gymnasium

Equipment
8 cones

Objectives
Students will work on several locomotor skills.

Setup and Description
Set up two lines of cones at opposite ends of the play area. Use creative division methods to break the class into four teams. Each team has two cones, one at the starting line and one at the other end of the area. Each team lines up at the starting cone. First, one student at a time skips to the far cone and back. Then one student at a time gallops to the cone and back. Then they hop, jump, leap, and so on. While one team member does a movement, other members chant the movement. For example, if a team member is leaping, the rest of the team chants "Leap, leap, leap."

Modifications
To help students learn the mechanics of a skip, have them say "step-hop" instead of "skip" when appropriate.

Locomotion Relays

Level
I and II

Area
Large playing space such as a gymnasium

Equipment
None

Objectives
Students will refine locomotor skills and improve cardiovascular fitness.

Setup and Description

Relays are classic activities that are limited only by your imagination. Make sure that the floor is clean, dry, and free of any objects that could cause injury. Use creative division methods to divide students into groups of four, five, or six.

Give the students a locomotor task. Students travel down the gym floor and back one at a time using the movement. The next player does not start until the previous one has made it back to the starting line and has tagged the next person.

After completing their portion of the relay, students walk, run, or jog around the perimeter of the play space twice and then sit down at the end of the line. The jogging or walking at the end of the task will keep them moving but also allow a little rest time before the next race.

Modifications
Use a variety of locomotor movements, such as walking, hopping, skipping, jumping, galloping, jogging, marching, or sliding.

Locomotion Square Dancing

Level
II and III

Area
Large playing space about half the size of a basketball court

Equipment
Square-dance music

Objectives
Students will work together in accomplishing a variety of locomotor square-dancing movements.

Setup and Description

Have students partner up using creative division methods and then spread out around the floor. When the music begins, they perform a certain locomotor skill, such as skipping. As they are skipping, tell them to do-si-do. They should then lock arms and skip around their square (circle of people) once. Then change locomotor skills.

Modifications

●● Use international folk music and discuss the cultural background of the music.

●● If you're having the students hold hands and they don't want to, they can hold onto different ends of a scarf or short rope instead.

Locomotor Cards

Level

I and II

Area

Large playing space such as a gymnasium

Equipment

Deck of cards; poster board or dry-erase board

Objectives

Students will refine locomotor skills and demonstrate that they can follow directions.

Setup and Description

Scatter the cards facedown in the middle of the play space. Write the following activities on poster board or on a dry-erase board for easy reference.

Chosen Card	Activity
2 through 5	Skip around gym
6 through 9	Hop on one foot around gym
10 through K	Gallop around gym
Ace	March around gym

Have the students jog around the gym until you signal them to go pick up one card. When they have chosen a card, they perform the correct activity as described in the previous list for a length of time to be chosen by the teacher.

Collect the cards and spread them on the floor again, then repeat the previous steps.

SAFETY NOTE

Make sure students do not slip on the playing cards. The cards should be in the middle of the floor and all activity should occur outside of the center.

Modifications

This activity could be made into a game of tag. The teacher could choose a movement card, for example "gallop," that would be It. After each person gets a card, say "Go" and the chase begins. Each person chases and flees using only the movement named on their card. The tagged person or persons become It.

Locomotor Circle

Level
I

Area
Large playing space such as a gymnasium

Equipment
Enough cones to create a large circle; lively music

Objectives
Students will learn how to perform different locomotor movements and how to distinguish among them.

Setup and Description
Set up cones in a circle around the gym. Explain how to do each locomotor skill and then start the activity. When you start the music, the students start jogging around the circle. Then shout out a locomotor skill that you want the class to do. The children execute this skill until you call out another skill. Use this activity as a warm-up; it should only last around five minutes.

Modifications
At random, tell the students to switch directions. It makes the exercise more fun and it also keeps the students focused.

Locomotor Line Tag

Level
I

Area
Large playing space such as a gymnasium or multipurpose room

Equipment
None

Objectives
Students will learn how to move safely throughout the play space using various locomotor skills.

Setup and Description
This is a fundamental movement activity that is noncompetitive. Most gyms or multipurpose rooms have a variety of lines on the floor, but if this is not the case, create lines using various colors of tape. Match colored lines on the playing area with locomotor patterns and let the children know what movement should be done for each line they're standing on. For instance, designate the white lines as walking lines, green as galloping, yellow as skipping, and red as running.

On your signal, students move on the lines wherever they like, but they must use the appropriate movement on the appropriate line. You can use music to enhance movement; when the music is playing, the children are moving and when the music stops, the children stop moving. Encourage the children to stay on the lines and complete the desired movement. They can move from line to line, but in doing so they must change to the appropriate movement. Remind students not to touch or run into each other.

Modifications

After the children get the idea of what they're supposed to be doing, designate one or more people to be It and travel in the appropriate manner while trying to tag fellow classmates. They must remember to perform the correct line movement.

Locomotor Tag

Level
I and II

Area
Large playing space such as a gymnasium

Equipment
None

Objectives
Students will demonstrate that they can perform a large variety of locomotor skills.

Setup and Description
Have the students spread out in the play space. Nominate one or two people to be It depending on class size and start the game by saying a locomotor skill to be performed. Everyone in the class does the skill, even those who are It. When students get tagged, they must complete a desired task (indicated by you) and then get back into the game. These tasks could be recite the alphabet, solve a mathematical equation, spell a word, and so on.

Modifications
- • Have the students balance something on their head, possibly a beanbag or an eraser, while they're moving around the area. If they drop the object, they must stop and put it back on their head before moving on. They cannot be tagged when they're putting the object back on their head.
- • Some students may need assistance with a variety of movements. Make sure you accompany any student who needs such help.

Me and My Shadow Stretching

Level
II

Area
Large playing space such as a gymnasium

Equipment
Enough tumbling mats to meet the needs and size of the class; soft music

Objectives
Students will perform various stretches and increase their flexibility while learning fun ways to stretch.

Setup and Description
Have the students partner up according to height and body size. One student does a stretch and the other person follows along and "shadows" the stretch. After you lead the students through a series of stretches, have each pair pick a stretch and see who can stretch the farthest.

SAFETY NOTE

Stress safety and proper stretching techniques you've already addressed in class and remind students that it is not safe to bounce during the stretch.

Modifications
You can partner up with anyone who is having difficulty or needs special attention due to a disability or limited flexibility. Use stretches that they can do and try to incorporate new ones. Encouragement is the key to improvement!

Partner Row

Level
II and III

Area
Large playing space such as a gymnasium, preferably with a wood or tile floor

Equipment
None

Objectives
Students will work cooperatively and increase their flexibility.

Setup and Description
Break the class into pairs using creative division methods. Partners then perform various stretches with each other. Students sit on the ground facing their partner, with the knees bent and the soles of their feet against the soles of their partner's feet. They hold hands with their partner. (Note: If students are uncomfortable holding hands with each other, pass out scarves or short ropes for them to hold onto.)

Using cooperation and a rowing motion, students try to move across the floor from one end of the play space to the other while doing a row stretch. To do this, one student must be straight legged while the other, with legs bent outward slightly, pushes the other student and herself. Provided there is enough space, all groups can do this activity at the same time.

Modifications

●● Work in pairs and do a stretch that will work for all students.

●● If students need extra help, let them sit on a scooter.

Pot of Gold

Level
I

Area
Large playing space such as a gymnasium

Equipment
2 mats; several playground balls (yellow would work best); 4 sets of 12 hula hoops (12 red, 12 blue, 12 green, 12 yellow); 4 large cards, each with a movement and its direction written on it (e.g., "Walk forward," "Walk backward," "Jump up and down," "Slide sideways"); 4 large cones; tape

Objectives
Students will demonstrate their ability to move around the gym in different directions without bumping into each other.

Setup and Description
Before class, arrange the equipment as follows:

On one half of the gym, spread out the mats so they lie parallel with each other, about 10 feet (3 meters) apart. Beginning at the end of one mat and ending at the other, lay the hula hoops of the same color close together in a row, arching them like a rainbow. Arch the next set just under the first row. Continue until you have four rows of hula hoops arching from one mat to the other. At the end of the mat

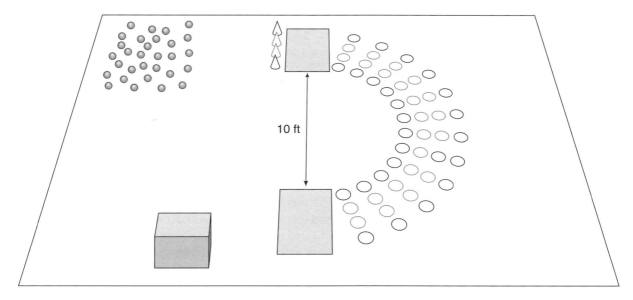

10 ft

in the empty half of the gym, place the big box of playground balls (the "pot of gold" at the end of the rainbow).

Tape one card to each cone. At the opposite end of the rainbow, place one cone by one color of the rainbow. For example, put "Walk forward" by the red rainbow, "Walk backward" by the blue, "Slide sideways" by the green, and "Jump up and down" by the yellow.

To begin the activity, scatter the playground balls around the empty half of the gym. At the teacher's signal, students pick up one ball and line up at the beginning of the rainbow (at the edge of one mat). Encourage students to move to a color of the rainbow where nobody is waiting. They then carry the ball and travel through the appropriate color of the rainbow using the appropriate movement designated by the cards taped to the cones. Once they reach the end of the rainbow, they put their ball into the pot of gold, go find another piece of gold lying on the floor, and repeat the activity traveling through a different section of the rainbow.

Modifications

You can use other colors of hula hoops based on the colors that you have, and you can use different movements other than those listed in this activity.

Relay Hoppers

Level
I, II, and III

Area
Large playing space such as a gymnasium

Equipment
2 cones for each group

Objectives
Students will learn all the components of a hop and will learn how to hop on either foot while also learning how to cheer for their team.

Setup and Description
Place cones about 20 feet (6 meters) away from each other, one cone as the starting point and the other as the turn-around point.

In order for this activity to work, all students must know how to execute a hop. Start the class by demonstrating correct hopping technique. Most children think that hopping is the same as a jump, only it's little and bunny-like. Explain that hopping is taking off on one leg and landing on the same one.

Emphasize to the students that this is not a race, but they're trying to perfect their hopping technique. Split the class into four groups using creative division methods and have them line up single file behind their starting cones. Each student hops all the way to the cone and back and gives the next person in line a high five. The next student continues until the line comes back around to the first student. The first student then hops down to the cone and back on the other foot.

Encourage the class to root for other people. It is also important for students to realize that everyone is a winner.

Modifications

- • Pay attention to the difference in hopping height and speed; there are all kinds of variations.
- • If hopping on one foot is difficult for the distance, consider switching feet at the far cone. You may address correct technique there as well.
- • Change the locomotor activity at the far cone.

Relay 'Round the Bases

Level
II and **III**

Area
Large playing space such as a gymnasium

Equipment
4 cones; 2 poly spots

Objectives
Students will use different locomotor skills to participate in a relay.

Setup and Description
Set up four cones to form a square about 30 to 50 feet (9 to 15 meters) per side, depending on the level of students. Place two poly spots inside the square on opposite sides. The poly spots are the bases. Divide the class into two teams; the two teams line up at opposite bases on the inside of the square. Teams compete at the same time. Students start inside the square and wait inside the square until it's their turn to run, but for safety purposes, they run outside the square. The first runner on each team makes one complete circuit around the outside of the cones. After returning to the line, the runner tags the next person in the line and moves to the end of the line.

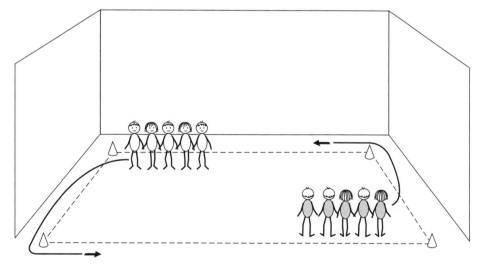

Modifications

- • Use different movements for each side of the square (e.g., run, gallop, leap, skip).
- • Mark more than one square and have more children moving at once.
- • Have four teams racing at the same time instead of two.

Roll 'n' Slide

Level
I, II, and III

Area
Large playing space with a flat surface such as a gymnasium

Equipment
Tennis ball for every two students; 2 cones

Objectives
Students will learn how to slide while rolling a ball.

Setup and Description
Set up one cone at one end of the room and one at the opposite end. Tell the class that they are going to be working on sliding. Demonstrate a correct slide and put the skill into words for auditory learners. Pair up the class using creative division methods and give each pair of students one tennis ball.

Students slide all the way down the length of the court while rolling the tennis ball back and forth to one another. Students should try to lead their partner with the ball by rolling the ball slightly ahead of their partner's intended path so a constant slide is used during the entire activity. Then they jog back to the end of the line and do the activity again except this time they switch sides. For example, if a student originally led with the right foot first, the left foot leads the second time. Using both sides ensures good locomotor skills on both sides of the body.

Modifications
This is a complex and physically challenging skill, so encourage the students; they may need it for this skill.

Scooter Obstacle Course

Level
I and II

Area
Large playing space such as a gymnasium

Equipment
Scooter for each student; 24 to 36 cones; active music that encourages fast movement

Objectives
Students will learn to maneuver around obstacles in a variety of body positions on scooters.

Setup and Description
Break the class into four to six groups using creative division methods. Place six cones or markers in a single line in front of each group of students. The cones should be spaced about 6 feet (2 meters) apart. One at a time, the students weave through the series of cones. The children can follow the person in front of them, but they should never get close enough to touch that person.

The first time through, students should sit on their scooters and push themselves through the line of cones with their hands and arms. The next time through, they can lie on their abdomen and push themselves through the cones with their hands and arms.

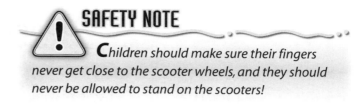

SAFETY NOTE

Children should make sure their fingers never get close to the scooter wheels, and they should never be allowed to stand on the scooters!

When students successfully accomplish the tasks, set up an obstacle course with cones for each group. The layout of the obstacle course is limited only by safety and your imagination. When you signal the students, they proceed through the obstacle course. Remember that more than one student can go through the group's obstacle course at the same time, but they must never get close enough to touch the person in front of them.

Modifications

Hold races through the cones with some friendly competition among teams.

Soap Bubbles

Level
I

Area
Large playing space such as a gymnasium

Equipment

Whistle; light and airy music (optional)

Objectives

Students will understand general and personal space while learning and refining a variety of locomotor skills.

Setup and Description

Discuss soap bubbles and how they float through the air until they touch something and pop. Tell students that today they will be bubbles. They should imagine a barrier around them that will not let them touch anyone or anything. On the whistle signal, they begin moving around as the teacher tells them what movements to perform, walking and then progressing to skipping, hopping, sliding, and so on. If they touch anyone or anything, they pop and have to go sit by you for a few seconds to get inflated. Remind students how to move safely through general space. You can play some light and airy music in the background.

Modifications

Sometimes bubbles come out of the blower attached to one another in groups of two or three. Have the students complete the same task after locking elbows in groups of two and three.

Spaceship Tag

Level

I and II

Area

Large playing space such as a gymnasium

Equipment

Hula hoop for each student; music or sound effects of spaceships blasting off and speeding through space (such as from *Star Wars* or *Star Trek,* for example)

Objectives

Students will learn how to move around the gym in their personal space.

Setup and Description

Scatter the hula hoops throughout the playing area. Have students walk to the hoops so that they all have their own hoop. They should stand inside the hoop and hold onto it with their hands, keeping the hoop parallel with the floor. The front part of the hoop should be touching the students' waist.

Have the students move in their self-space without touching others, emphasizing that their hoop is their spaceship and should not be touching any other spaceship. They walk around the playing area in their spaceship, making sure not to bump into anyone or anything. If their spaceship bumps into another spaceship, they must sit down inside the spaceship with their hands on their knees. They cannot get up and walk until you gently tap them on the head. (Remember that the children need to become active again as soon as possible.)

At first have the students move slowly around the gym. With successful practice, allow the students to gradually increase their walking speed. In addition, encourage them to move in different pathways and at different levels (heights from the floor) and perform various locomotor movements.

Modifications

- • • When the students are successful at moving around without bumping into each other, turn the game into a type of walking tag. Two or three students are It. While remaining in their spaceship, they try to tag other students. When they tag another player, they say "Spaceship down." Tagged students sit in their spaceship and any of the other students other than the taggers can free them by gently tapping them on the head and saying "Spaceship up." Change the taggers frequently.

- • • As the students are playing the game, assign different locomotor skills.

- • • If you do not have enough hula hoops for everyone, you can pair up students and put them in the same spaceship. They must cooperate to move together.

Take Me Out to the Ball Game

Level

I and II

Area

Large playing space such as a gymnasium

Equipment

"Take Me Out to the Ball Game" song

Objectives

Students will practice locomotor movements such as skipping, galloping, hopping, jumping, and so on while using their imagination.

Setup and Description

This activity includes several different aspects of a baseball game at a collegiate or professional baseball park. Students move around the floor imitating different aspects of the game—fans, the mascot, fielders, batters—and then put it all together.

• • **Fans:** Say, for example, "We are at the ballpark. What kinds of things do you see the fans doing?" While playing the music, have the students demonstrate how they would act as a fan.

- Standing up and sitting down
- Yelling and clapping
- Jumping for a foul ball

Students can use a certain number of locomotor skills (chosen by you) and can move from low to high levels (height from the floor) at any time. Some actions are high or above the shoulders and others are low or below the knees. Have the children experiment with various levels while moving.

• • **Mascot:** Tell students, "Act like your favorite mascot!" Students perform movements that their favorite mascot would perform. Make sure that the movements are appropriate and not offensive to anyone.

• • **Players:** Say, "Now we're Major League Baseball players. Who do you play for and what position to you play? We're infielders or outfielders. What kinds of actions are we going to be doing?" Students should be in the ready position for their chosen action.

- Squatting as a catcher
- Fielding a ground ball
- Running to tag a base
- Throwing the ball
- Pitching
- Diving for a ball
- Jumping to catch a fly ball
- Jumping on the wall
- Fielding a ground ball
- Throwing a long way

• • **Batters:** Next, say "We are now batters! Show how a batter swings and how he hits the ball." Children can pretend to run bases, but they have to watch where they are going! How would they swing the bat or run if they were hitting a

- bunt,
- home run,
- pop fly, or
- ground ball?

• • **Everything:** Finally, tell students, "Now put it all together!" Students can be any position on the field, a batter, or a fan. The choice is theirs.

Modifications

Change the sport to football, soccer, hockey, curling, or whatever works with your class—the choices are limitless.

What Do You See?

Level
I

Area
This activity can be played in a gym, multipurpose room, or outside

Equipment
Brown Bear, Brown Bear, What Do You See? book by Eric Carle and Bill Martin, Jr.; 4 cones to mark boundaries of a rectangle or square for the playing area

Objectives
Students will practice locomotor movements such as skipping, galloping, hopping, jumping, and so on while using their imagination.

Setup and Description
Have students spread out in the activity space. Tell them that you are going to read them a story and they are going to act it out. Begin to read the book, giving time between each animal for the students to complete each movement. For example, the opening line in the book is "Brown Bear, Brown Bear, what do you see?" Have students demonstrate with movement and noises what a bear looks like. Discuss the different locomotor movements a bear would use.

Modifications
Have the students perform the movements along predetermined pathways (lines on the floor).

Chapter 2

Cardiovascular Activities

In these activities, the emphasis is on cardiovascular fitness. When you exercise, your heart, lungs, and circulatory system get a workout. Working these systems vigorously and regularly is what improves your cardiovascular fitness. If you sit around all day and aren't doing anything physical, your heart does not have a chance to get healthy and you will have poor cardiovascular endurance.

Several aspects are involved in improving and maintaining the cardiovascular system. First, the heart rate must be raised to a specific level. The precise level depends on many factors, but generally, the heart rate should be around 140 to 150 beats per minute. Second, the heart rate should remain elevated for 15 or more minutes. Third, this type of exercise should be performed at least two times a week to maintain cardiovascular fitness or three times per week to improve cardiovascular fitness.

Virtually all of the activities in this section emphasize fun and high activity. Many of them move very fast and you must be sure to supervise each game with safety in mind.

The key to appropriate activity selection is choosing activities based on the abilities of the students in the class. The levels listed for the activities in this chapter are merely recommendations; you must use discretion in choosing activities according to your students' abilities. In general, level I activities are appropriate for kindergarten and grade 1; level II activities are appropriate for grades 2 through 3; and level III activities are appropriate for grades 4, 5, and 6.

Aerobic Circle

Level
  I and II

Area
  Large playing space such as a gymnasium

Equipment
  Music with a strong 4/4 beat

Objectives
  Students will demonstrate many skills while developing cardiovascular endurance.

Setup and Description
  Have players form a large circle, spacing themselves at arm's length from each other. When you point to someone, that player comes to the middle of the circle to lead the class through an activity of their choice for 16 counts. As they're doing the activity, encourage all the other students to be thinking of what activity they'll lead. Duplications are acceptable but not encouraged. Here are some examples of activities:

- Jogging—Clap hands above the head, behind, or in front.
- Sailor jumps—Jump with one leg forward and the other back while swinging arms in time to the music.
- Jumping jacks—Jump legs and arms apart sideways and then together.
- Combo jacks—Alternate jumping jacks and sailor jumps.
- Side kicks—Kick legs from side to side and wave hands.

•• Seat kicks—Kick the buttocks.

•• Mule kicks—Kick behind with straight legs.

•• X jumps—Jump to cross and uncross ankles.

Modifications

If you think your students might have a hard time coming up with activities on their own, write activities on cards and hand them out.

Barker's Hoopla

Level

II and **III**

Area

Large playing space such as a gymnasium

Equipment

4 hula hoops; 16 to 20 beanbags

Objectives

Students will work together to accomplish a task while improving or maintaining their cardiovascular fitness.

Setup and Description

Place one hoop in each of the four corners of the playing area. Leave about 25 to 30 feet (8-9 meters) between hoops. Place five or six beanbags in each hoop.

Break the class into four equal teams using creative division methods. One team should stand behind each hoop, or their home base. The object of the game is for players to steal beanbags from other hoops and return them to the hoop that is their home base.

In playing the game, these rules must be followed:

•• Players can take only one beanbag at a time, and they must take it to the home base before returning for another one.

•• Players can take beanbags from any hoop.

•• Players cannot throw or toss beanbags to the home base; they must carry the beanbags over the vertical plane of the hoop before releasing them.

•• No one can protect the home base or its beanbags with any defensive maneuver.

•• When you give the stop signal, players must freeze immediately and release any beanbags in their possession.

Modifications

Players must skip or use another designated locomotor movement.

Capture the Football

Level
III

Area
Large playing space such as a gymnasium

Equipment

2 footballs; 2 hula hoops; 2 folding mats, colored pinnies or shirts for half the class

Objectives

Students will demonstrate teamwork and encouragement while experiencing the training benefits of cardiovascular fitness.

Setup and Description

Unfold the mats and place them at opposite ends and in opposite corners of the playing area. The mats will be the jail for each end. Place the footballs in the hula hoops on opposite ends of the floor near the middle of the end line. Break the class into two teams using creative division methods and send each team to one side of the gym. One team puts on pinnies.

Players can run anywhere in the room. The object is to run into the opposition's playing area, steal the football, and return with it to the other side of the playing area without being tagged. If players are tagged by an opposing team member while attempting to capture the football, they immediately go to jail and stand on the mat. To return their jailed teammates to the game, team members must come into the opposition's playing area and tag them without being tagged themselves.

Modifications

•• This game could include more than one football placed in different areas of the playing space. In order to win, teams must retrieve all footballs safely.

•• Depending on the size of the class, you can make the field shorter or longer.

•• You can substitute belts and flags for pinnies.

Card Conditioning

Level
II and III

Area
Large playing space such as a gymnasium

Equipment

Deck of playing cards (2 decks for a big class); 4 cones; 4 posters (1 spade poster, 1 heart poster; 1 diamond poster; 1 club poster)

Objectives

Students will learn how the heart helps them function while also learning to follow directions.

Setup and Description

In each corner of the room place a cone with a spade, heart, diamond, or club sign on it. Each sign represents one of the four types of playing cards, which each represents a particular exercise:

- Spades represent jumping jacks.
- Hearts represent crunches.
- Diamonds represent push-ups.
- Clubs represent jumping.

Give each student one card. Students should hold the card facedown until you say go. Then the students look at their card to see what they have drawn. Every numbered card represents how many repetitions of each exercise they must do, and all face cards count as 11 repetitions. For example, a jack of diamonds means a student has to do 11 push-ups.

When students are done with the first card, they have to bring the card back to you and get another card. Each student should draw five cards and do five different exercises. Hopefully, every child will do all of the four exercises at least one time.

Modifications

Ask the students to hold on to their five cards. After everyone is done, look at the students' cards and figure out who has the best poker hand. The child who has the best hand gets the Big Heart award for the class period—a special award you create for positive reinforcement (other examples could include the Hustle award or the Fast Feet award).

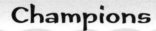

Champions

Level
II and **III**

Area
Large playing space such as a gymnasium

Equipment

8 to 10 cones to adequately mark a rectangular playing area (if you are in a space without lines such as those on a basketball court)

Objectives

Students will work on cardiovascular fitness, running for speed, and proper running technique.

Setup and Description

If your play area does not have the necessary lines (e.g., end line, free-throw line), use cones instead. A championship on a basketball court goes as follows:

- Start on the end line and run to the nearest free-throw line and back.
- Run to half-court and back to the end line.
- Run back down to the farthest free-throw line and back.
- Run down to the end line.
- Run the length of the court and back.

Modifications

- Have the students dribble basketballs or soccer balls while running the course.
- Use other locomotor activities.

Circle Tag

Level
I

Area
Large playing space such as a gymnasium

Equipment
General fun music

Objectives
Students will raise their heart rate for cardiovascular health while working cooperatively with each other.

Setup and Description
Break the class into groups of seven using creative division methods. Six members of the group join hands and form a circle. The seventh person, who is outside of the circle, is the tagger. The group then designates one person in the circle as the target. The object is for the group to move in a circular pattern to keep the target person away from the tagger. The group can't run away from the tagger; they must remain in place and move in a circle. The tagger can't go under or over the circle but must run around it to catch up to the constantly moving target. It will be difficult (but not impossible) to catch the target.

When the target gets tagged, the students trade places. A new student becomes the target. Switch up positions if the person who is It cannot tag the target after one minute.

Modifications
Make the groups larger or smaller to make the activity more or less challenging according to the needs and abilities of the class.

Clothespin Tag

Level
II and III

Area
Large playing space such as a gymnasium

Equipment
3 clothespins per student; music that would encourage a fast pace

Objectives
Students will combine chasing, fleeing, and grasping while raising their heart rate for cardiovascular health.

Setup and Description
This game is an alternative to simple running. It is a type of tag that includes an extra element of grasping clothespins. Every student in the class starts off with three clothespins pinned to the back of their shirt. If students can't put on their own clothespins, they can help each other put them on. They can't put clothespins

on the front of the body or on the legs, arms, head, and so on; they must place the clothespins on the upper back in plain view.

The point of the game is to sneak up behind other students and quickly remove their clothespins. If they get one, they attach the acquired clothespin to their own shirt. The person with the most clothespins at the end of the game wins.

> ⚠ **SAFETY NOTE**
>
> *This game can get exciting and must be supervised with safety in mind. Students are not allowed to grab body parts to stop a player. Clothespins must be removed by only grasping the pin.*

Modifications

Have the students try to grab the clothespins with their nondominant hand.

Color Tag

Level
I, II, and III

Area
Large playing space such as a gymnasium

Equipment

8 to 10 cones or enough to adequately mark the playing area

Objectives

Students will learn or reinforce a variety of locomotor skills and raise their heart rate for cardiovascular health.

Setup and Description

Using cones, mark out two safe zones, one at each end of the space. When students are on or behind this line, they cannot be tagged. Pick two students to be It and have them stand in the center of the court or playing area. All the other students line up along the line marking the safe zone. The two students who are It call out a color. Anyone with that color somewhere on their body (e.g., clothes, eyes, hair) must run to the other side of the playing area and enter the safe zone.

If students are tagged, they must sit down with their legs crossed and they are now seated taggers. If someone runs by them, they must stay seated, but they can extend their arms to tag the runner. If the taggers want to have everyone run, they call out "Color tag" and everyone runs. To reduce chaos, wait until all the students on one side run completely through the playing area to the other safe zone before allowing any students to return to the original safe zone.

Modifications

- Use a variety of locomotor movements that challenge the children.
- When people are tagged, they help tag others, but they must hold on to the part of the body that was tagged.

Crazy Colors

Level
I and II

Area
Large playing space such as a gymnasium

Equipment

36 note cards (6 each with the color "red,""green,""purple,""orange,""yellow," or "blue" written on them); 36 small cones (6 each of red, green, purple, orange, yellow, and blue); upbeat music at least 4 to 5 minutes long

Objectives

Students will learn about and improve their cardiovascular fitness.

Setup and Description

Scatter cones around the activity area as far apart as possible. Under each cone, place one note card of a different color (i.e., do not place a red card under a red cone). Students spread out in the activity area. When the music begins, they jog to any cone, read the color on the card beneath cone, replace the card under the cone so that the next person does not see the color on the card, and then jog to a cone of that same color (e.g., if green is written on a card, the student jogs to a green cone). Students continue moving from cone to cone until the music stops.

At the end of a minute or so, stop the music. Have students feel their heart and how fast it is beating. Remind them that their heart loves it when they are active like this. Call out a new locomotor movement for children to use, challenge them to move to as many cones as possible, and begin the music again.

After repeating the activity a few times, have the children sit in a group. Discuss why their heart was beating so fast and how being active is important to keep their heart healthy. Ask students to name other activities that are good for their heart.

Modifications

- Have students move in different directions (e.g., forward, backward, sideways).
- Challenge children to see how many cones they can go to in a specific time span. Or, have them count how many total cones they go to throughout the whole activity.
- For some fun confusion, write the colors on the cards in a color that is different than the word. For example, write "Green" using a red marker. This really makes students read the words carefully!

Dice Stations

Level

I and II

Area

Large playing space such as a gymnasium

Equipment

Pair of dice for each station; note card with an activity written on it for each station

Objectives

Students will raise their heart rate for cardiovascular health while performing various calisthenics.

Setup and Description

Set up various stations throughout the gym floor. You can have as many stations as you deem necessary to fit the size and abilities of the class. Put a pair of dice and a note card that has a specific action on it (e.g., sit-ups, push-ups, jumping jacks, squats) at each station. Using creative division methods, break the class into groups of four.

Each group starts at a different station and rolls the dice. The group performs the number of exercises on the dice and completes the activity together. After the students have gone through all the stations, ask them how they feel. Do they notice anything different about how their bodies feel? Discuss heart rate and breathing. Tell them how these types of activities will increase their cardiovascular endurance.

Modifications

Hang a large poster in the room showing the heart, lungs, and circulatory system so that you can trace the flow of the blood through the body as you discuss the concept of cardiovascular fitness.

Elbow Tag

Level

III

Area

Large playing space such as a gymnasium

Equipment

Music that would create a fast-paced mood (optional)

Objectives

Students will improve their spatial awareness in an exciting, fast-moving cardiovascular activity.

Setup and Description

Using creative division methods, pair up the students. The partners stand side by side. One person puts his left hand on his left hip bone while bending the elbow. The other partner puts her right hand through the hole made by the bent elbow of her partner. The players put their outside hands on their own hip bones, making another hook. This process is called hooking elbows.

Teams spread out away from each other. Appoint one pair of students to be It. These two students unhook elbows. One student is the chaser and the other is the chasee. Give the chasee three seconds to get away and then allow the chaser to attempt to tag the chasee. The chasee tries to elude the chaser by running around, behind, and in front of the other pairs who are spread out all around the play space. If the chaser tags the chasee, they reverse roles.

At any time during the chasing, the chasee can hook an elbow onto an elbow of one person standing around the room. When the chasee hooks onto another person, the student on the opposite end of the chain is now the chasee (e.g., if the chasee hooks on the left side of the chain, the person on the right side of the chain unhooks elbows and runs from the chaser, trying to find another chain to hook onto). This quick-moving game continues until you say stop.

Modifications

• • Depending on the number of students in the class, there can be several chasers and chasees.

SAFETY NOTE

Adding more chasees and chasers makes the game a little more hectic, and players must be conscious of their surroundings so they don't run into each other.

• • To make it more interesting, you can tell the chaser and chasee to reverse roles at any given time.

• • Have the tagger and chasee perform certain locomotor movements.

• • Players are safe from being tagged when they hold their nose with the left hand and at the same time hold the toes of their left foot with the right hand.

Endurance Challenge

Level
I, II, and III

Area
Large playing space such as a gymnasium

Equipment
Jump rope for every two students; 8 to 10 cones, or enough to mark out the playing area

Objectives
Students will learn how to elevate their heart rate and keep it elevated for an extended period of time.

Setup and Description
This activity demands high levels of endurance as the children will be very active. Place cones around the gym to mark a large rectangular area (approximately 40 by 60 feet [12 by 18 meters]) for the runners. Inside the cones scatter the jump ropes so that students will not hit each other when jumping rope. Break the class into pairs using creative division methods. One student in the pair goes inside the cones with the jump ropes and the other is the first runner around the cones.

The student in the middle has four tasks to complete—jump rope, sit-ups, push-ups, and jumping jacks. The student in the middle will pick one of the tasks to perform while the other student runs two laps around the cones. (If the students cannot run two laps, a combination of running and walking is allowed.) At the completion of the two laps, the students change places with their partners. Now the person who was inside the cones is running and the person running is doing an activity inside the cones. This rotation continues until each student has completed eight laps and all four tasks.

After finishing the activity, it is important to have the children walk several laps in order to gradually bring down their heart rate.

Modifications

●● There are several modifications for this game. For example, you could have the students walk instead of run and choose different activities to complete inside of the rectangle.

●● You could do this activity in a multipurpose room; the running area would probably be smaller, but the activity would still be effective.

Fire and Ice

Level
I and **II**

Area
Large playing space such as a gymnasium

Equipment
2 soft red balls and 3 soft blue balls that are 4 to 5 inches (10-12 centimeters) in diameter (Gator Skin balls work great); 8 to 10 cones to mark the boundaries of the playing space; upbeat music

Objectives
Students will play the game with accuracy while developing their cardiovascular endurance.

Setup and Description
Three students have blue balls (ice) and two students have red balls (fire). Everyone else is free and can run wherever they want. The game begins when the music is turned on. The ice people try to freeze the free people by tagging them with their blue ball (fire people cannot be tagged by the ice people). Throwing the balls at the free people is not allowed; ice people must tag others with the ball.

When an ice person tags a free person, the free person becomes frozen (stands still with both hands on head). The fire people try to free all of the frozen players by handing their ball to a frozen person. The person receiving the fire ball must say "Thank you." If he doesn't say thank you, he stays frozen and the fire person goes to free someone else. If the person does say thank you, he takes the ball and become a new fire person. The person who unfroze him becomes a free person and begins moving around the playing area. The fire balls keep getting passed on and on, but the ice people stay ice people until you stop the music, which means the game is over.

Modifications

●● Change the locomotor activity to prevent boredom and to challenge the students' movement capabilities.

●● You can have more fire students and ice students to accommodate a larger class size.

Fried Egg Tag

Level
I

Area
Large playing space such as a gymnasium

Equipment
Fast music that creates an upbeat mood

Objectives
Students will raise their heart rate for cardiovascular health while improving their ability to dodge and evade through cooperative play.

Setup and Description
Talk to the students about heart rates, pulses, and how to take a pulse. The object of this game is to have students complete a physical activity at a high enough level to raise their heart rate.

Designate two students as It. At your command, the game begins. When students are tagged, they must pretend to be a fried egg sizzling in a pan by lying on their back and kicking their legs and moving their arms. The students continue to do this until a person who is not It touches the students who are a fried egg. The students are now free to begin playing again. Frequently change the students who are It. Play music to help signal when the students should be active and when they should stop.

Modifications
Change the locomotor activity to enhance the game and prevent boredom.

Go Tag

Level
II and III

Area
Large playing space such as a gymnasium

Equipment
None

Objectives
Students will develop strategies and quick decision-making skills while playing a fast-moving chase game.

Setup and Description
To begin this game, everyone stands in a line and every other player faces an opposite direction; for example, the first player faces west, the second faces east, the third faces west, and so on. After all of the players are facing the correct direction, they squat or kneel down. The person at one end of the line is the runner and runs around the others. He may run either clockwise or counterclockwise around the line and he may change directions at any time.

The person at the other end of the line is the chaser and is trying to tag the runner. However, though the chaser can go in any direction at the beginning, once she has started, she cannot change directions. Instead the chaser can tap any squatting or kneeling player, shout "Go," and change places with that player. Those who are squatting or kneeling should be encouraged to cheer and work together in order to capture the runner, but they can never touch or grab the runner. The person who finally tags the runner becomes the new runner and the next person at the end of the line becomes the chaser.

Modifications

- • Use different locomotor movements to complete the task.
- • Have more than one runner and chaser at a time. This will be a little confusing but will create more excitement.

Gobble Blob

Level
II and **III**

Area
This activity can be played in a gym, multipurpose room, or outside

Equipment
If lines are marked on the playing area, no equipment is needed; if no lines exist, 4 cones will be needed to mark the court.

Objectives
Students will practice their running, fleeing, chasing, and dodging skills as they practice a variety of locomotor movements.

Setup and Description
One person starts out as It (the blob) and tries to tag others. When someone is tagged, they must hold hands with the person who is It and become part of the blob. As more people are tagged, the blob gets bigger and bigger. The two people on the ends with free hands are the only ones who can tag others. The game is over when the last free person becomes part of the blob.

Modifications

As the game goes on and the blob gets larger, break the students up into groups of no less than two students per group. They continue to tag the students, only now they're in groups of two, three, four, or more.

Jumping Jack Tag

Level
I, II, and III

Area
All or half of a basketball court, depending on class size

Equipment
None

Objectives
Students will increase their heart rate for cardiovascular health.

Setup and Description
Students spread out in the play area. Depending on the size of the class, designate three, four, or five students to be It. When you tell them to begin, they run to tag their classmates. Once students have been tagged, they must stop and do 15 jumping jacks. When they have finished performing their jumping jacks, they stand with one hand in the air. Once a classmate comes by and gives them a high five, they are free to rejoin the game. The objective is for the taggers to tag all other students so that everyone has stopped with one hand raised.

Modifications
If the class is large and the area is small, divide the class into two groups using creative division methods. Half of the class can play jumping jack tag while the other half walks or runs laps around the perimeter of the space. Be sure to rotate groups.

The Lone Ranger Strikes Again!

Level
I, II, and III

Area
Large playing space such as a gymnasium

Equipment
Long jump rope for every three students

Objectives
Students will work together to accomplish a task while combining several locomotor movements.

Setup and Description
Using creative division methods, divide the class into groups of three. All three stand side by side and hold onto a long rope to make a chariot. On your cue of "Giddyap," each chariot begins galloping through the play area without touching

anyone else. On your cue of "Whoa," the chariots stop and the horse, or the student in the middle of the three, begins jumping inside the long rope as the turners jump inside the rope at the same time. On "Giddyap" cue, the children rotate positions and the chariot is off again.

Modifications

For more talented students, have the rope turners step into the rope as they're turning it and jump along with the horse.

Mousetrap

Level

I

Area

Large playing space such as a gymnasium

Equipment

None

Objectives

Students will work together as a team while playing a game of chasing and fleeing.

Setup and Descriptions

Break the class into two equal teams using creative division methods. One team forms a circle and joins hands. The other team stands outside of the circle. The circle is the mousetrap and the others are the mice.

When you call "Go!" the mice skip around the circle clockwise. When you yell "Open!" the students forming the trap raise their arms, forming arches. This gives the mice a chance to run in and out of the trap. All mice must move in and out of the trap; they cannot simply stay outside the trap. At your discretion, yell "Snap!" The mousetrap drops their arms, trying to catch some mice in the circle. The mice that are caught have to join the circle. The game continues until there are no mice left. When the game is over, switch roles and play again.

Modifications

Have students practice a variety of locomotor movements.

Obstacle Course

Level

I, II, and III

Area

Large indoor playing space such as a gymnasium

Equipment

Mats; jump ropes, cones, hula hoops, and other objects for creating an obstacle course; microphone (optional); the *Rocky* soundtrack

Objectives

Students will learn the value of working hard to overcome adversity as well as how physical activity can be fun.

Setup and Description

Set out numerous objects all over the gym in a challenging yet fun obstacle course. Design the course with the abilities and skill levels of the class in mind. Make sure that you anticipate any dangerous spots on the course and reinforce those areas with mats.

Explain to the class that you are looking for competitors who want to be the next Rocky. (You may have to tell the students who Rocky is.) Tell them that the activity is good for the heart and that you want to see them try their hardest. Also tell them that all you are asking is for them to do their best and that this is not a race.

The object of the game is to complete the course using correct technique for the different skills. Go over the layout of the course with the class before you start the activity, and make note of the fact that there is enough equipment in each section so that two people can easily go through the sections at the same time.

Have the students get in line and start in groups of two. Announce students individually on the microphone (if you have one) in order to motivate them even more. Allow 20 seconds after the pair has begun before announcing the next contestants. Have fun and the students will work hard. Feel free to readjust areas of the course if they are too difficult for the class or too dangerous to complete.

Modifications

The obstacle courses are limited only by your imagination and the skill level of the students. Let your imagination fly, but remember to keep it safe!

Plastic Bag Toss

Level
II

Area
Large playing space such as a gymnasium

Equipment
Plastic grocery bag for every two students

Objectives
Students will improve or maintain their cardiovascular health by running and catching plastic bags thrown in the air.

Setup and Description
Using creative division methods, divide the class into two equal groups and have the groups form two lines facing each other. The students partner up with the person directly across from them. Give a plastic grocery bag to each student in the first line. On your signal, each student with a bag throws it in the air, trying to get the most hang time. The students in the other line run to catch their partner's bag before it hits the ground. Meanwhile, the throwers run to the other side and become the catch-

⚠ SAFETY NOTE

It's best to have the students run past their partner on a specific side to make sure that they do not run into each other. For example, tell the students to pass each other on their partner's right side.

ers for the next round. Move the lines one step farther back each time and see how far they can run before the bag hits the ground.

Modifications

Give each person a bag, which means that each partner will throw and catch at the same time. This activity allows partners to progress at their own rate. If they catch the bags successfully, they keep moving farther apart; if not, allow the partners to remain closer together.

Pumpkins in the Haystack

Level
I

Area
Large playing space such as a gymnasium

Equipment

6 large collapsible tumbling mats; different colored paper pumpkin for each student

Objectives

Students will elevate their heart rate for cardiovascular health while enjoying a Halloween activity.

Setup and Description

Place the mats upright, slightly flexed at the seams, so that they are standing on their sides. Someone should be able to stand behind the mats when set up properly. Place about six mats around the room. There should be enough distance between the mats so that the students can run between and around them. Hand out the pumpkins to the students.

Designate one color as It. All other students hide behind a haystack (mat). The game begins when you call out one of the colors. Students with that color of pumpkin must move from one haystack to another without being tagged by one of the children designated as It. Students can travel anywhere in the gym. Be sure to give all colors a chance to be It.

All students must stay on their feet and not knock over the mats. When children knock over a mat or slide on the floor, they must perform 10 push-ups or sit-ups. Similarly, when they are tagged, they must do 10 repetitions of a designated exercise and then enter the game again.

Modifications

- If you are in a small space or the room has several obstacles in it, you can use different objects as haystacks and only have a few students participate at a time. Other students can help call out colors.
- Play Halloween music for an added effect.
- You can modify this game to fit other holidays.

Pyramid Relay

Level
I, II, and III

Area
Large playing space such as a gymnasium

Equipment

4 volleyballs per group; as many as 8 cones to adequately mark the playing area (if lines are not already marked on the floor)

Objectives

Students will increase cardiovascular endurance and work on sprinting while carrying objects.

Setup and Description

The playing area should be a large rectangle with lines or cones marking the ends or baselines of the area. These lines mark the beginning and ending of the race area. At one baseline, stack volleyballs in a pyramid with three on the bottom and one on top. Break the class into groups of four using creative division methods. Each group lines up on the baseline at one end of the playing area in line with a stack of volleyballs.

At the command of "Go," the first person in each group sprints down, grabs one ball, sprints back, and hands it off to the next person who, while holding the first ball, runs down, picks up another ball, and runs back to hand off two balls to the third person. The third person, while holding the first two balls, runs down, grabs the third ball, and hands off the three balls to the last person. The last person runs down to the other end while holding on to the three balls, grabs the last ball, and then runs back to hand off the four balls to the next person.

That person runs down with all the balls, drops one ball, and sprints back to hand off the other three balls. The next person runs down and drops one more ball. This continues until the last person runs down with one ball. That person has to set the pyramid back up and sprint back to sit down with their team. If the pyramid falls down, the team has to fix it.

Modifications

If children's hands are too small and arms aren't long enough to hold four balls, provide large plastic bags for them to carry the balls in.

Red and White

Level
II and III

Area
Large playing space such as a gymnasium

Equipment

As many as 8 cones to adequately mark the playing area (if lines are not already marked in the space)

Objectives

Students will enhance or maintain their cardiovascular system.

Setup and Description

The playing area should have a center line and two end lines at opposite ends of the floor that are the safety zones (use cones to mark the lines if necessary). Separate the class into two teams using creative division methods. One team is the red team and the other is the white team.

To start the game, each team lines up on their side of the playing area within 3 feet (1 meter) of the designated center line. The teams are facing each other. When you yell "Red!," the red team retreats as fast as they can to their designated safety zone, which is behind them. The white team tries to tag as many of the red team as possible. If caught, the players must switch sides. When every player has either been caught or made it to the safety zone, the activity starts over.

Modifications

Have the students complete a variety of locomotor movements when retreating to their safety zone.

Relay Race

Level
I, II, and **III**

Area
Large playing space such as a gymnasium

Equipment
8 to 10 cones, or enough to adequately mark the playing area

Objectives
Students will compete against one another while raising their heart rate to maintain or improve cardiovascular endurance.

Setup and Description

Relay races are as old as the hills, but they never fail to create excitement. There are as many types of relays as there are teachers; relays are limited only by your imagination. Numerous pieces of equipment can be used in relays and students can compete with various locomotor skills. When developing relays, let your imagination run wild!

In this particular relay, use creative division methods to split the class into teams of four, five, or six (each team should have the same number of students). Each team lines up single file at one end of the room. Place one cone next to each team, marking the beginning spot, and one cone at the other end of the gym, marking the end of the race area.

At the command of "Go," the first student in each line runs to the other end of the room, around the cone, and back. When she arrives back at the beginning, she tags the next person in line to run the same race. When the students have completed the run, they sit down so that everyone knows who gets done first. Continue until all team members have run the race.

Modifications

Have students jump rope while running to the end and back, dribble basketballs, or perform various locomotor movements. Challenge the students' abilities and skills.

Run the Gauntlet

Level
I and II

Area
Large playing space such as a gymnasium

Equipment
Jump ropes, cones, hula hoops, and other objects for creating an obstacle course

Objectives
Students will increase their cardiovascular endurance while working on a number of locomotor skills.

Setup and Description
Set up a pathway or obstacle course. Make sure to incorporate a number of different skills. For example, you can set up hula hoops and have students hopscotch through the hoops. Then make an imaginary pond by laying jump ropes on the ground and make your students hop over the pond. Next, set up cones in a zigzag pattern and tell students to run in between the cones. Then tell the students to skip to the next cone, where there is a hula hoop about 5 feet (1.5 meters) away. The students have to jump from the cone into the hula hoop and then run to a pile of jump ropes, where they have to jump rope 15 times.

Modifications
You are the best person to analyze your students' skill levels, so set up the obstacle course to focus on students' needs. If they are weak in jumping skills, for example, then develop parts of the course that focus on jumping skills. Challenge your students!

Shadow Tag

Level
II and III

Area
This activity can be played in a gym, multipurpose room, or outside

Equipment
If lines are marked on the playing area, no equipment is needed; if no lines exist, 4 cones will be needed to mark the court; pinnies (optional)

Objectives
Students will practice their running, fleeing, chasing, and dodging skills as they practice a variety of locomotor movements.

Setup and Description
Choose one player to be the shadow chaser. The shadow chaser steps on the other players' shadows to make a tag. Players who are tagged become It as well. The same process continues until all the players have had their shadow stepped on. Because confusion may result, it may be a good idea to give the It players colored shirts or pinnies to distinguish them from the untagged players.

Modifications
Players may be required to tag another shadow with their nondominant foot or hand. If desired, when a person is It, you could give them a ball that bounces and have them tag other shadows with the bouncing ball instead of the foot.

Sharks and Minnows

Level
I

Area
Large playing space such as a gymnasium

Equipment
None

Objectives
Students will improve cardiovascular fitness while performing specific locomotor movements.

Setup and Description
This is a tag game where the majority of the students are classified as minnows and a select few (about 5 students out of 30) are sharks. Choose the sharks yourself, rotating players when a new game begins. The minnows move around in one area while performing specific locomotor movements like walking, running, skipping, hopping, jumping, and galloping. The sharks line up in the middle of the gym, and on your signal, the minnows try to run from one end of the court to the other without being tagged. When they safely reach the other end, the minnows wait for the command to begin again. When minnows get tagged, they become sharks and help tag others.

Modifications

Students could line up at opposite ends of the room and the tag game becomes a one-on-one chase game. The shark at the front of the line runs out and tries to tag the first minnow in line while the minnow is trying to get to the other end of the floor. The tagged minnow becomes a shark and goes to the end of the shark line and the shark assumes the role of the minnow. After playing the game for a while, send out more than one shark at a time.

Squirrels in the Trees

Level
II and III

Area
Large playing space such as a gymnasium

Equipment
None

Objectives
Students will work together while competing in a chasing and fleeing game.

Setup and Description

Using creative division methods, break the class into groups of three with the exception of one student. The first two students in each group join hands, representing a hollow tree, while the third student stands between them, representing a squirrel. The student who isn't part of a group is a squirrel without a home and stands in the middle of the floor. At your signal, all the squirrels must change trees. The homeless squirrel attempts to get a tree during the change. Trees should spread out over a large area if possible. After a short period, squirrels and trees change positions.

Modifications

Have more squirrels and fewer trees. When squirrels are not in a tree, they go to the side of the playing area, complete a designated number of exercises, and start playing the game again.

Streets and Alleys

Level
II and III

Area
Large playing space such as a gymnasium

Equipment
None

Objectives
Students will develop strategies in a fleeing and chasing game and will make directional changes upon command.

Setup and Description

All students are set up in a pattern shown in the streets mode (see figure *a*). Students should stand next to each other in rows and gently raise their arms. When all students' arms are extended, they should move sideways away from each other so that only their fingertips touch the fingertips of the person on each side of them. Then, upon your command, everyone turns to the right or left. This is the alleys position (see figure *b*). To get the correct distance from each other, they follow the same procedure.

Choose one student to be the runner (R) and another to be the chaser (C). The runner and chaser must run through the open spaces. When the streets turn into alleys, the runner and chaser will have to run in a different direction. Call out first one (e.g., streets) and then the other (e.g., alleys) to make it difficult for the chaser to catch the runner. When the runner is caught, both runner and chaser join the lines in place of two other children chosen by you.

Modifications

- Have more than one game going on at once to get more children in a highly active mode.
- If only one game is going on at once, you could use pinnies in order to have more than one chaser and runner.

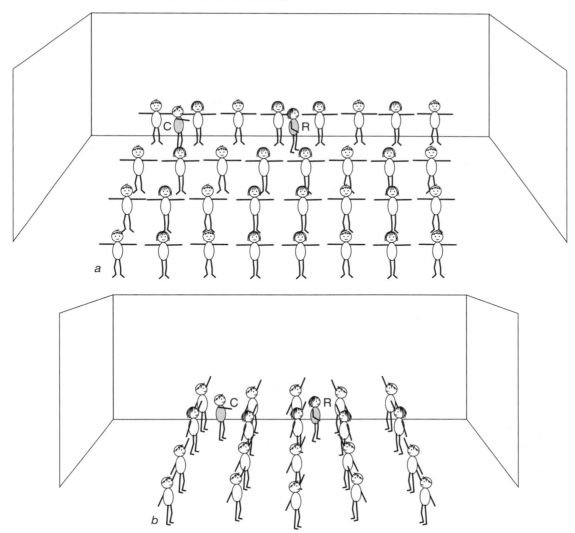

Stuck in the Mud

Level
II and III

Area
Large playing space such as a gymnasium

Equipment
Enough pinnies or colored shirts for half of the class

Objectives
Students will work together as a team to accomplish the goal of tagging all members of the other team.

Setup and Description
Using creative division methods, divide the class into two teams. Give one of the teams the colored shirts. On your command of "Go," the teams try to tag all the members on the other team. When students are tagged, they are "stuck in the mud" and must stand still with their hand in the air. To get out of the mud and begin playing again, another person from the same team must run by and give the stuck student a high five.

Modifications
- Using creative division methods, break the class into multiple sets of ball-throwing partners and tagging partners. Standing and facing each other approximately 6 feet (2 meters) apart, partners toss a fluff ball underhanded to each other. At the same time, two other students are playing tag. To escape from the tagger, runners can approach the partners and try to catch the fluff ball. If the runner succeeds, the student who did not catch the intended pass becomes the new target of the tagger and the runner begins playing catch with the student who threw the ball.
- Instead of high fives, have the children say thank you or do something else that frees them from the mud.

Touchdown

Level
II and III

Area
Large playing space such as a gymnasium

Equipment
2 small objects that can be hidden in the hands; approximately 8 to 10 cones to mark the boundaries if no lines are available

Objectives
Students will combine cardiovascular activity with teamwork and strategies.

Setup and Description
The playing area should be marked with two parallel lines about 60 feet (18 meters) apart. Break the class into two teams using creative division methods.

Each team stands on one of the parallel lines so that the teams face each other. One team huddles and decides which two players will carry the two objects to the opponent's goal line. The team moves out of the huddle and lines up like a football team or just spreads out on the starting line.

On your signal, the players run toward the opposing team's goal line with all players holding their hands closed as if carrying one of the objects. On the same signal, the opponents also run forward and tag as many of the opposing players as possible. When tagged, players must stop and open both hands to show whether or not they have the object. If the player carrying the object reaches the goal line without being tagged, she yells, "Touchdown!" and scores a point for her team. If the player carrying the object is tagged, she gives the object to you, and the other team tries to score using the same procedure.

Modifications

• • Offer more than two objects to carry, depending on the size of the class.

• • Change the locomotion movement—have them skip, hop, jump, and so on instead of running.

Turkey Tag

Level
I and II

Area
Large playing space such as a gymnasium

Equipment
2 large feathers roughly 6 to 10 inches (15-25 centimeters) long; big sheet of butcher paper with the words "I am thankful for . . ." written at the top and enough crayons so that children won't have to wait to use one; 8 to 10 cones, or enough to effectively mark the playing area

Objectives
Students will enjoy Thanksgiving in a new way while working on cardiovascular fitness and expressing their thankfulness.

Setup and Description
Use the cones to mark out a large rectangular area where the game will be played. The area can be as large as 40 by 60 feet (12 by 18 meters) for the younger children. Place the butcher paper and the crayons on the floor away from the game. If you are in a gym, have the students line up on the sideline of the basketball court. If not, have the students line up in a straight line.

Choose two people to be the turkeys and give each turkey one of the large feathers. All students go inside the rectangle and the game begins. The turkeys try to tag the other students with the feathers. If the students are tagged, they have to go to the side of the room and write down one thing that they are thankful for on the butcher paper. If the students cannot spell the word they're thinking of, have them draw a picture instead. Once students finish writing what they're thankful for, they go back into the game. After a while, switch the turkeys.

Modifications

• • Change the locomotor activity—for example, students skip instead of run.

• • Change the number of turkeys.

• • Hang the butcher paper on the wall so that students don't have to sit down to write on the paper.

Ultimate Frisbee (Modified)

Level
III

Area
Large playing space such as a gymnasium or field

Equipment
Frisbee; enough pinnies for half of the class

Objectives
Students will stay active for a long period of time, work together as a team, learn how to throw a Frisbee to a moving target accurately, and follow directions.

Setup and Description
Before you play this game, make sure students already know how to throw and catch a Frisbee while in a stationary position. Split the class into two large groups using creative division methods and give one team pinnies or colored shirts. The game begins when the team without the pinnies throws the Frisbee to the other team. The person who catches the Frisbee can take no more than three steps before throwing the Frisbee to a teammate. In order to retain possession, a team must successfully throw and catch the Frisbee without letting it hit the ground. The team keeps passing the Frisbee in an attempt to get the Frisbee to the other end of the field.

At the same time, the other team tries to intercept the Frisbee or block a pass. If the team in possession of the Frisbee drops a pass, the Frisbee goes to the other team at the point where it was dropped. If the Frisbee goes out of bounds, it goes to the other team wherever it went out of bounds. All players are free to move wherever and however they want if they do not have the Frisbee, but once they get possession of the Frisbee they can only take three steps in any direction. The Frisbee must be thrown over the goal line and caught for a point to be scored. This game can go until one team scores a certain number of goals.

Modifications
The great thing about this game is that almost anyone with any level of skill can play it. To modify the game for players with lower skill levels, make the playing field smaller or use a smaller Frisbee.

Chapter 3

Flexibility Activities

Flexibility refers to the range of motion of a given joint or body part. Many physical activities demand a specific range of motion, and sometimes people cannot participate or improve their skills in them due to a lack of flexibility. Not only should we focus on improving flexibility in various joints, but once flexibility has been developed we should also focus on maintaining it.

Some people believe that unless they're performing specific exercises for a specific joint, then they're not enhancing their flexibility. This is not necessarily true. We can maintain and even improve joint flexibility by participating in an exercise or activity program. The following activities focus on improving flexibility through specific exercises as well as maintaining flexibility through various forms of movement.

The key to appropriate activity selection is choosing activities based on the abilities of the students in the class. The levels listed for the activities in this chapter are merely recommendations; you must use discretion in choosing activities according to your students' abilities. In general, level I activities are appropriate for kindergarten and grade 1; level II activities are appropriate for grades 2 through 3; and level III activities are appropriate for grades 4, 5, and 6.

Back Bends

Level
II and III

Area
Large playing space such as a gymnasium

Equipment
Tumbling mats

Objectives
Students will learn how to safely execute a back bend while understanding how flexibility relates to doing a back bend with ease.

⚠ SAFETY NOTE

When dealing with gymnastics, safety is of the utmost concern. A back bend can be potentially dangerous if done incorrectly. Ask a student who takes gymnastics to come to the front of the class and do the back bend. After the student does a back bend, break down the skill for safety purposes. Have beginners do the modified back bend first, or a bridge. This is done by having students lie on their backs and bend their knees with their feet flat on the floor. They then take their hands and place them on the floor next to their ears. As the teacher gently lifts and spots each student at the low back, students push up their bodies by pressing down on their hands and feet.

Setup and Description
Explain the importance of the back and how it bends. Discuss how the initial bend of the back bend takes place in the shoulders, not in the lower back. Also teach the class to lead with the arms, not the head. If both of these things are done correctly, the rest of the back should bend in a safe manner. Tell the students that the more flexible the back, the better the back bend.

Have the students start from a standing position rather than from the floor. Then tell them that you want them to do five back bends. Make sure that you are in full view of the entire class; even after telling the class what to do there will still be students who didn't listen.

Modifications
To begin the activity, have students do back bends from a starting position of lying on the floor.

Body Alphabet

Level
I, II, and III

Area
Large playing space such as a gymnasium

Equipment
None

Objectives
Students will increase their flexibility, practice the alphabet, and work with others.

Setup and Description
Break the class into groups of four using creative division methods. Give every group a letter that the students must try to make with their bodies. The students can be either standing or lying on the floor. Have the students try to guess what letters the other groups are making.

Modifications

- • If the students are young and do not know the alphabet very well, put the letters on a card or poster to remind them what the letters look like.

- • Change the focus of the activity and have the students make shapes with their bodies that represent flowers, trees, rocks, or even states or nations.

- • If students with disabilities are unable to participate, have them try to guess first what letter each of the groups are making.

Circuit Stretching

Level
I and II

Area
Large playing space such as a gymnasium

Equipment
None

Objectives
Students will work on flexibility as well as cardiovascular endurance.

Setup and Description
A circuit could be defined as somewhere where many items come together to form a basic, functioning unit. In this case, a variety of stretches come together to improve flexibility. Have the students spread out. Call out a locomotor movement that students must perform. After the students have been performing the skill for a while, call out "Circuit!" and demonstrate a stretch. The students should then stop and perform the stretch. After holding the stretch for approximately 15 seconds, continue by calling out another locomotor skill.

Modifications
This activity could be incorporated into a warm-up to get the students ready for a vigorous activity.

Cold Stretch

Level
II and III

Area
Large playing space such as a gymnasium

Equipment
Piece of cold taffy candy or Tootsie Roll for each student

Objectives
Students will learn the importance of warming up muscles before stretching them.

Setup and Description
Refrigerate the candy before class and then give each student a piece of cold candy. Ask the students to try to stretch the taffy. They won't be able to because it is cold. Next have the students move around holding the piece of taffy in their hand or putting it in their pocket. After moving for about five minutes, ask them to stretch the taffy. Now that the candy is warm it is easier to stretch. Explain that this is the same principle for appropriately stretching their muscles. That is why they move first when they come to physical education class.

Modifications
Use this activity during a sit and reach fitness test. Show them how much better their scores are after warming up and stretching first.

Crab Walk

Level
II and III

Area
Large playing space such as a gymnasium

Equipment
None

Objectives
Students will work on flexibility and strength of the shoulders, quadriceps, and back while learning new movements.

Setup and Description
Students squat down and reach back with their arms, putting both hands on the floor without sitting down. With the head, neck, and body level, students should walk forward, backward, and sideways. Make sure that students' hips do not sag to the floor; the body needs to stay level.

SAFETY NOTE
⚠ *For most children, this is a difficult task and they will tire quickly. Start with short periods of time and work up to longer periods.*

Modifications
Once students are able to do the crab walk for longer periods of time without tiring, have them play tag while crab walking.

Dice Stretching Stations

Level
I and II

Area
Large playing space such as a gymnasium

Equipment
Note card for each station; 3 dice for each station; relaxing music that would be soothing to the mind and body

Objectives
Students will improve their flexibility while working on math skills and working as a team to complete a task.

Setup and Description
Determine how many stretching stations are appropriate for the class size; there should be one station per group of students and groups should have no more than five people. Come up with a different stretching exercise for each station, write the exercises on note cards, and place one note card at each station.

Break the class into the same number of groups as stations using creative division methods and send each group to a station. Each group rolls three dice and performs the stretch that is listed at that station for the number of seconds that the dice add up to. The group then moves to a different station after completing the stretch for the appropriate length of time.

Modifications
- If some students might have difficulty with the stretches, post modified versions at each station. Partner those students with another student who will help them accomplish the stretch.
- If the class is older, have them use more dice, or use an arithmetic function (5 + 6 = 11, 5 − 2 = 3, and so on) to determine the number of seconds they must hold the stretch.

Elephant Walk

Level
I

Area
Large playing space such as a gymnasium

Equipment
None

Objectives
Students will work on flexibility while acting like an animal.

Setup and Description
Have students find their own personal space. They should bend forward at the waist, clasping the hands together to form a trunk. The end of the trunk should

swing close to the ground. Students should walk in a slow, deliberate, dignified manner, keeping the legs straight and swinging the trunk from side to side. They can stop and throw water over their back with the trunk.

Modifications

You could add music to this activity. "Baby Elephant Walk" by Henry Mancini would be a nice treat for younger children.

Exercise Band Exploration

Level
II and III

Area
Large playing space such as a gymnasium

Equipment

Dyna-Band or other resistance band (see appendix) for each student (match band resistance to each student's capabilities)

Objectives

Students will show that they can use Dyna-Bands appropriately and safely to work on flexibility.

SAFETY NOTE

*E*mphasize that there should be no horseplay when using the bands, in particular snapping them at others!

Setup and Description

Give all students a Dyna-Band and then have them find their own personal space. With the bands, they can do all types of stretching and strengthening. The students can stretch out the muscles of the legs, arms, and chest. This is a great exercise for many students with disabilities.

Modifications

Have the students stretch their bands in beat to music.

Fitness Foursquare

Level
II and III

Area
Large playing space with foursquare courts if possible

Equipment

Foursquare court for every four or five students and plastic floor tape; playground ball for each court; die for each court; piece of paper and pencil for each court or dry-erase board and marker

Objectives

Students will incorporate fitness into the game of foursquare by performing a variety of exercises.

Setup and Description

The foursquare courts can be any size to meet the needs of the class, but they usually consist of one big square divided into four 3-by-3 foot (1-by-1 meter) squares. If you don't have access to such courts, you can tape them off on the floor. Have students suggest six fitness strengthening exercises such as sit-ups, push-ups, squat thrusts, and so on. Number the exercises and write them on the dry-erase board or have students write them on the paper at their court. Review foursquare rules.

Foursquare is a classic game of pushing a ball into one of the four squares on the court. In doing so, each player is trying to hit a shot into another person's square so that the person cannot return it. After the serve, play continues until someone makes a pass to another person's square that the person cannot return.

Before each serve, the student in the head square (identified by you) rolls the die. The students in all the squares must perform the exercise from the list that corresponds with the number on the die. Once these exercises are completed, the server may serve. When someone is out, that student rotates to the next square. If there are five students per court, the student in line enters the court and the die is rolled again. All students, even those who are momentarily out of the game, should complete the exercises.

Modifications

For students with disabilities, make the squares wider and the ball larger in order to increase the success rate.

Flexibility Stations

Level
I and II

Area
Large playing space such as a gymnasium

Equipment
Cone and piece of paper for each station; stopwatch; tape

Objectives
Students will stay moving while working on various components of flexibility.

Setup and Description

Set up cones in a large circle. Tape a piece of paper to each cone after writing on the paper the activity to be performed at that particular station. Use creative division methods to split the class into as many groups as you have stations and start each group at a different station. Demonstrate the movements for the students for clarity and precision of performance.

At your signal, each group performs the flexibility activity listed at their station for 30 seconds. When you give the signal again, they get up and move clockwise to the next station.

The exercises for the stations are limitless. Use your imagination. Some examples include the following:

- • Front lunges
- • Side lunges

- • Little circles
- • Big circles
- • Toe touches (stand up with feet a little farther than shoulder-width apart and arms straight out to the side, then bend at the waist with legs straight and touch the left toe with the right hand and then alternate with left hand to right toe)
- • Push-up walks (stand up with legs straight, bend down, and touch the ground in front of the toes; then walk the hands down until in the push-up position, do a push-up, and then walk the feet all the way up to the hands, and repeat)

Modifications

Offer modified activities or additional help to students who have trouble with the movements so they can stay with their group. For example, students in wheelchairs may need help moving to each station if they cannot push themselves, and students who are sight impaired may need help moving from station to station.

Forward Rolls

Level
II and III

Area
Large playing space such as a gymnasium

Equipment
Tumbling mats

Objectives
Students will learn about the importance of flexibility to movements in life such as the forward roll.

SAFETY NOTE

Forward rolls can be dangerous if the head is not supported correctly throughout the roll. Emphasize that students should tuck the chin to the chest and should not land the body weight on the head or neck.

Setup and Description

The forward roll, or somersault, is important for flexibility, and flexibility is required to do a perfect roll. Have the class sit down and watch a demonstration before they try to do a forward roll.

Students start from a standing position and then squat with bent knees and flexed ankles and hips. The hands are the first part of the body that should touch the ground. Students place their hands on the floor next to the feet, tuck the chin to the chest, push off with the toes, and roll forward to get the body through the roll, pushing off with their hands to bring the rest of the body around. When done correctly, the body will roll all the way up to a standing position.

Either you or a talented student must demonstrate this movement. Show the students how to spot their partner properly and pair up each child in the class with someone of equal size.

Modifications

Have students perform forward rolls side by side, two, three, or four people at a time.

Hoop Travel

Level

II and III

Area

Large playing space such as a gymnasium

Equipment

1 or 2 hula hoops per group

Objectives

Students will learn to work together and will use shoulder and hip flexibility.

Setup and Description

Students form a circle with hands connected. One person breaks hands, puts a hula hoop over their shoulders, then grasps hands again so that the hoop now rests on the arms of the joined hands. Next the students try to pass the hula hoop around the whole circle without breaking hands by getting it over their head, around their lower body, and onto the next person. To accomplish this, students may toss the hoop over their head first and then slide it down over their body to the next person or step through the hoop first and then pass it over their head to the next person.

After they have practiced this, add another hula hoop directly across from the person with the first hoop. Both halves of the circle are now racing to get their hula hoop to the other side of the circle. Both hoops should be going in a clockwise direction. The first team whose hula hoop reaches the opposite side wins!

Modifications

● ● Have some students face the inside of the circle and some face the outside of the circle.

● ● Increase the number of hoops. You can have as many hoops in the circle as you have people. Students should try not to let the hoops pile up on them.

Human Chain

Level
II and III

Area
Large playing space such as a gymnasium

Equipment
10 to 20 tennis balls

Objectives
Students will increase their flexibility and work cooperatively.

Setup and Description
Break the class into groups of seven using creative division methods. Have them line up side by side with a little room in between. The last person in the line should be standing on the sideline, or home line, of the gym. Scatter the tennis balls about 8 to 15 feet (2.5 to 4.5 meters) from the end of the lines.

On your signal, each group must work cooperatively to stretch out and make the chain longer while the end person keeps at least one foot on the home line. The person on the front of the line picks up a ball, takes it to the home line, and goes to the end of the line. Each line tries to collect as many balls as possible.

Modifications
Start with smaller groups of three or four and then gradually increase the size of the groups as they become more successful. Eventually have the entire class working to accomplish the task, all working and stretching as one.

Limbo

Level
I, II, and III

Area
Large playing space such as a gymnasium

Equipment
Broomstick or other long stick for each group; tumbling mats; Caribbean music

Objectives
Students will participate in a challenging activity while working on lower back and hip flexibility.

Setup and Description
Break the class into several groups (no more than six per group if possible so that no one will have to wait long for a turn) using creative division methods. In each group, two students hold either end of a broomstick at chest height. Mats should be placed under the broomstick. Start the music and have students go under the stick one at a time by leaning backward. Anyone who touches a knee, elbow, hand, or other body part to the floor is out. After each child has gone through once, the students holding the stick lower it a few inches. The game continues until only one student is left.

The first two students who are out trade places with the two students holding the stick. That prevents eliminated students from sitting on the sidelines and it gives everyone a chance to go under the stick. Remember to begin new activities quickly so that no one remains out for long.

Modifications

- Use ropes instead of sticks.
- Depending on the length of the stick or rope, have two or more students go under it at the same time.

Line Up, Stretch Out

Level
I, II, and III

Area
Large playing space such as a gymnasium

Equipment
None

Objectives
Students will line up at the door at the end of class in an orderly fashion while demonstrating their knowledge of movement concepts, bones, muscles, and fitness components.

Setup and Description
As a closure activity at the end of class, have students freeze and perform a muscle stretch of their choice. Then direct the students to line up near the door in an orderly fashion as they get ready to leave the classroom. You can have them line up according to the following directions, or you can make up your own directions depending on the activity you choose for them to do at the end:

- Line up if you are stretching your biceps.
- Line up if you are stretching your quadriceps.
- Line up if you are doing a stretch involving the low back.
- Line up if you are stretching at a low level.
- Line up if you are stretching your body in a twisted shape like a pretzel.
- Line up if you are stretching at a high level.
- Line up if you are stretching your triceps.

Modifications

- If students are having trouble responding correctly, keep the list of directions shorter. Students respond more efficiently if the directions are clear and concise.
- Include cardiovascular activities or other activities on the list.

Muscle Stretch

Level
II and III

Area
Large playing space such as a gymnasium

Equipment
Tumbling mats

Objectives
Students will practice stretching their muscles.

Setup and Description
This makes a good warm-up or cool-down activity. Use a creative group division technique to get the students into pairs. Instruct students to find a spot on a mat and wait for instructions. Then discuss the basic muscles as follows and demonstrate the stretches:

- • Quadriceps—Holding onto a partner's shoulder in a standing position, flex your knee and grab the foot behind you with the same hand (i.e., right hand to the right foot). Pull the heel toward the buttocks and hold.
- • Chest, shoulders, and biceps—Lift your arms slightly up and back behind you. Your partner should grab your wrists and gently stretch these major muscle groups.
- • Triceps—Lift your right arm above your head, grab the right elbow with your left hand, and slightly pull down.
- • Gastrocnemius—Lean forward against a wall with both hands, keeping one or both heels on the ground. You can stretch both calf muscles at the same time or alternate one at a time.
- • Hamstrings—Sit on the floor with both feet together and legs straight. Reach out and touch your knees with your hands while your legs remain straight. Slowly move down to touch your calves, ankles, toes, and beyond.

Show the students what to do and have them copy you. Then quiz them by just telling them the muscle to stretch.

SAFETY NOTE

Stretching all of the major muscle groups is important to lifelong fitness and wellness. In order to prevent injuries, basic fundamentals of stretching must be adhered to. For example, stretch slowly to the point of mild discomfort and hold it there for 15 seconds.

Modifications
Have students do stretches to relaxing music.

Partner Hop Stretch

Level
   III

Area
   Large playing space such as a gymnasium

Equipment
   None

Objectives
   Students will demonstrate that they can use teamwork to accomplish a goal while increasing their flexibility.

Setup and Description
   Students pair off using creative division methods. Partners should face each other. Both lift up their right leg and their partner grabs it at the ankle with their left hand. Now both are standing on one leg (left). In this position they can slowly hop on the left leg while stretching out the hamstring. Students should let go of each other's ankles if one or both begin to fall. Make sure both legs get stretched, and monitor this activity carefully for safety.

⚠ **SAFETY NOTE**
   This is a potentially dangerous activity. It should never be done as a race or competition.

Modifications
   Instead of hopping, students simply stand and get a good stretch.

Partner Stretching

Level
   II and III

Area
   Large playing space such as a gymnasium

Equipment
   None

Objectives
   Students will demonstrate that they can work together and appreciate the concept of teamwork while improving their flexibility.

Setup and Description
   Students pair off using creative division methods; they should be in same-gender pairs. One student lies supine (on their back) on the ground. The partner stands next to the student on the ground, takes the right leg, slowly pushes it back until a slight resistance is felt in the hamstring, and holds it for 15 seconds. Then switch to the other leg. In order to prevent injury, partners should be in complete communication with each other during this process.

SAFETY NOTE

Make sure the students understand that this type of stretching is different from individual stretching. Having a partner help you stretch adds a potentially dangerous outside force to the stretch that wasn't involved in individual stretches and they must be careful.

Next, the partner takes the student's right leg, pushes the knee up to the abdomen, and holds the stretch for 15 seconds. Then switch to the other leg. After completing both stretches, the students switch places.

Modifications

Types of stretches are limited only by safety and your imagination. Focus on stretching all of the major muscle groups. Other stretches could include the following:

- Sitting in a straddle facing each other, students reach out and grab their partner's hands and *slowly* stretch each other by alternately leaning backward.
- Students sit next to their partner's extended legs, grasp their partner's toes and ball of the foot, and *slowly* pull the ball of the foot toward the knee.
- One student stands behind the other. The student in back grasps the wrists of the person in front and *slowly* pulls the arms back and up to stretch the shoulders.

Pretzels

Level
I, II, and III

Area
Large playing space such as a gymnasium

Equipment
Customized spinner from a board game; colored or numbered circles that match the spinner; plastic floor tape

Objectives
Students will increase their flexibility.

Setup and Description

This activity is similar to the classic board game of Twister. It may work best with a small class or on a day when several students are absent. Make your own spinner or customize one from a board game so that the spinner points to circles to show students where to stand during the activity. Set up several game stations by taping colored or numbered circles on the floor. Make enough stations so that there are no more than five students per station.

Tell students to take off shoes for this activity. Using creative division methods, split the class into groups of five according to gender (i.e., it is better if each station has all boys or all girls). Players start on each side of the playing area. After the spin, each player moves the teacher-designated hand or foot to the correct circle. Play continues as students work on flexibility and balance. When players fall or cannot move to the designated circle, they are out of the game for no more than 4 minutes.

If there are several students, set up several different stations. Remember, the more games on the floor, the more people can participate. You could set up a tournament where the losers at one station play the losers of another station and the same with the winners. You could even make a round-robin tournament if you wish, but be careful not to focus only on the winners. (In a round-robin tournament, each team would compete against every other team, one at a time.) If not all students can participate at once, play the game for five minutes before giving other students an opportunity.

Modifications

If some students are physically unable to participate, they can be the designated spinners.

Shadow Stretching

Level
II and III

Area
Large playing space such as a gymnasium

Equipment
None

Objectives
Students will show appreciation for the importance of flexibility and will demonstrate that they can work together.

Setup and Description
Students pair off using creative division methods. One student starts performing a stretch and the other student mirrors the stretch. Then the students switch.

Modifications
Have the students sit in a large circle with enough space between one another to stretch. One at a time, have each student lead a stretch.

SAFETY NOTE

Remind students that stretching all of the major muscle groups is important. In addition, basic fundamentals of stretching must be adhered to in order to prevent injuries. For example, stretch slowly to the point of mild discomfort and hold the position for 15 seconds.

Simon Says "Stretch"

Level
I and II

Area
Large playing space such as a gymnasium

Equipment
None

Objectives
Students will stretch muscles in legs and arms while playing a fun game.

Setup and Description

Students should stand in their own personal space but stay close enough to hear and follow directions. When you say "Simon says" and a stretch, students should perform the stretch. If you only say the stretch, students should not perform the stretch; if they do, they're out of the game and should do the stretches to the side of the game. Continue until only one person is left in the game.

Examples of stretches are toe touches, spread the feet wide, stretch to the left, stretch an arm across the body, both hands reach toward the ceiling, lunge forward, and so on. The variety of stretches is limited only by your imagination.

Modifications

• • Begin by letting students stay in the game even if they mess up. After they get the hang of it, have them leave the game and do the stretches to the side.

• • Increase the speed or frequency of stretches to make the tasks more challenging.

Sit and Reach

Level
III

Area
Large playing space such as a gymnasium

Equipment
Sit and reach boards or tumbling mats and masking tape

Objectives
Students will measure their flexibility.

Setup and Description

Make sure that the students have warmed up and stretched before you begin. Students place their right foot up against the sit and reach board and bend their left leg so that their left foot touches the inside of the knee of the right leg. Then they place one hand over the other, lean forward, and push the lever on the top of the board. Record their measurements. Students should do this three times and then switch legs.

Modifications

If you do not have sit and reach boards, you can use mats. Mark the mats with tape that has lengths marked on the tape and put the mats on the floor. The lengths should be measured in inches or centimeters. Students slightly straddle the marks and proceed just as with the boards only both feet are stretched out in front of them and so they will only do the stretch three times total.

Valentines for the Heart

Level
I, II, and **III**

Area
Large playing space such as a gymnasium

Equipment
Box of popular children's valentines

Objectives

Students will participate in a fun warm-up activity that creates a positive atmosphere on Valentine's Day and promotes flexibility.

Setup and Description

Before class, write fitness activities on the inside of the valentines. The activities should fall under the categories of flexibility, cardiovascular endurance, and muscular strength and endurance, such as 10 partner sit-ups or 15 jumping jacks.

As the students enter the activity area, tell them you have special valentines for them. Hand the valentines out to the students. Students read the card, perform the fitness activity safely, and then trade cards with another student. Make sure students complete the full range of motion with each of these exercises so the emphasis is on flexibility. Continue the activity as long as you like.

Modifications

Don't limit the number of exercises. The larger the variety, the better the overall flexibility work and warm-up will be. Keep the activities safe, but otherwise the selection is limited only by your imagination.

Veggie Values

Level
I

Area
Open playing space (can be large or small depending on class size)

Equipment
Posters of different vegetables

Objectives
Students will work on their flexibility and balance.

Setup and Description
Show the pictures of vegetables and make sure the students know what the vegetables are. Explain the importance of vegetables as they relate to proper nutrition. After discussing the importance of vegetables, students should spread out into personal space. Then they should pick which vegetable they want to be and try to shape their body into that vegetable. For example, if they choose carrots, they could stretch long and tall on the floor with their hands spreading out above their head like a carrot with the greenery still attached. Two students could get together and form an oblong shape like a potato. Three or more students could get together and form a head of broccoli. Use your imagination!

Modifications
Students unable to get into the necessary positions should help other students instead.

Chapter 4

Balance Activities

According to Pangrazi, "Balance demands that different parts of the body support the weight or receive the weight" (2004, p. 301) while doing a variety of stationary and movement activities. Many times, balance is one of the forgotten parameters of motor development, and leaders of children's activities do not take the time to teach specific activities directed toward improving balance. This approach is dangerous in that if balance is not specifically taught, children's balancing skills do not mature equally. Specific balance activities must be taught to provide equal development opportunities for all children. This chapter's activities are based on that premise.

The key to appropriate activity selection is choosing activities based on the abilities of the students in the class. The levels listed for the activities in this chapter are merely recommendations; you must use discretion in choosing activities according to your students' abilities. In general, level I activities are appropriate for kindergarten and grade 1; level II activities are appropriate for grades 2 through 3; and level III activities are appropriate for grades 4, 5, and 6.

Balance Beam

Level
II and III

Area
Large playing space with lines on the floor such as a gymnasium (mark lines with chalk or tape if necessary)

Equipment
Balance beam that is 6 to 12 inches (15 to 30 centimeters) off the ground; tumbling mats

Objectives
Students will develop their balancing skills.

Setup and Description
Before starting the activity, discuss the easiest way to keep balance. Some hints are to put the hands out to the side and keep the eyes on the end of the beam or line or to tighten the abdominal and gluteal muscles.

Start students off on a line on the gym floor. After successfully completing the task on the floor, move the activity to the balance beam. Students begin slowly walking across the line or beam. If students are having an easy time with this activity, progress to dip steps, where the foot dips down on either side of the beam and touches the bottom of the beam. Students can also perform arabesques, where one leg is straight and the other is raised behind the body while the chest is up. Progress to turning a half-circle (180 degrees) on the beam and facing the opposite direction. Many different activities can be done on the beam. Use your imagination, but keep it safe.

Modifications
After students have practiced several basic skills, they can develop short routines by combining at least four separate movements. These movements should flow into a consistent routine. Students should develop and practice routines on lines on the floor before attempting them on the beam.

Balance Beam Barrage

Level
III

Area
Large playing space with lines on the floor such as a gymnasium (mark lines with chalk or tape if necessary)

Equipment
Balance beam that is 6 inches (15 centimeters) off the ground; small foam balls; tumbling mats

Objectives
Students will increase their static balance and dodge objects while staying in one position.

Setup and Description
In this activity, students stand on a line or balance beam while other students try to hit them with small foam balls. Start the activity on one of the lines on the floor, and after successfully completing the task on the floor, move to the balance beam.

Approximately two-thirds of the class stands on a balance beam in a static position. The other students stand approximately 20 feet (6 meters) from the balance beam and throw the balls *underhand* trying to hit a student on the balance beam. The students on the balance beams are allowed to duck or catch the balls that are thrown at them. If they catch the ball, they must toss it back into play. If they fall off the balance beam, drop an attempted catch, or are hit by a ball, they trade places with the person who threw the ball. Play continues until the teacher stops the action.

⚠ SAFETY NOTE

Balls are not to be thrown overhand. When losing their balance, students on the beam or lines should never grab a person next to them to keep their balance. If students do not want to be on the balance beam or line and have balls thrown at them, that's OK. They should just throw balls the whole time instead.

Modifications
Increase or decrease the distance between balancers and throwers. From larger distances, throws could be overhand.

Balance Beam Relay

Level
I, II, and III

Area
Large playing space such as a gymnasium

Equipment
Low-level balance beams no more than 12 inches (30 centimeters) off the ground (the more beams the better so that more people can stay active); tumbling mats; beanbag for each balance beam

Objectives

Students will improve their static balance.

Setup and Description

Break the class into an appropriate number of teams using creative division methods. Teams should have 10 to 12 members so that there will be 5 or 6 students on each end of the beam. Half of the team lines up at one end of their balance beam and half lines up at the other end. The object of the game is for players to walk across the balance beam one at a time with a beanbag on their head and hand off the beanbag to the teammate waiting at the end of the beam. If the beanbag falls off while walking on the balance beam, students must begin their turn over again. The relay continues until all members of the team have crossed the beam.

⚠ SAFETY NOTE

Be sure to place tumbling mats under the beams in case of falls. Remind students that they shouldn't go too fast and should be careful when walking on the beams.

Modifications

Some students with disabilities may not be able to walk on a balance beam without falling from it. Allow these students to walk next to the beam while balancing the beanbag on a body part that is easier than the head, like the hand.

Balance Shuffle I

Level
II

Area
Large playing space such as a gymnasium

Equipment

Balance beam about 6 inches (15 centimeters) off the ground; plastic floor tape

Objectives

Students will focus on balance while using their peripheral vision and sense of where their body is in relation to another person.

Setup and Description

Pair students up using creative division methods. Mark the ends of the balance beam with one line 12 inches (30 centimeters) from each end. One child stands on one end of the beam and the other at the opposite end. Children start and finish behind the lines at opposite ends.

Each child walks to the center of the beam. When both reach the middle and face each other, they must trade places without falling off. When they switch they travel to the mark on the opposite end of the beam before turning around. In short, each child travels to the opposite end of the beam and back without falling off or touching any body part to the ground.

Modifications

After some of the students have mastered this skill with a single partner, increase the number of people on one board. They complete the same task, only with more people involved.

Balance Shuffle II

Level
II

Area
Large playing space such as a gymnasium

Equipment

Low-level balance beam no more than 12 inches (30 centimeters) off the ground or a 2-by-4-inch (5-by-10-centimeter) board lying on the ground—the more beams the better so that more students can stay active

Objectives

Students will be aware of where their body is in relation to the ground and the students they are going to walk over.

Setup and Description

Position two students in the middle of the beam about 4 feet (1.2 meters) from each other, and position one student at each end of the beam. They can stand on the beam to begin with but may need to squat down. The students at the end of the beam must go to the other end. They must climb over the students bent over on the board and they must get by the other student coming at them. This activity takes tremendous concentration. If at any time students touch the floor, they must start over.

Modifications

Start with just one student in the middle of the board and just one student going from one end to the other, making this a progressive activity.

Balance the Stick

Level
II and III

Area
Large playing space such as a gymnasium

Equipment

Stick approximately 3 feet (1 meter) in length and no more than 1 inch (3 centimeters) in diameter for each student

Objectives

Students will balance a stick with body parts while realizing the importance of balance.

Setup and Description

Have the students find their own personal space on the floor. Students then come up, get their own stick, and return to their personal space. First, they balance the stick on the open palm of their right hand. Then they complete the same task in the left hand. Tell students that if they focus their eyes on the top of the stick instead of their hand, they'll be able to balance it more easily.

Modifications

Once all students can do this activity, make it more challenging:

- • • Have them switch hands by gently tossing the stick up in the air.
- • • Have them balance the stick on a fingertip. Or have them bend an elbow, hold the flexed arm out to the side parallel to the ground, and balance the stick on top of the flexed arm.

Balloon Balance

Level
I, II, and III

Area
Large playing space such as a gymnasium

Equipment

Balloon for each student

Objectives

Students will balance objects with their body and practice spatial awareness.

Setup and Description

This is a good warm-up activity. Give every student a balloon. They should balance the balloon on their head or another body part as they move around the room. Make sure that the students have plenty of room to move around without running into anyone else.

Modifications

To make sure everyone participates, use larger objects (bigger balloons) because not all children will be able to handle the smaller balloons.

Beanbag Balance

Level
I

Area
Large playing space such as a gymnasium

Equipment

Beanbag for each student

Objectives

Students will balance the beanbag on different body parts while performing different movements.

Setup and Description

Give each student a beanbag. Then demonstrate ways of balancing beanbags on different body parts. Have the students spread out and find their own personal space. On your signal, they begin walking while balancing the beanbag in the palm of their hand. While the activity continues, you can call out different body parts to balance the beanbag on, and if the students are really skilled, call out different locomotor movements.

Modifications

Have the students work at different levels (i.e., high, medium, and low) while balancing the beanbag.

Beanbag Line Game

Level
I and II

Area
Large playing space with lines on the floor such as a gymnasium (mark lines with chalk or tape if necessary)

Equipment

Beanbag for each student; music that encourages a fast pace

Objectives

Students will improve their balance.

Setup and Description

Students should each pick a line on the gym floor and then place a beanbag on their head. On your signal, they try to walk on their line while balancing the beanbag on their head. They may only change lines when another line intersects the line they are on. If their beanbag falls off, they must stand still until a classmate comes along, bends down, picks up the beanbag, and places it back on their head. Start and stop the music as needed to start and stop the activity.

Modifications

- If students are unable to walk and balance the beanbag at the same time, they can try sitting while balancing it on their head and thus work up to walking.
- Have the students play tag while balancing beanbags on their heads.

Blind Balance

Level
I and II

Area
Large playing space such as a gymnasium

Equipment

None

Objectives

Students will develop their balancing skills.

Setup and Description

This activity makes a great warm-up for other balancing activities. Have students get into their own personal space. They begin by raising their right leg and trying to balance on the left leg, seeing if they can hold it for five seconds. Then they hold the other leg up and see if they can balance on that leg as well.

Next, the students shut their eyes and balance on one leg, seeing if they can hold this position for five seconds. Then students perform an airplane, where one leg is straight out behind them and their other leg is slightly bent. They lean forward so that the torso is more horizontal and keep their heads up. They also spread their arms out like airplane wings. When their eyes are closed you can also have them touch body parts with their hands.

Modifications

- • • Time the activity. How long can the students stay balanced with their eyes open and their eyes closed?

- • • Have the students balance on wobble boards (see appendix).

- • • If some students have trouble with this activity, let them try it while standing on a thick mat.

Body Shapes

Level
I

Area
Large playing space such as a gymnasium

Equipment
Music that is calming but still encourages movement (optional)

Objectives
Students will improve their balance and be able to differentiate among shapes by making shapes with the body.

Setup and Description
Create a list of shapes for students to make. Examples might be "While sitting on your bottom, make a circle," "While standing on one foot, make a triangle shape with a partner," and "With both feet on the floor, show what a tree looks like on a very windy day." Have students get in their own personal space. Play music in the background while they attempt to make the shapes.

Modifications
Come up with a theme for the day and have students come up with ideas of actions and shapes that follow the theme.

Book Balance Relay

Level

II and III

Area

Large playing space with lines on the floor such as a gymnasium (mark lines with chalk or tape if necessary)

Equipment

3 books for each group of five or six students

Objectives

Students will balance objects on various body parts.

Setup and Description

Break the class into groups of five or six using creative division methods. Have them form straight lines down the long part of the court (lines on the baselines). Pass out books to the first three people in line (having more books allows more people to be active).

First, balancing the book on the top of their head, students must walk all the way to the other end of the gym and back without dropping the book or touching it. When the first person in line gets a designated distance (10 to 15 feet [3 to 4.5 meters]) away from the person in front of them, the next person can start. If the book falls, the student must go back to the beginning and start again. When students successfully make it down and back without dropping the book, they hand the book to the next person in line and go to the end of the line. After all the groups have gone, do the race again with students balancing the book on another body part.

Modifications

• • Allow students to balance larger or smaller objects.

• • Make the relay race shorter so they don't have to walk as far.

Counterbalances

Level
I, II, and III

Area
Large playing space such as a gymnasium

Equipment
Tumbling mat for each group

Objectives
Students will improve static balance while working together as a team.

Setup and Description
In this activity, students will balance in positions that they would not normally be able to maintain without help of others.

Pair the students up by similar body size. Have students attempt these positions:

- Face each other, hold wrists, lean back, and move in a circle.
- Let go of one wrist and lean back, switch to the other wrist, and repeat.
- Sit down and face each other, grab each other's hands, and pull each other to a standing position.
- Lean into each other while standing back to back.
- Sit on an "air chair" while leaning against one another.

Modifications
Divide the students into groups of three and then four, and have them try to accomplish the same goals.

Hopscotch

Level
I, II, and III

Area
Large playing space such as a gymnasium

Equipment
Masking tape, sidewalk chalk, or hula hoops; beanbag for each hopscotch court

Objectives
Students will hop on one foot and keep their balance.

Setup and Description
Create several hopscotch areas with sidewalk chalk (if outdoors) or masking tape or hula hoops (if indoors). If so desired and with permission from the appropriate people, hopscotch courts can be painted on a safe area of the parking lot or on the playground. Try to have no more than four children per court so that there will be less standing around.

Students line up and hop in each square on one foot. The next time, students hop on the other foot in each square. Then give the first person in line a beanbag. Students toss the beanbag in a square, and then on their way through, they hop on one foot in each square except the one with the beanbag in it, pausing and picking up the beanbag without falling down or losing their balance.

Modifications

For added difficulty, have students spin around once when they are going through the course or have them cross their legs in two of the squares.

Hula-Hoop Hug

Level
II and III

Area
Large playing space such as a gymnasium

Equipment

Hula hoop for each group

Objectives

Students will use strategy and teamwork to get their team to stand on only one foot inside a hula hoop.

Setup and Description

Break the class into small groups of eight or nine students using creative division methods. Give each group one hula hoop, which they should place on the ground. At your signal to begin, each group tries to find out how many people they can get standing on one foot inside the hula hoop for as long as possible. Start with two people in the hoop, then three, then four, then five, and so on. The students will find out how hard it is to keep their balance and the balance of those around them as the groups get larger and there is less space inside the hoop.

Modifications

To increase the difficulty, have students hold one person off of the ground in the center of the hula hoop while everyone else stands on one foot. The person standing in the middle bends the arms and holds the elbows tight against their sides. The group can then slightly lift the middle person off the floor by placing their hands under the person's bent elbows.

Line Travel Cooperation

Level
II and III

Area
Large playing space with lines on the floor such as a gymnasium (mark lines with chalk or tape if necessary)

Equipment

None

Objectives

Students will learn how to cooperate with other students and how to keep their balance while moving.

SAFETY NOTE

The key to this activity is for students to keep their balance while working cooperatively to move around each other. Some students may think this is a combative activity, but it's a cooperative activity. Make sure students are safe and do not hurt each other.

Setup and Description

Students will travel along the line markings on the gym floor. When they encounter another person, they have to pass the person by working together. Students are not allowed to step off the line, but they can swing around the other person, squat down and climb over, or use other ways to get to the other side. They should use their imagination but keep it safe.

Modifications

- •• Have students partner up and coach each other around the lines on the floor.
- •• Add an element of tag in which one or two people are It and try to tag the other students, who can walk only on the lines. When one student on a line blocks another, the two must cooperate to get around each other and continue moving before they get tagged.

Palm Push

Level
II and **III**

Area
Large playing space such as a gymnasium

Equipment
None

Objectives
Students will learn techniques to keep their balance in an ever-changing situation.

Setup and Description

Pair the students up by similar body size. They should stand facing each other. Both partners put their hands at shoulder level and extend their arms slightly with elbows slightly flexed. The partners' palms should meet with the fingers pointing to the sky. In a series of pushes and relaxed arm motions, the objective is to get the other player to take a step forward or backward. Hands should stay connected and pushes should be moderate, never causing the other student to fall down. Grabbing the other student's hands is not allowed.

Modifications

- •• Have students do the activity with closed eyes. This will show the students how sight is used to maintain balance. If they start to fall, they should open their eyes.
- •• Change the palm-to-palm connection so that the fingers of the hands are pointing to the ground.

Partner Hopping

Level
II and **III**

Area
Large playing space such as a gymnasium

Equipment

Enough tumbling mats to meet the needs and size of the class; circus music (optional)

Objectives

Students will coordinate hopping movements for short distances and move in different directions.

Setup and Description

This activity involves three progressive balancing combinations that partners perform together. Using creative division methods, divide the class into pairs.

1. Students face each other and extend the right leg forward to be grasped at the ankle by their partner's left hand. Partners hold right hands and hop on the left leg. Music can be the cue for when to stop and start hopping. Teachers should use their discretion when deciding how long to play the music, factoring in the skills of the students.

SAFETY NOTE

In these activities, students could easily fall to the floor. Instruct students that if they begin to fall they are to let go and fall away from their partner. Correct demonstrations and safety instructions are essential.

2. This is a more difficult task. Students stand back to back, lift one leg backward, bend the knee, and have the partner grasp the ankle. Then they hop as before.

3. Students stand side by side with inside arms around each other's waist. They lift the inside foot from the floor and hop on the outside foot. This is similar to the classic three-legged race, but legs are not tied together.

Modifications

- Students run a short relay race while balancing.
- Students travel through a short obstacle course while balancing.
- Students pick up beanbags while balancing.

Push and Pull Pairs

Level
III

Area
Large playing space such as a gymnasium

Equipment
Tumbling mats

Objectives
Students will balance while standing on one leg and while being pushed and pulled.

Setup and Description
Break the class into pairs using creative division methods. The two students stand on the mats on one leg, join right hands, and try to push or pull each other off balance. The student who stays balanced on one leg without falling over or putting the other foot down is the winner. Don't forget to do the activity standing on the other leg and holding left hands. Make sure that there are adequate tumbling mats and that the students are matched up by size and ability. Have the other students surround the mats and make sure that the two engaged in the activity do not fall outside of the mats. You could have up to five groups going at a time, depending on mat space.

SAFETY NOTE

This activity is mildly combative, and safety should be addressed. When students begin to fall, encourage them to let go of the other person's hands so they don't pull their partner on top of them as they fall.

Modifications
- • Have students stand on both legs instead of one.
- • Have students do the activity from a sitting position; the one who best maintains balance wins.

The Snake

Level
I

Area
Large playing space such as a gymnasium

Equipment
10 or more cones to effectively mark the playing area

Objectives
Students will follow pathways while weaving in between cones without bumping into other students or cones.

Setup and Description
Place at least 10 cones 3 feet (1 meter) apart in a line or lines. You can set up as many as five different lines. Ask the students if they have ever seen a snake and

how they move. Demonstrate how snakes weave in and out, and then tell them that today they are going to pretend that they are snakes.

Students line up in groups of five behind one of the rows of cones. The person in front is the head of the snake and everyone behind this student is the body. They must weave in and out of the cones just like the person in front of them. When they reach the end, they should turn around and start moving back the same way, being careful not to bump into another student or cone.

At times during the activity, yell "Stop!" All students should freeze where they are and try to maintain their balance. Some students may be on one foot and others may be on both feet.

After they are able to perform the activity as described, have groups compete against each other to see who can go through the cones without touching a cone or bumping into another student. Next, have the entire class line up and start moving about the gym together as one big snake. Observe to see that the students are moving in and out of the cones while following the person in front of them. Watch to make sure they do not bump into other students or the cones. Finally, ask the students what sports use weaving movements.

Modifications

- • • Have students partner up and help each other through the cones.
- • • Increase the distance between cones so students in wheelchairs can pass through more easily.

Stork Stand Tag

Level
I, II, and **III**

Area
Large playing space such as a gymnasium

Equipment
Two-thirds as many paper plates as there are students in the class

Objectives
Students will learn how to balance on one leg.

Setup and Description

Scatter numerous paper plates all over the floor. Tell the class that they are going to play a kind of tag game that improves balance. Choose one or more students to be It, then explain the rules of the game. Stork stand tag works like most other tag games in that there is a base; however, in this game every plate is a base. When stu-

SAFETY NOTE

⚠ *P*aper plates can slide on the floor, so make sure the students slowly approach the plate and are not running full speed when they try to step on the plate.

dents are on a plate, they must be balancing on one leg. Students can be tagged if they are off the plate or if they're not standing on one leg. If the other leg touches the ground, students must run on to another plate and risk being tagged. If someone is tagged, they trade places with the tagger. This activity helps students practice static balance while increasing cardiovascular endurance as well.

Modifications

• • Halfway through the activity, ask students to start balancing on their other leg instead so they can develop the skill on both sides of their bodies.

• • Use poly spots (which don't slide as much) instead of paper plates.

• • As the game progresses, take away some of the poly spots or paper plates.

Stork Stand Test

Level
III

Area
Large playing space such as a gymnasium

Equipment
Stopwatch

Objectives
Students will test their ability to maintain their balance in a static position.

Setup and Description

Students should stand on both feet and put their hands on their hips or in front of their chests. Then they lift one leg and place the toes of that leg against the inside of the other leg at the knee. On your command, students raise their heel and balance as long as they can while you start the stopwatch. When the heel touches the ground or the leg comes away from the other leg, they're done. When everyone has finished, test the other leg.

Modifications

Have students perform the same task but with their eyes closed.

Toy Story Statues

Level

I and II

Area

Large playing space such as a gymnasium

Equipment

Music, possibly the *Toy Story* soundtrack (optional)

Objectives

Students will practice the skill of freezing and keeping their balance in different shapes.

Setup and Description

Ask students if they've seen the movie *Toy Story*. Discuss the toys that belonged to Andy, the little boy (including Buzz Lightyear the astronaut, Woody the cowboy, Ham the pig, and Mr. Potato Head, among others). Remind them that the toys could move and talk except when a real person could see them.

Explain that they will be moving around like the toy that you call out, but when you say "Andy's coming!", everyone has to freeze in a shape like the toy might make. First, though, they'll need to practice making the shapes. Have students spread out and find their own personal space, and then guide them through the following:

- Make a statue like Buzz might make. How are his arms and legs? Yes, straight. Make a Buzz shape with your body all the way on the floor . . . partly on the floor . . . up in the air.
- How would Woody look? Yes, floppy and loose. How would Woody look all the way on the floor? What about when he's partly on the floor?
- What about Ham? Yes, he would make an angular shape, using all his body parts on the floor.
- What about Mr. Potato Head? Yes, he is a wide shape. How would Mr. Potato Head look if he were all the way on the floor? Standing up?

Once everyone has practiced making the shapes, call out a toy. Challenge students to move around like the toy might move; then call out "Andy's coming!" Students should freeze in a shape the toy might make. Challenge them not to move! When you say "He's gone," students can begin to move again. Continue to call out other toys and having them freeze when you say "Andy's coming!"

You may wish to pinpoint the shapes that different students make so that they can see what others look like. Be sure that students are not just imitating the toy (i.e., making noises, moving the exact same way all the time), but that they are moving using the shape the toy would make.

You can also put on music; have students move around using any movement, meaning they don't have to move like a toy. When you call out a toy's name, they must freeze in a shape that toy might make. Make sure they hold the freeze until you call "All clear!"

Modifications

This same concept can be used with other popular movies, such as the *Star Wars* series, the *Harry Potter* series, and others. For example, students pretending to be *Harry Potter* characters can freeze as if blasted by a spell from an evil wizard, or students pretending to be *Star Wars* characters can be frozen in carbonite like Han Solo.

Chapter 5

Eye-Hand Coordination Activities

Photo courtesy of Speed Stacks, Inc.

E ye–hand coordination includes an immense number of activities, also called manipulative activities, for all levels and abilities. Improving eye–hand coordination not only allows students to be more successful in some sporting activities, but recent research on brain function and learning indicates that it also has a direct correlation to improved handwriting and reading skills. This chapter includes a variety of movement activities that develop eye–hand coordination.

The key to appropriate activity selection is choosing activities based on the abilities of the students in the class. The levels listed for the activities in this chapter are merely recommendations; you must use discretion in choosing activities according to your students' abilities. In general, level I activities are appropriate for kindergarten and grade 1; level II activities are appropriate for grades 2 through 3; and level III activities are appropriate for grades 4, 5, and 6.

Ball of Glass

Level
I

Area
Large playing space such as a gymnasium

Equipment
Soft foam ball or fluff ball for each group

Objectives
Students will develop eye–hand coordination through a cooperative activity.

Setup and Description
In this game students pass a ball with different actions and different body parts. Break the class into groups of no more than six using creative division methods. Have each of the groups form a circle and give them one ball per group. Students toss the ball underhanded to each other in no particular pattern. This is a cooperative game and not competitive; good, catchable tosses should be made.

When the students get the hang of this and become more successful, encourage them to catch and toss the ball in a variety of ways: underhand, overhand, behind the back, two-handed, and so on. Sometimes a person may choose to pass the ball using only the head and one finger. The next person may choose to pass the ball using only the chin and neck. The person receiving the ball has to receive it the same way it was given.

Since this is not a competitive game, it's never really over, but encouragement of experimentation is critical.

Modifications
- • Add a second tossing object to each group.
- • Before tossing the ball, students must call out the name of the student who will receive the ball.

Ball Toss and Catch

Level
   II and III

Area
   Large playing space such as a gymnasium

Equipment
   Tennis ball for every two students

Objectives
   Students will improve eye–hand coordination through throwing and catching.

Setup and Description

This activity is relatively simple in the beginning, but it ends with challenging catching and tossing activities. Pair students up using creative division methods and give each pair a tennis ball. They should face each other about 5 feet (1.5 meters) apart and toss the tennis ball back and forth. Next they should bounce the ball back and forth to each other.

⚠ **SAFETY NOTE**

Tell students that this is a cooperative and not a competitive activity; consequently, they should not throw the tennis balls with much force. Also, they should throw the tennis ball so that the partner can catch it.

   Next, the partners decide on a key word. Then one partner turns around facing away from the other person. The partner with the ball tosses the ball toward the partner and at the same time says the key word to notify the partner to turn around and catch the ball. They should vary the throws high, low, left, and right. Last, one partner slowly jogs away from the partner with the ball. As the partner is running away, the other partner throws the ball and uses the key word to tell the partner when to look for the ball to catch it over the shoulder.

Modifications

Make sure to work on both sides of the body, catching and tossing with both the dominant and nondominant hands and over the dominant and nondominant shoulders.

Ball Toss Copycats

Level
   III

Area
   Large playing space such as a gymnasium

Equipment
   Soft bouncy ball for each student; poly spot for each student (optional)

Objectives
   Students will develop eye–hand coordination.

Setup and Description

Break the class into pairs using creative division methods and give each student a ball. The two students stand a few feet apart from each other and pass their ball to

their partner with their right hand. The students will pass at the same time. If necessary, put poly spots on the floor showing where the ball should bounce.

First, partners should do the bounce pass, passing with their right hand and catching with their left. After they have done the bounce pass for a while, they should pass with their left hand and catch with their right hand. Then switch to the chest pass, continuing to pass with one hand and catch with the other.

Modifications

Have the students move farther apart from each other to enhance the challenge.

Balloon Strike

Level
III

Area
Large playing space such as a gymnasium

Equipment

Tennis racket, badminton racket, or pickle ball racket for each person or group of two; balloon for each person or group of two

Objectives

Students will practice teamwork while striking an object into the air with an implement.

Setup and Description

Give each student or group of two students a racket and a balloon. Students place the racket in their dominant hand and hit the balloon up in the air, working on high and low hits. Students try to keep the balloon in the air and not let it touch the ground. Then have the students do the same activity with their nondominant hand. Students can also work with both hands on the racket.

Next, gather students in groups of three or four using creative division methods and have them work on keeping one balloon in the air as a group. Then, depending on their skill level, add two, three, or even four bal-

⚠ SAFETY NOTE

Obviously, with multiple balloons and striking objects in the same vicinity, there is an increased risk of students hitting each other with the rackets. Make sure the students stay spread out, and supervise the groups with safety in mind.

loons at once that they should keep in the air at the same time. Remember that children should work on both sides of the body in order to improve eye–hand coordination, so make sure that the students still use their dominant and nondominant hands.

Modifications

Break the class into five teams of equal number using creative division methods and have them line up single file behind a boundary line. One member from each team must bat the balloon across the room to another boundary line and then back to pass it off to the next teammate in line. The balloon must not touch the floor; if it does, the player must return and start over. Players may use any body part to bat the ball.

Balloon Sweep

Level
III

Area
Large playing space such as a gymnasium

Equipment

Broom for each group; cone for each group; balloon for each group

Objectives

Students will make a simple eye–hand coordination activity much more difficult by holding an object in their hand.

Setup and Description

Break the class into several teams of no more than four, five, or six using creative division methods. Each team stands in single file at the starting line. Place a cone on the goal line about 40 feet (12 meters) away directly in line with each team. Give a broom and balloon to the starter of each team. Starters place the balloon on the floor at the starting line.

On your signal, the starters sweep the balloon to their team's cone, circle it, and continue sweeping the balloon to the starting line. As soon as they cross the line, they hand the broom to the second player, who places the balloon directly behind the line and starts sweeping. The previous sweeper goes to the end of the team's line. The first team to complete the cycle and have its players in the original positions wins the game.

Modifications

Change the location of the hands on the broom. For example, if the right hand was on the top of the broom, students place the left hand on the top.

Balloons

Level
I and II

Area
Large playing space such as a gymnasium

Equipment
Large balloon for each student

Objectives
Students will improve their eye–hand coordination with activities involving slow-moving objects.

Setup and Description
Balloons can be very exciting to young students. They are colorful and easy to handle. They move slower than a ball and thus can be tracked easier. Striking skills, volleyball games, kicking upward, and even beginning racket skills become easier with balloons. Inexpensive and yet practical, balloons, beach balls, and slow-motion balls should be a part of every elementary curriculum. Here are some sample activities:

- Hit the balloon to self using various body parts.
- Continue consecutive hits with body parts.
- Jump and hit using one hand.
- Hit the balloon up, jump, and catch it.
- Contact the balloon above the head and then below the waist.
- Hit the balloon underhand, overhand, and sidearm.
- Hit the balloon forward and keep walking.
- Hit the balloon back and forth to a partner.
- When ready, do all of the previous activities using a heavier ball.

Modifications
Have the students develop a variety of activities or strikes with the hands into a routine that they can show to the rest of the class.

Basketball Bustle

Level
III

Area
Large playing space such as a gymnasium

Equipment
Basketball for each student

Objectives
Students will increase eye–hand coordination through basketball activities.

Setup and Description

Give every student a basketball and have them spread out all around the space and listen to your directions while holding the ball. You can make up your own routines based on various basketball skills you want to work on, but here are some examples:

- Students place the ball on the ground. Using one hand, they roll the ball around one leg and then use the other hand to roll the ball around the other leg.
- Students do a figure eight around both legs.
- Students bring the ball up to their knees and rotate the ball around their knees, then switch directions.
- Students do the same thing around their torso.
- Students "dribble" the ball from hand to hand above their heads, then dribble it in front of their chest, then in front of their legs, and then down to the ground.
- Students hold the ball between their legs at knee level, lightly toss it up, place their arms behind their legs as the ball is in the air, catch the ball, and throw it up again catching it the way they began.
- Students do the spider, where they bend down and dribble the ball between their legs. They must dribble it two times in front of their body, then through their legs, two times behind their body, and so on.

Use your imagination in challenging the students.

Modifications

You may need to use smaller basketballs for younger children. Also, smaller children may not be able to do some of the activities, so allow for them to do them the best they can.

Bat Ball

Level
III

Area
Large playing space such as a gymnasium or outdoor field

Equipment
High-density foam ball; 4 baseball or softball bases for each game of 10 players

Objectives
Students will improve eye–hand coordination through catching and striking a moving object.

Setup and Description
Break the class so that there are teams of five students using creative division methods. Set up fields with four bases 30 to 50 feet (9 to 15 meters) apart in the same diamond pattern as a baseball or softball field. There will be more than one game being played at the same time. This allows more participation. Designate

which teams are playing each other and have the teams of five spread out over the playing areas. Batting teams should line up a safe distance from the home base.

Pitchers lob the ball so that it bounces once before it reaches the batters, who hit the ball with the fist and forearm. Once players hit the ball, they run around all the bases and back home as in baseball. Everyone on the fielding team must touch the ball by passing it to one another and then the fielding team must throw the ball to another teammate at home (the catcher) or run and beat the runner back to home plate. If the runner gets home first, then the batting team scores a point.

In order to keep play moving quickly, after only one out the fielding and batting teams switch. The batter gets as many chances as needed to put the ball in play. Make sure that everyone gets a chance to bat and the batting orders alternate boys with girls.

Modifications

If teams have no trouble getting everyone to touch the ball, then have them touch the ball in the order of youngest to oldest players or in alphabetical order by the fielders' last names.

Beanbag Toss

Level
I

Area
Large playing space such as a gymnasium or outdoor field

Equipment

3 beanbags for each student; 1 hula hoop for every 3 to 5 students

Objectives

Students will concentrate on throwing their beanbag through a target.

Setup and Description

There are several ways to play this game. One way is to put the hula hoops down on the floor and practice tossing the beanbag into the hula hoop. Another way is to hang the hula hoop from the ceiling or from the basketball hoop and have the students throw the beanbag through it. The distance they stand away from the hoop depends on the overall ability of the class.

Modifications

- • You may need to challenge the students more by swinging the hula hoop back and forth while students throw through the moving target.
- • Students could throw into a box instead of a hoop.
- • Change the distance they throw or change the way they throw by having them throw overhand, underhand, or sidearm passes; with the dominant and nondominant arm; behind the back; and so on.

Blind Man's Hand

Level
II and III

Area
Classroom, gymnasium, or outdoor playing space

Equipment

2 quarters; 2 small balls no bigger than 6 inches (15 centimeters) in diameter

Objectives

Students will learn how to react to what the eyes see and put a chain reaction of hand squeezes into motion in an activity of teamwork and cooperation.

Setup and Description

This is a fun game that depends on reaction time and eye–hand coordination. No speaking is allowed in this game, so it rests on touch and sight. Break the class into four groups using creative division methods. Groups 1 and 2 will play against each other and groups 3 and 4 will play against each other. Each game requires one quarter and one ball.

Teams should line up facing each other, and then students sit on their knees on the floor facing a member from the opposite team about 5 feet (1.5 meters) in front of them. Place the quarter at one end between the two lines and the ball at the other end between the two lines. Every person on each team should join hands with their teammates next to them. All players except the two students at the end of the line with the quarter should have their eyes closed.

The two students at the end of the line flip the quarter and watch carefully to see if it lands heads or tails. If the quarter lands tails up, the students flip the quarter again. When the coin lands heads up, the student at the end squeezes the hand of the person next to them, who then squeezes the hand of the next person and so on until the squeeze, or message, reaches the last person in the line. The student at the end then tries to grab the ball before the member of the opposing team does. The person who grabs the ball first rotates to the end of the line with the quarter. The team that loses does not change positions.

Modifications

Add a penalty to the game when the quarter lands on tails and a team leader falsely sends a message and it reaches the end of the line. For example, the penalty could be the loss of a point or the performance of some exercises.

Boxing Glove Relay

Level
III

Area
Large playing space such as a gymnasium

Equipment

Pair of boxing gloves for each team; 6 sticks that are 6 inches (15 centimeters) long for each team; enough cones or ropes to mark off a 60-foot (18-meter) square

Objectives

Students will gain a greater appreciation for the use of their fingers and hands while improving eye–hand coordination.

Setup and Description

Mark off a 60-foot (18-meter) square on the court with cones, lines, or ropes. Break the class into teams of no more than six using creative division methods. Place six sticks per team at the other end of the playing area and give each team one pair of boxing gloves. The teams then form single-file lines, ready for a relay race. The two teams are side by side with the first person in line wearing the boxing gloves.

On the signal to start, the first player of each team runs to the other end of the floor, picks up one of the sticks, returns and drops it at the starting line, and gives the gloves to the next person in line. This continues until everyone has run down, picked up a stick, and returned it to the starting line. The first team to finish wins. At the end of the race, make sure to mention the value of fingers and hands.

Modifications

Have the students go to the other end of the floor in a variety of locomotor patterns. How about some skipping, walking, hopping, jumping, or crawling?

Captains and Tanks

Level
II and **III**

Area
Large playing space such as a gymnasium

Equipment

Blindfold for every two students; soft, throwable object like fluff balls for every two students

Objectives

Students will cooperate with each other in an exciting activity that involves throwing and dodging.

Setup and Description

Break the class into pairs using creative division methods. Give each pair one blindfold and two soft, throwable objects. Each pair has a sighted person who cannot touch any of the objects and a blindfolded person who throws, retrieves, and tries to avoid being hit by the objects. The sighted person can give unlimited verbal instructions but may not physically assist the blindfolded partners. The goal for each pair is to throw an object and hit a blindfolded player from another twosome. Hitting a sighted person is meaningless. If a hit occurs, the two partners swap roles and resume action.

Modifications

Change the requirements so they cannot use any form of the English language. Foreign languages and non-English signals are acceptable.

Card Toss

Level

I, II, and III

Area

Large indoor playing space such as a gymnasium

Equipment

Trash can for each team; deck of cards for each team; plastic floor tape or some other method of marking lines

Objectives

Students will learn to accurately throw an object that has an unpredictable flight.

Setup and Description

Set up each trash can and draw or mark a line for students to stand behind. Break the class into equal teams of no more than six using creative division methods. The teams sit or stand in semicircles around a trash can. Each team divides a pack of cards equally among the members. While standing behind the line, team members take turns trying to toss a card into the container. When all the cards have been tossed, they count the cards inside the container. The team with the most cards in the container wins the game.

Modifications

Decrease the size of the opening of the container, thus making it more difficult to get the card into the container.

Catching Animals

Level

I

Area

Large indoor playing space such as a gymnasium

Equipment

Beanbag animal (or another soft object) for every two students; hula hoop or poly spot for each beanbag animal; fun music

Objectives

Students will develop eye–hand coordination while perfecting locomotor skills.

Setup and Description

Scatter the hula hoops or poly spots around the playing space and place one beanbag animal inside each hoop. Break the class into partners using creative division methods.

When the music starts, call out a locomotor movement, and students travel side by side with a partner performing the movement. When the music stops, the partners go to opposite sides of the nearest hoop, take approximately five steps back from the hoop so they are about 15 feet (4.5 meters) from each other, and toss the beanbag back and forth. When the music starts again, students return the beanbag to the hoop or poly spot and the movement continues. Change locomotor skills each round.

Modifications

You can use any object if necessary to make the activity more difficult. Try catching and tossing in a variety of different ways, such as high and low tosses, behind the back, underhand, overhand, sidearm, and so on.

Circus Rounds

Level
I

Area
Large indoor playing space such as a gymnasium

Equipment
Variety of equipment such as (but not limited to) hula hoops, a variety of differently sized and shaped balls, flying discs, ropes, and sticks, depending on the stations you choose to develop; whistle

Objectives
Students will improve eye–hand coordination through a large variety of tossing, catching, and movement activities.

Setup and Description
Set up various stations around the play space. The stations should include any necessary equipment and note cards that indicate what the students should do at each station. The stations you choose are strictly up to your goals and imagination. Students work at each station for two minutes, staying on task for the full two minutes. Blow a whistle to signify the end of the two-minute period. After the two minutes are up, the students move to the next station.

Here are just a few ideas of different stations you might include:

- Jump roping
- Crawling like a crab
- Bouncing a tennis ball with a racket
- Tapping a balloon with the hands around half of the gym
- Bouncing a basketball
- Throwing a tennis ball in the air and catching it before it bounces
- Throwing a Frisbee to a partner

Modifications
Have students make up the various stations. Children are very imaginative and come up with some great ideas.

Cleaning House

Level
I and II

Area
Large playing space such as a gymnasium

Equipment
15 or more fluff, foam, or soft playground balls; volleyball net

Objectives
Students will work on throwing and catching skills.

Setup and Description
Break the class into two equal teams using creative division methods. The students on each team randomly spread out on their side of the net. As evenly as possible, divide the balls between the two sides. The object is for each team to keep throwing balls over the net to the opponents' side so that when the time limit is up the other team will have as many balls as possible. The time limit is unknown to the players so they do not hoard the balls and throw them over at the last possible moment.

A game is played in four quarters of three minutes each. At the end of each quarter the balls on each side of the net are counted. The totals for all four quarters are added together and the team with the lowest number wins the game.

Modifications
This game can be played anywhere; there does not have to be a net. You could just place cones across the gym to form a dividing line instead.

Corner Wiffle Ball

Level
II and III

Area
Large playing space such as a gymnasium

Equipment
16 poly spots; 4 Wiffle bats; 4 Wiffle balls (preferably of different colors); 4 batting tees or large cones; whistle

Objectives
Students will learn to move safely around a crowded space while working cooperatively and improving eye–hand coordination.

Setup and Description
Wiffle ball is just like regular baseball except for a few differences in equipment. In this activity, four different games of Wiffle ball are going on at once, so you will need to set up four small fields with the home bases located in the four corners of the gymnasium. You can use the corners of the basketball court for this if the court

is marked on the floor. Place the poly spots, or bases, appropriately with base paths of 20 to 25 feet (6-8 meters) in length.

Break the class into eight different teams using creative division methods. Two teams go to each field. Because a tee or large cone is used for batting, there is no pitcher or catcher. Each field has a different colored ball for easy identification.

SAFETY NOTE

The idea behind playing multiple games at the same time is to have few or no students standing around. Baseball is notorious for this; however, with four games people will be running everywhere chasing balls. Teach the children to turn and look before chasing after a ball. Reinforce this idea throughout the game and supervise with safety in mind.

Teams will not have nine players each like regular baseball, so everyone will play multiple positions and consequently must be ready to move all over the field. Place the balls on the batting tees, and when you are ready, use a whistle to start play. The first player on the batting team hits the ball off of each tee and the fielding begins. When play is stopped on each field, the ball is placed on the batting tee again. No play begins again until you blow the whistle.

The batting team only gets one out, so exchanges from hitting to fielding occur frequently. If a team has all of its members on base and no one has made it home to bat again, then the team batting switches out to defense. This game can be quite chaotic with four balls flying around. Remind players that they may only touch the colored ball that their game is playing with. If another ball comes into their field, they must leave it alone.

Modifications

Ideally you want to have no more than four people per team, so make as few or as many games as you need to keep the children active.

Deck Tennis

Level
III

Area
Large playing space such as a gymnasium

Equipment
6-inch (15-centimeter) deck ring for each court; a long rope or badminton net to string across the middle of the court; standards to hold the net up; plastic floor tape

Objectives
Students will develop cooperative skills in a quick-moving eye–hand coordination activity.

Setup and Description
Break the class into two teams using creative division methods. If there are more than eight players on a team, create more than one game and divide the class into multiple teams. In this game a large court of 12 by 40 feet (4 by 12 meters) is needed depending on the skill level of the children—the higher their skill level,

the larger the court. As in volleyball, each team goes to one side of the court and spreads out.

The object of the game is to toss the ring back and forth across the net without letting it touch the ground. Choose who will begin play. Play begins with an underhanded toss from behind the baseline. Servers continue to serve until their team fails to return the ring. Players may not change hands to throw the ring; whatever hand was used to catch the ring must be used to throw the ring. The ring must land inside of the boundary lines. Students may not hold the ring for more than three seconds before throwing it, and the ring must be thrown so that it travels parallel to the ground or turns end over end. The thrower is not allowed to feint a throw. Points are scored as in volleyball, with rally scoring (either team may score a point regardless of whether they served).

Modifications

To make the game more challenging, you can have fewer people on each side so the players have to cover more space. To make it easier, have more players per team. However, the latter creates less activity for each player, so be careful that players aren't spending too much time standing around.

Flag Belt Favorites

Level
II and **III**

Area
Large playing space such as a gymnasium

Equipment
Belt and 2 flags for each student

Objectives
Students will use grasping and pulling skills in chasing and fleeing games.

Setup and Description

The following activities are a variety of chasing and fleeing games. When these types of games are played, frequently there are arguments among the children on whether or not they were tagged. When each student wears a belt with two flags attached to it by Velcro, these arguments are eliminated because players can tell instantly if they've been tagged or not by whether their flag has been pulled.

Here are some sample activities where belts and flags can be used.

Steal the Flag

Students remove both flags from their belt and place one flag in the tail position behind their body. The other flag is placed on the side of the playing space out of the way. Flags cannot be covered by shirts or tucked deep in the waistband of the players' pants. Assign partners using creative division methods and the game begins. Using lots of faking and feinting with no pushing, shoving, or grabbing, students try to snatch the flag from their partner's back.

Alley Dash

Break the class in half using creative division methods and assign each team a flag color (probably red and yellow). One team breaks into two parallel lines 6 feet (2 meters) apart, forming an alley. One at a time, members of the other team run through the alley while the students in the lines try to snatch the flags from the running person. Players cannot be grabbed or pulled; only flags can be pulled. Runners cannot hide or hold onto their flags.

Flag Battle I

Break the class in half using creative division methods and assign each team a flag color (probably red and yellow). On your signal, both teams start running around the play area. Yellow players try to snatch flags off the red players' belts and vice versa. If players lose both flags, they must move off the court and replace the flags on their belts. When a teammate runs by and gives them a high five, they can return to the game. After a duration chosen by the teacher, count flags to see which team collected the most. Players cannot be grabbed or pulled; only flags can be pulled. Runners cannot hide or hold onto their flags.

Flag Battle II

This game is the same as Flag Battle I except that there are no teams; students compete for themselves. When both flags are pulled, players must move to the side of the playing area, perform 25 sit-ups (or another exercise designated by you), replace the flags on their belts, and return to the game.

Frisbee Golf

Level
III

Area
Large outdoor playing space

Equipment
Frisbee for each student; homemade golf scorecard for each student; sticks with flags on them to mark the holes

Objectives
Students will practice strategies and skills related to catching and throwing Frisbees.

Setup and Description
Before participating in this activity, students must have a solid foundation of skills in accurately throwing the Frisbee. Frisbee golf is played much like regular golf.

Locate a large playing area. Mark out a nine-hole course as imaginatively as you wish, and create and distribute scorecards. Give each student a Frisbee. Students throw their Frisbee from a specified teeing area. After all players have teed off, they move to their Frisbee and make their second toss. The player has holed out when their Frisbee lands in a specified area of the course (hitting a tree, landing inside a circle, or landing in a basket of some kind). Students record their scores on the scorecard for each hole.

Modifications
Have the students make up their own courses. In groups of three, four, or five, they agree on the layout of the hole to be played and then tee off. Don't forget to encourage them to add "water hazards" or "sand traps" to increase the difficulty of the game.

Hands Up, Hands Down

Level
II and III

Area
Large playing space such as a gymnasium

Equipment
2 to 4 quarters

Objectives
Students will develop improved eye–hand coordination and strategies for hiding objects from an opposing team.

Setup and Description
This activity could be used for a warm-up. Separate the class into two equal groups using creative division methods. The two groups should face each other while each sitting in a semicircle on the floor. Choose which group goes first. The team that is not chosen hides their eyes. Everyone on the other team opens their hands. Two, three, or four of the team members will receive and hide two, three, or four

quarters. The number of coins is based on the size of the group; larger groups need more coins to hide.

At your command of "Hands up," everyone in the coin-hiding group closes their fists to hide the coins and raises their closed hands into the air. On this same command, everyone on the other the team opens their eyes. At the command of "Hands down," everyone in the coin-hiding group places palms down on the floor, trying not to let the coins drop too loudly. As they do so, the other team listens carefully to see if they can find out who has the coins.

Once all hands are down, the other group picks one person on the other team who they think has the coins. The choosing team has three or four opportunities to pick the students who are hiding the coins; the number of choices depends on how many students are in the class and how many coins have been hidden. It's usually best to allow one more guess than the number of coins hidden.

Modifications

Finding the coins is sometimes difficult. If needed, start with a smaller number of students in each group and fewer coins.

Horseshoe Hoopla

Level
II and III

Area
Large playing space such as a gymnasium

Equipment
10 soccer balls, 10 tennis balls, 10 Frisbees, and 10 footballs; 8 cones

Objectives
Students will improve eye–hand coordination by tossing or throwing objects of various sizes and shapes with various amounts of force.

Setup and Description

In this activity, students throw various objects in an attempt to get the object as close as possible to the cone. Place cones in a variety of locations on the floor. Using creative division methods, separate the students into groups of two.

One member from each pair throws the object toward the cone and then switches with the other member. The students throw or toss the object from approximately 20 feet (6 meters) and see which one gets closer to the cone. Obviously, the more cones you have the fewer people will be standing around. Students score a point when their object lands closest to the cone. After both members of each pair have thrown at that cone, it is time to move to the next and throw a different object. At the end, the pairs add up their points. Whichever pair has the highest number wins.

Modifications

Pick a large variety of objects in different shapes and sizes that will challenge the students.

Hot Potato

Level
I, II, and III

Area
Large playing space such as a gymnasium

Equipment
Soft, bouncy ball for every two students

Objectives
Students will learn the correct way to pass a ball and to keep their eye on the ball while performing a variety of locomotor skills.

Setup and Description
Before participating in this activity, students should already know how to perform chest passes and bounce passes. To be more efficient, you can set up the activity so multiple groups can participate at the same time.

Pair up students using creative group methods. Students should line up along the baseline of a basketball court about 5 feet (1.5 meters) across from one another. The students should face each other and lightly jog from one end of the floor to the other and back while at the same time passing the hot potato (ball) back and forth to each other with a chest pass. Instruct them to go slow, stay under control, and make correct and efficient passes. After they have successfully completed chest passing, they should do the same with bounce passes.

Modifications
While continuing the chest and bounce passes, change the locomotor movement. For example, have the students skip, gallop, or slide. You can use your imagination here.

Hot Potato Tag

Level
I and II

Area
Large playing space such as a gymnasium

Equipment
Playground ball or basketball for every two students; peppy music that encourages movement

Objectives
Students will improve their eye–hand coordination.

Setup and Description
Pair up the students and have them take five to eight giant steps away from one another. Give each pair one ball. When the music starts, the students throw and catch the ball. When the music stops, the person with the ball runs (or walks, grapevines, skips, hops) carrying the ball and the other chases. If tagged before the music starts again, the student carrying the ball dribbles the ball three times and

then becomes the tagger. When the music starts again, the two go back to throwing and catching as before, though in a different part of the playing area.

Modifications

Use balls of different sizes to allow for adaptation to various catching and tossing skills for each class. You can also use different objects to throw and catch. Depending on throwing and catching ability and space, the distance between the catcher and thrower can increase or decrease.

Juggling Partners

Level
II and III

Area
Large playing space such as a gymnasium

Equipment
4 beanbags or tennis balls for each student

Objectives
Students will work with a partner and learn to juggle successfully.

Setup and Description
Break the class into partners using creative division methods. Partners stand across from each other no more than 6 feet (2 meters) apart. One student will toss the ball underhand to her partner across from her with her right hand. The partner will catch the ball with the left hand, transfer it to the right hand, and underhand toss it back to his partner. Start with one ball. When the team can successfully toss and catch one ball, add a second ball, then a third ball, and then a fourth.

Modifications
- Partners can bounce the ball to each other instead of tossing it.
- Create groups of five or seven. After a tossing pattern has been established, add a second ball, then a third, and so on.

Juggling Scarves

Level
I, II, and III

Area
Large playing space such as a gymnasium

Equipment
3 scarves for each student; active music or circus music

Objectives
Students will learn to juggle using basic juggling techniques.

Setup and Description
The object of this activity is to learn the basics of juggling using scarves, which are easier to catch, they float in the air, and they do not drop as quickly as denser

objects. Break the class into pairs using creative division methods and give each student three scarves.

Teach the children how to juggle by using the following sequence. Begin by showing students how to toss up one scarf with the left hand and catch it with the right. Say "Up-catch" or "1-2" on the movements. After students master up-catch or 1-2, move on to two scarves. Explain that they will always catch a scarf with the hand that did not toss it. Holding one scarf in each hand, toss the scarf in the left hand to be caught with the right hand. Remind the students that the right hand now needs to get rid of its scarf so it can catch the scarf tossed by the left hand. The saying now is "Up-up-catch-catch" or "1-2-3-4." Model the movements, and give students ample time to master them.

Once they can juggle two scarves, it is time to move on to three. Start with two scarves in the left hand and one scarf in the right hand. Remind the students that they need to get rid of a scarf before they can catch the other one. Toss up one scarf from the left hand, toss up the scarf from the right hand, catch the first left-hand scarf with the right hand, toss up the other left-hand scarf, and catch the scarf that was originally in the right hand with the left hand. Continue the tossing and catching sequence. The saying now is "Up-up-catch-up-catch-up-catch-up."

After the students can juggle three scarves, have them work on a juggling routine. Have the students experiment with their skills working from simple tosses to more advanced patterns. Incorporate more scarves into the routine when ready. You may also have one person in each pair perform a juggling sequence. The partner then repeats the sequence. Use music to keep the pace of juggling.

Modifications

If you don't have juggling scarves, use lightweight plastic grocery bags instead. As skills increase, change the objects. Try beanbags, tennis balls, or even one scarf, one beanbag, and one tennis ball.

Nervous Wreck

Level
I and II

Area
Large playing space such as a gymnasium

Equipment
1 or 2 soft foam balls or fluff balls for each group

Objectives
Students will develop eye–hand coordination through a competitive activity.

Setup and Description
Break the class into groups of no more than six using creative division methods. All students in each group stand in a circle with their hands at their sides. One student moves into the center of the circle, holding a ball. That student can underhand throw the ball at any member of the circle, who must then try to catch it. However, the center student can simply pretend to throw the ball instead without actually releasing it, faking the throw. If the catcher puts hands up to catch what turns out

to be a fake throw, that person is declared a "nervous wreck" and exchanges places with the center student.

Modifications

Put two balls in the action. This will make it more difficult to focus on just one ball. It will not only help with the development of eye–hand coordination, but with peripheral vision as well.

Over the Shoulder

Level
II and **III**

Area
Large playing space such as a gymnasium

Equipment
Tennis ball for every two students

Objectives
Students will be challenged to find the ball as it comes from behind them and to catch it.

SAFETY NOTE

Throws should be underhanded, lofted, and soft and should not hit the catcher's head. In addition, all groups should be tossing in the same direction. Throwers all need to be on the same side and catchers all need to be on the same side.

Setup and Description

Use creative division methods to divide the class into partners. The partners stand one directly in front of the other about 5 feet (1.5 meters) away. The person in the back (the thrower) has a tennis ball, and the other (the catcher) turns around away from the thrower partner. The thrower lobs the ball over one of the catcher's shoulders and the catcher tries to catch the ball as it comes from behind and over the shoulder.

Modifications

- • Use a bigger ball like a foam football or soccer ball. After the students master this ball, have the throwers toss the ball a bit farther, requiring the catchers to jog before they can catch it. This represents a route a football player would run.

- • Have one of the students in each pair lie on his stomach with his head away from his partner, who is standing behind him. As the standing player says "Now," she tosses the ball high enough into the air for the person lying on the ground to pop up to a standing position, turn around, and track and catch the ball.

Over-Under Relay

Level
II and III

Area
Large playing space such as a gymnasium

Equipment
Playground ball for each relay team

Objectives
Students will develop teamwork skills while competing in an exciting relay.

Setup and Description
Using creative division methods, separate the class into teams of eight. Each team lines up single file in relay formation. Give the first player in each line a ball. At your signal to start, the first player passes the ball over his head to the second player, who passes it between her legs to the third. Team members pass the ball over and under the whole length of the line. Upon receiving the ball, the last player runs forward to the front of the line and starts the ball again. This continues until students are back in their original position in the line.

Modifications
Have more than one ball going at once in each line. Players must pay attention to the location of all the balls to keep the activity going.

Paddleball and Jacks

Level
II and III

Area
Large playing space such as a gymnasium

Equipment
Paddleballs for half the class; jacks sets for half the class

Objectives
Students will develop their eye–hand coordination with two timeless activities.

Setup and Description
Group students up according to the number of jacks sets and paddleballs available and hand out the paddleballs and jacks. Half of the group can play jacks for a few minutes while the other half practices with the paddleball, then switch groups. Remember to explain how to play jacks and paddleball, as many students may not be familiar with the games. You can increase the difficulty by making the jacks group pick up as many jacks as they can on one toss and creating a competition for the paddleball group.

Briefly, the paddleball consists of a small paddle with a broad face and a handle. A ball is attached to the face of the paddle by a 2.5-foot (76-centimeter) rubber band. The objective is to hit the ball off the paddle with enough control and direction so the ball comes back to the paddle and as many consecutive hits can be obtained as possible.

Jacks is a game that involves a small ball and 10 metal or plastic pieces with prongs on them that rest on the ground. Players toss the jacks on the ground, and after looking at the location of the jacks, they gently toss the ball in the air with the dominant hand. After it bounces once, they collect one jack in their dominant hand and catch the ball before it bounces again. This continues until all jacks have been picked up one by one. Then players toss the jacks again, this time picking up the jacks two at a time, then three at a time, and so on until all of the jacks are picked up at once.

Modifications

- Have the students complete the tasks with the nondominant hand.
- Have the students play jacks in teams of two. One person bounces the ball and the other collects the jacks.

Poison Ball

Level
III

Area
Large playing space such as a gymnasium

Equipment
Large cage ball (see appendix) 25 to 35 inches (63-89 centimeters) in diameter; 20 playground or foam balls; plastic floor tape

Objectives
Students will increase their aiming and throwing skills in a game that involves throwing objects at a moving target.

Setup and Description
Create a goal line across each end of the playing area. Separate the class into two groups using creative division methods and divide balls equally between teams. Place the poison ball (cage ball) in the center of the playing area. Each team tries to hit the poison ball and knock it across the opposite team's goal line. Players may not hold the balls or go out into the playing area to retrieve them. No one may touch the poison ball to keep it from crossing the line. Direction or movement of the poison ball may only be changed by hitting the poison ball with another ball. If many balls get stuck in the middle, stop the play and appoint someone to go and throw the balls back to the players of each team. When the poison ball crosses a goal line, play ceases and a point is awarded to the team who caused it to cross the line.

Modifications
Have more than one poison ball on the floor and increase the number of throwing balls. You could also use a variety of throwing balls (sizes and shapes).

Quiet Ball

Level
I

Area
Large playing space such as a gymnasium

Equipment
Soft foam ball or fluff ball for each group

Objectives
Students will improve their eye–hand coordination through a competitive activity.

Setup and Description
Break the class into groups of at least eight using creative division methods and give each group a ball. Each group chooses a judge who will decide which students are out according to the rules of the game. Once the game starts, no one is allowed to talk or they will be eliminated from the game. Students softly toss the ball to each other in any order they choose. Tosses should be underhanded.

Before beginning, remind students one more time there are three ways to get out: Talking, dropping the ball, or not throwing the ball to the target person. If someone tries to catch the ball and fails, that person must sit down on the floor. If the throw is a poor throw or doesn't make it to the proper target, the thrower sits on the floor. The last person standing is the winner and becomes the judge for the next game.

Whenever a judge points at a student, that person is out and must sit down. No arguments are allowed. (The new games will start quickly, so there should not be any problems here.)

Modifications
- • Students must call the person's name before tossing the ball.
- • Add another ball into each group. This may be difficult, however, for level I children.

Ruler of the Squares

Level
II and III

Area
Large playing space such as a gymnasium

Equipment
Playground ball, volleyball, or foam ball; plastic floor tape

Objectives
Students will work on eye–hand coordination by throwing and catching.

Setup and Description
Mark off several courts using the tape; there should be one court for every five or six players. Each court should have four squares in it making one large box. Number each square, 1 through 4. Each individual square should be about 3 feet (1 meter), making each court 6 feet (2 meters) in length.

Break the class into groups of five or six using creative division methods. One player is in each square with a maximum of two players waiting to play at each court. Play begins when one player drops the ball to the floor within their square and then hits it to a square next to or diagonally across from them. The ball must hit the floor within that square and then the student in that square must hit the ball on the first bounce to any square other than the square from which it came. Players may hit the ball with one or two hands, but they cannot hold or catch the ball. Players must have at least one foot in their square whenever hitting the ball.

When players miss the ball or hit it out of the court, they go to the end of the waiting line. The person who hit the shot that could not be returned is now the ruler. The first player in line moves into the fourth square, which is now open, and the remaining players move clockwise toward the ruler's square. The player who remains in the ruler's square the longest is the winner.

Modifications

Set up a tournament to make the game more challenging and exciting.

Scooter Sink

Level
II and **III**

Area
Large playing space such as a gymnasium

Equipment
1 scooter per team; 6 bowling pins per team; foam soccer ball for each team; tumbling mat for each team; plastic floor tape

Objectives
Students will improve eye–hand coordination and throwing skills by throwing from an unusual position—sitting down.

Setup and Description
Lay out floor mats at one end of the gym and set up bowling pins on top. Break the class into teams of five using creative division methods. Each team lines up single file at the opposite end of the gym from the bowling pins and mats. Explain that each mat and pins represent a battleship. The students must try to sink each ship by knocking down all its pins with a ball.

Mark a line approximately 15 feet (4.5 meters) away from the battleships. This is the line that the students cannot cross. One person from each line scoots out to the line and throws one ball at the pins. Afterward, the thrower retrieves the ball and goes to the end of the team's line so that the next person can go. The first team that knocks down all their pins yells "We sank the ship!" and wins.

Modifications
- · · If some students are only able to throw a limited distance, move the line closer for them. You can also give them a larger ball or give them more shots.
- · · In order to speed up play, have one person from each line stand behind each battleship and return the thrown balls to the other players.

Shoe Relay

Level
III

Area
Large playing space such as a gymnasium

Equipment
None

Objectives
Students will participate in a quick recognition activity that requires dexterity and recognition skills.

Setup and Description
Split the class into four teams using creative division methods. Each team puts their shoes into one big pile about 30 feet (9 meters) away so that all shoes from all teams are in the same pile. Mix up the shoes.

At your signal, one person from each team races to the pile. After finding the right shoes, putting them on, and tying them, the student runs back to the team and the next person in line can go. Remind students that there is no throwing of other people's shoes outside of the pile.

To promote more activity, you may want to have three or four piles of shoes and, therefore, more students being active at the same time.

Modifications
To increase the difficulty, have a peer lead a blindfolded teammate through the activity only by verbal instructions.

Spoonball Relay

Level
II and III

Area
Large playing space such as a gymnasium

Equipment
Plastic spoon for each group; table-tennis ball for each group

Objectives
Students will complete a difficult eye–hand coordination activity under the duress of a race.

Setup and Description
Break the class into groups of no more than five using creative division methods. The groups line up single file for a relay race. One at a time, the players must balance the ball in the spoon and quickly walk to the designated turning line and back, passing the ball and spoon to the next person in line. If the ball rolls off, players may replace it with the free hand. This relay can be made more difficult if the ball is picked up without help from the free hand.

Modifications

Shorten the course and blindfold the person holding the spoon. The next person in line is the blindfolded student's verbal guide. Guides cannot touch the person with the spoon; they can direct the student with words only.

Sport Stacking

Level

I, II, and III

Area

Large playing space such as a gymnasium

Equipment

Set of Speed Stacks (see appendix) for every student or every two students

Objectives

Students will improve quickness and eye–hand coordination by stacking Speed Stacks cups using both their left and right hands.

Setup and Description

Give each student a set of 12 Speed Stacks cups and have them sit on the floor, facing you. Ask them to make three nested stacks of three cups each, and put the remaining three cups behind them to be used later. The three stacks should be in a horizontal line in front of each student, about 12 inches (30 centimeters) apart.

Working from left to right, the students use both hands to "up stack" each stack of three cups. The right hand leads, picking up the top cup and placing it next to (and touching) the two remaining nested cups. The left hand then follows, picking up the second cup and placing it on top of the two base cups, forming a three-cup pyramid. Ask the students to repeat this process with the other two stacks. This produces what's called a 3-3-3 in an up stacked position, and the students are now ready to "down stack" each stack.

Again, working from left to right and leading with the right hand, each student pulls the top cup down and to the right so that it falls (or nests) onto the bottom right base cup. Using the left hand, each student then picks up the left base cup and places it over the two nested cups. This forms what's called a down stack of three cups. Ask the students to repeat this process with the other two pyramids, and they're back to a down stacked 3-3-3, right where they started.

After the students have practiced basic up stacking and down stacking of a 3-3-3, have a race. Students start by placing both hands flat on the floor in front of their down stacked 3-3-3. At your signal, the students up stack from left to right and down stack from left to right, raising their hands when finished. During the race, watch the students to make sure that they use both hands and they stack the cups properly.

Modifications

Teach the students the additional sport stacking patterns below. For more detailed stacking instructions, contact Speed Stacks, Inc. (see appendix).

- 3-6-3 stack: Working from left to right, students up stack the first 3, the middle 6 (using the 3-2-1 method), and the last 3. Then they return to the beginning and down stack each in this same order.

- Cycle stack: Students start with a 3-6-3, form a 6-6, form a 1-10-1, and end with a 3-6-3.

Spud

Level
II and III

Area
Large playing space such as a gymnasium

Equipment
12-inch (30-centimeter) playground ball

Objectives
Students will practice dodging and fleeing in a cooperative eye–hand coordination activity.

Setup and Description
Have the class form a circle and number off. Designate one person to be in the center. Choose a locomotor movement for the students to perform around the circle.

The child in the center throws the ball in the air and yells a number. The person assigned to this number runs toward the ball and catches it while the others run away from the circle. After catching the ball, the person yells "Spud!" Everyone freezes and the person with the ball rolls the ball toward another person, trying to hit the feet. If the roll is successful, then the hit person is It and tosses the ball in the air, calling out the next number. If the roll is not successful, then the roller must start the game again by tossing the ball into the air. Stress that once "Spud!" is yelled, no moving of the feet is allowed.

Each time students' feet are hit by a rolled ball, the person who was hit gets one letter (S, P, U, and then D). Players keep track of their own letters. If necessary, keep a scorecard with everyone's name on it and the letters achieved. Once someone spells SPUD, the game is over and a new game begins.

Modifications
Students stand in a circle with one in the center holding a cane (yardstick). One end of the yardstick is on the floor with one fingertip holding up the other end. The person in the middle is It. She calls out the name or a designated number of someone in the circle and then lets go of the cane. The called person must run up and catch the cane before it hits the floor. If he doesn't catch it, he is now It. If he does catch the cane, the person who is still It calls another name.

Streamers

Level
I, II, and III

Area
Large playing space such as a gymnasium

Equipment
Streamer for each student (streamers may or may not have sticks attached to one end)

Objectives
Students will use creativity in movement while performing an eye–hand coordination activity.

Setup and Description

This activity exercises the arms, shoulders, and trunk while students hold streamers in their hand. The following are some suggestions for streamer activities. Of course, you are not by any means limited to these activities alone.

- Rainbow: Starting position is with the arms by the side. In a four-count exercise, the right hand swings out from the side and moves up across the top of the head as the body bends to the left.
- Swoop (Toe Touches): Starting position is with the arms extended above the head. In a two-count exercise, bend at the waist and let the hands swoop down past the ankles as far back as possible and return to the starting position.
- Figure 8: Execute a figure 8 in front of the body.

Students should be allowed to experiment and play with their streamers in order to develop their creativity.

Modifications

Have the students watch a brief segment of an Olympic rhythmic gymnastics competition where streamers are used. This will definitely spark some creativity.

Tee Ball

Level
I

Area
Large playing space such as a gymnasium or outdoor field

Equipment

5 or 6 tee-ball stands or large cones; 5 or 6 Wiffle bats; 40 Wiffle balls

Objectives

Students will demonstrate safe conduct while hitting a ball off a tee.

Setup and Description

Break the class into groups of five or six using creative division methods. Each group will be hitting off of the batting tee. Emphasize

- proper placement of feet in relation to the ball,
- correct hand placement on the bat,
- correct striking technique, and
- keeping the eye on the ball during the process of hitting.

One group will simultaneously hit balls off the tees while the other students are out in the field catching or fielding the balls. Balls should be rolled back to the hitting tees. Rotate the hitters out after a while so the fielders can bat also.

Modifications

Shrink the playing field so the students are closer, or use a bigger ball or a bigger bat to help students hit and field the ball.

Tennis Exploration

Level
III

Area
Large playing space such as a gymnasium

Equipment
Tennis racket for each student; beanbag for each student; tennis ball for each student

Objectives
Students will learn a little about the game and skills of tennis.

Setup and Description
Provide all students with a tennis racket, a beanbag, and, when skills progress enough, a tennis ball. A variety of activities can help students learn more about the skills of tennis. Here are a few examples that help create racket control:

- Beanbag Toss—With the racket in one hand and beanbag in the other, toss the beanbag and catch it on the racket strings.
- Beanbag Flip—Start with beanbag on the racket strings, flip it up in the air, and catch it on the strings.
- Red Light—Balance the beanbag on racket strings. On the cue of "Red light," stop, and start on "Green light." Walk in general space and try to keep the beanbag balanced on the racket. More advanced students may use balloons or balls.
- Beanbag Catch—Start with the beanbag on the racket strings, and toss it to a partner who catches it on the racket strings.
- Using a soft ball (a fluff ball or foam tennis ball), tap it straight up in the air to self; allow one bounce on ground.
- Using a soft ball, tap it straight up in the air to self; allow no bounces.
- Using a soft ball, alternate hitting sides of racket.
- Alternate hitting a soft ball with the right and left hand.
- Walk and dribble the ball on the ground with the racket.
- Walk and hit the ball in the air with the racket.
- Using hands only, no rackets, rally the ball (hit it back and forth) to a partner. Then hit ball against the wall using hands, alternating hits with the partner.
- Do the previous exercise with rackets.
- Drop the ball to yourself, slightly in front of your body so that you can hit it, or have a partner start the ball with an underhand pass, and hit forehand to the partner, who must catch the ball to score a point. After 5 points are scored, switch places. Continue until one person reaches 21 points.

Modifications
Watch the children carefully; many of them may be ready to move on quickly to using a tennis ball in working with their skills.

Tennis Slap

Level
III

Area
Large playing space such as a gymnasium

Equipment
Enough tennis balls to keep the students active (at least 1 tennis ball for every two children); plastic floor tape

Objectives
Students will enhance their eye–hand coordination through bilateral striking of a tennis ball with the hands.

Setup and Description
Mark out some small tennis courts. The number and size of courts depends on the size and abilities of the class—for example, if you have 25 children, try to mark out at least four to six courts so that four to six children can rotate in and out on each court. Tennis Slap is played like regular tennis, but instead of using a racket, students use either hand. Points are earned in the same fashion as they are in tennis.

Modifications
If students are having a difficult time hitting a tennis ball, play the game with larger balls such as beach balls. It's harder to control the specific direction they go in, but they're easier to hit.

Terminator Ball

Level
II and III

Area
Large outdoor playing space

Equipment
Hoop, barrel, or net for a target; 4 bases; ball of your choice for the students to throw; hoop (or jump rope formed in a circle) for every four students

Objectives
Students will develop eye–hand coordination.

Setup and Description
Set up the bases as in baseball. Students can choose how far apart the bases should be or you can designate the distance. Each playing field should have a hoop on the ground where the pitcher would be standing.

Separate the class into groups of four using creative division methods. Each group of four will play their own game on their own field to keep more students active and fewer standing around. Within each group, there is one thrower, two fielders, and one terminator. The terminator stands inside the hoop. Terminators can take one foot out of the hoop, but otherwise they can't move outside the hoop. Place the target (barrel, net, or hoop) 15 feet (4.5 meters) from the terminator, but this distance can be shortened if needed.

To start the activity, the batter throws the ball anywhere in the field (behind, forward, sideways). Encourage throwers to throw to open spaces where players aren't standing and to use proper throwing technique by using opposition and trunk rotation to increase the distance of their throw. The thrower then runs around all four bases and continues until the fielders throw the ball to the terminator, who in turn throws it into the target for the out.

Stress the importance of quality throws by the terminator since the terminator cannot leave the hoop. For the most accurate throws, the terminator should follow through when releasing the ball. If the fielders have trouble with throwing the ball to the terminator, the thrower should continue around the bases several times. If students are keeping score, the score can be the number of bases the thrower touched before the ball went into the target. If the terminator's throw doesn't go into the target, the fielders must retrieve and throw to the terminator and try again. The fielders must spread out for good coverage. After one thrower has a turn, another person in the group gets a turn as thrower. Make sure that players in other games don't touch any ball but the one they're playing with.

Modifications

Change the distance between the bases and the length of the throws.

Tower Tumble

Level
II and **III**

Area
Indoor playing space

Equipment
Several sets of wooden tower pieces (such as Jenga) so that there are no more than four people per game

Objectives
Students will apply strategy to a physical eye–hand coordination activity.

Setup and Description

This activity challenges dexterity, creativity, and strategy and could be used as a warm-up activity. Start by explaining the game of Tower Tumble to the class. The game involves using fine-motor skills. The object is to remove pieces of wood from the tower and place them on the top of the tower without the tower falling down. Players cannot take a piece from the top two rows of the tower. Each person takes one piece at time.

Place the Tower Tumble games on a level surface, preferably the ground. Have students sit in a circle around the game and take turns clockwise around the circle. When the tower falls, the game is over. Restack the tower and do it again, provided there is enough time.

Modifications
All moves during the game could be done with the nondominant hand.

Z-Ball Bounce

Level
II and **III**

Area
Large playing space such as a gymnasium

Equipment
Z-ball (see appendix) for every two students

Objectives
Students will react to and catch a ball that bounces erratically.

Setup and Description
Break the class up into pairs using creative division methods. Warn the class that these balls do not bounce like normal balls. Have each group spread out around the room. Then one person tosses the ball underhanded with a little loft on the toss. After the toss, the other partner tries to catch the Z-ball off one bounce. The catcher's knees should be slightly flexed to enhance movement and catching.

After a few trials, combine with another pair of students. Form a circle with the group of four. This time students alternate bouncers and try to catch the Z-ball off one bounce again. Then they try catching the Z-ball after two bounces. Activities involving the Z-ball really challenge skills already learned with a regular ball. This activity teaches students to expect anything and be ready to catch whatever comes at them.

Modifications
All catches and throws could be made with the nondominant hand.

Chapter 6

Eye-Foot
Coordination
Activities

Coordinating the feet with the eyes is sometimes quite difficult, especially for level I and some level II children. A tremendous number of activities focus on this skill, and combined with modifications and your imagination, you can develop many units of instruction. This section focuses on activities that assist in the development of this important motor skill.

The key to appropriate activity selection is choosing activities based on the abilities of the students in the class. The levels listed for the activities in this chapter are merely recommendations; you must use discretion in choosing activities according to your students' abilities. In general, level I activities are appropriate for kindergarten and grade 1; level II activities are appropriate for grades 2 through 3; and level III activities are appropriate for grades 4, 5, and 6.

Balloon Stomp

Level
I, II, and III

Area
Large playing space such as a gymnasium

Equipment
Deflated balloon for each student; 4-foot (1-meter) string for each balloon; peppy music

Objectives
Students will work on eye–foot coordination and use their peripheral vision while dodging and evading.

Setup and Description
Give each student a balloon and a string attached. Have the students blow up the balloon and tie it off. Then they should tie one end of the string to the end of the balloon and the other end to their shoelaces. When the music starts, they move around the room at any speed they want. At the same time, they try to stomp on others' balloons and pop them while trying to prevent their own balloon from being popped.

When a balloon is popped, that player is out and must stand on the perimeter of the game. If a person comes close enough to the perimeter, students who are out can take one step into the game area and stomp on that person's balloon. When there are fewer students left in the game, move the perimeter in as necessary.

Modifications
Break the class into pairs using creative division methods and have half the students (one in each pair) tie a 4-foot (1-meter) string around their ankle. Tie a small balloon to the end of the string. Partners must keep their arms linked at all times, with the player with the balloon on the right. Together they try to protect their balloon while trying to step on and break other students' balloons. The last pair with a full balloon wins.

Beanbag Pass Relay

Level
II and III

Area
Large playing space such as a gymnasium

Equipment
10 beanbags per team, but this number could vary at teacher's discretion

Objectives
Students will pass a beanbag using their feet.

Setup and Description

Break the class into three teams using creative division methods. Each team forms a line that begins at one end of the playing area and extends toward the other end of the playing area. Students must pass a beanbag down the line using only their feet. There are two ways this can be accomplished.

In the first method, which is the easier method, all students in the line lie flat on their back with their feet at the next person's head. The first person picks up a beanbag with their feet and passes it to the next person using only the feet to drop the beanbag onto the person's chest or into their hands. That person then places it between the feet and passes it to the next person using the same technique. If someone drops the beanbag, it goes back to the first person in line. After passing the beanbag, each player gets up and goes to the end of the line. Students keep passing the beanbag until their team reaches the other end of the playing area. The first team to reach the end wins the game.

The second, more challenging method is set up the same way as the first method; the only difference is in the way students pass the beanbag. Students lie flat on their back with their feet at the next person's head. The first person picks up a beanbag with the feet and passes it to the next person. The second person in line lifts the feet and legs above and behind the head to receive the beanbag.

Modifications

- Add more beanbags.
- Use larger balls instead of beanbags. Generally, the larger the ball, the easier it is for students to get their feet around it.

Fitness Kickball Challenge

Level
I and II

Area
Large playing space such as a gymnasium or outdoor field

Equipment
8 to 10 soccer balls; 4 bases

Objectives
Students will work on eye–foot coordination and cooperation.

Setup and Description

Kickball is not usually known for high levels of physical activity, but the main focus of this noncompetitive version is physical fitness. Break the class into two teams

using creative division methods. When on offense or kicking the ball, students run the bases as in normal kickball, only they do not stop until they cross home plate. The defense only corrals the kicked balls back to you or the pitcher. Defensive players cannot throw or tag out runners on the base paths. They must run the ball back to the pitcher, but in doing so they must also hand the ball off to other teammates so that at least four people are involved.

All players kick the ball on offense twice and then teams rotate. In this game there are no losers. Everyone wins since physical fitness is the ultimate goal.

Modifications

Incorporate different locomotor skills for the defense and offense to perform rather than just running the bases.

Foot Bowling

Level
I, II, and III

Area
Large playing space such as a gymnasium

Equipment
30 bowling pins; 3 playground balls; plastic floor tape

Objectives

Students will practice eye–foot coordination in kicking a ball to knock down bowling pins.

Setup and Description

In this game, students try to knock down all of the bowling pins by kicking a playground ball instead of rolling it with their hands and arms. Mark off some bowling lanes with the floor tape, one lane per five or six children. Set up three sets of 10 bowling pins. Break the class into three or more groups using creative division methods. Students take turn bowling, and when one person is bowling the others are setting up the pins and returning the ball to the bowler. Everyone gets two chances to knock all of the pins down, just like in bowling. It is up to you to keep score, or they can just play among themselves without keeping score.

Modifications

- • Spread the pins farther apart to make it harder to knock them down.
- • Ask the students to control their kicks to hit certain pins or parts of the bowling alley.
- • Move pins closer for students with disabilities.

Foot Dribble Relay

Level
I and II

Area
Large playing space such as a gymnasium

Equipment
Soccer ball for every three students; bucket for every three students

Objectives
Students will improve cardiovascular fitness and eye–foot coordination at the same time.

Setup and Description
Break the class into groups of three using creative division methods and have them line up at one end of the gym. Students dribble the ball with their feet to the bucket at the other end of the gym. They pick up the ball, put it inside the bucket, and complete three sit-ups or abdominal crunches. Students then take the ball out of the bucket, dribble it back, and pass it to the next person in line. The first team to have all of its players complete the relay wins that round.

Modifications

- • Play music to keep the excitement high.
- • Let students who are waiting in line stay active by jumping rope.
- • Add eye–hand coordination to the activity by having the children dribble basketballs.
- • Use fitness activities other than sit-ups.

Foot Juggling

Level
I, II, and III

Area
Large playing space such as a gymnasium

Equipment
Balloon for each person

Objectives
Students will improve eye–foot coordination using an object that floats slowly and is easy to track.

Setup and Description

Give each student a balloon. After finding their own personal space, students keep the balloon in the air using only their feet and knees. Following are some suggestions for the activity:

- Use the right foot only.
- Use the right knee and foot only.
- Use the left foot only.
- Use the left knee and foot only.
- Use both feet only.
- Use both knees only.

Bring the entire class together and form a tight circle. Students must attempt to keep all of the balloons in the air at once. If you find that the group is too big, break it into groups of no more than eight using creative division methods. Each group forms a circle and keeps the balloons in the air using only their feet or knees.

Modifications

This concept can be expanded into relay games. Students can progress to soccer balls or Hacky Sacks.

Foot Pass

Level
I and II

Area
Large playing space such as a gymnasium

Equipment

Big ball (a beach ball would work well)

Objectives

Students will work on eye–foot coordination while passing a big ball in a circle.

Setup and Description

All the students sit in a circle and then lie on their backs with their feet in the air. The students pass the ball with their feet to the next person in the circle; everyone must touch the ball. After it has gone around the circle a couple of times, they can move the ball anywhere in the circle, all while still lying on their backs.

Modifications

- Have two balls going around the circle at the same time.
- Students stand instead of lie on the ground.
- Use high-density foam deck rings.

Four-Corner Kickball

Level
I, II, and III

Area
Half of a basketball court

Equipment
Soccer ball

Objectives
Students will develop eye–foot coordination and kicking skills.

Setup and Description
Using creative division methods, break the class into four groups and have them line up on the lines in the four corners of half of a basketball court. Put the ball on the floor in front of one student. The student kicks the ball with the right foot to any person in the line to the right. After kicking the ball, the student joins the line that received the ball. After mastering this, reverse the direction and instruct students to kick with their left foot.

Modifications
Add two or three soccer balls rather than just one.

Four-Wall Big Ball

Level
II and III

Area
Large playing space such as a gymnasium or outdoor field

Equipment
Big ball such as a cage ball (24 inches or 61 centimeters), a very large beach ball, or a partially deflated 12-inch (30-centimeter) playground ball; 4 cones

Objectives
Students will learn how to kick a ball and why it is important to know how to kick a ball with correct technique.

Setup and Description
Set up a square that has four 15-foot (4.5-meter) sides, using a cone to represent each corner. Break the class into four equal groups using creative division methods. Each group goes and sits on one side of the square. Number the children off on each team; in other words, each team will have players numbered, for example, 1 through 9.

Call out one or two numbers, say "Go," and drop the ball into play. The players with those numbers come off their lines and try to kick the ball past an opposing team. Players score a point every time they kick the ball past another team, and they lose a point every time the ball passes by their own team. The first team to score 5 points wins the game. The team that is being kicked toward may try to block the ball if they wish.

SAFETY NOTE

Be careful when playing this game. Don't choose a ball that is too heavy for younger children to kick. Remind students that although it is a competition, they are playing with a very large ball and should take it easy.

Modifications

- Use multiple balls in the game.
- Have students make all kicks with the nondominant foot.
- Have the students move in a crab position (moving on hands and feet with the abdomen facing the ceiling).

Guard the Trash Can

Level
II and III

Area
Large playing space such as a gymnasium

Equipment
4 soccer balls; 2 large plastic trash cans

Objectives
Students will improve basic soccer skills with instep and outside the foot kicks. The guards of the trash cans will enhance their peripheral vision while preventing the ball from hitting the can.

Setup and Description
Break the class into two groups using creative division methods. Have the two groups form circles and put a trash can inside each circle. Then nominate one person from each group to guard the trash can and throw two soccer balls into the circle. The object is for students to hit the trash can with the ball by kicking it with the instep, toe, or outside of the foot. The guard tries to prevent balls from hitting the can. If someone does hit the trash can, that person becomes the new guard.

SAFETY NOTE

Remind students not to kick toward the face and to kick one ball at a time.

Modifications
- Add two or three guards per can.
- Use a bigger target or a bigger ball.
- Make the playing area smaller and just use one ball in a circle.
- Stack blocks or pins instead of using a trash can. When the pins are knocked down, the task has been accomplished.

Hacky Sack

Level
II and III

Area
Large playing space such as a gymnasium

Equipment
Hacky Sack for each student

Objectives
Students will work on eye–foot coordination and cooperation with others.

Setup and Description
Hacky Sack is a great eye–foot coordination activity that can involve a tremendous number of progressions limited only by the students' imagination. The objective is to pass the sack in the air from one person to another with a variety of kicks.

Each student must be able to perform the basic kicks off the instep of the foot, the inside of the foot, the outside of the foot, the top of the knee, and the upper torso. Students can practice these kicks with a partner, in small groups, or by themselves.

To begin, break the class into pairs using creative division methods and have students stand a couple of feet apart. One student places the Hacky Sack on one foot and tosses it in the air, and the other student tries to catch it with one foot. Students should try to catch the Hacky Sack with their dominant foot so that it lands right at the base of their toes on the top off the foot. They need to curl their toes up and make a little spot for the ball to land. Then they should lift the foot up, forcing the ball into the air, and hit it with the inside of their foot to their partner.

After practicing this, the next step is to practice kicks off the inside of the foot and the outside of the foot and then off the flexed knee. Practice can continue alone, with a partner, or in small groups.

Modifications
To encourage success, have the students count and report how many times they're able to kick the sack and keep it in the air.

Hopping Patterns

Level
   II and III

Area
   Large playing space such as a gymnasium

Equipment
   Plastic floor tape, music that encourages lots of activity

Objectives
   Students will improve eye–foot coordination while learning patterns of movement.

Setup and Description
   Mark off a series of ladders on the floor using pieces of tape or a collapsible ladder that you can lay on the floor. The length should be about 10 feet (3 meters) with the rungs about 12 inches (30 centimeters) apart. The first student in line hops a basic pattern from spot to spot, and then everyone else repeats the pattern. Increase the complexity of the patterns (e.g., figure eights, out-in-out). Use the music to help the students keep the beat.

Modifications
   - • Break the class into pairs using creative division methods. Partners hook elbows and attempt the activity together.
   - • Use larger landing areas to make the activity easier.

Human Foosball

Level
   III

Area
   Gymnasium

Equipment
   Soft foam ball; pinnies or colored shirts for half the class; 2 soccer goals or enough cones to effectively mark the goals

Objectives
   Students will use eye–foot coordination while working together with others.

Setup and Description
   Break the class into two teams using creative division methods. Give one of the teams the pinnies to distinguish teams. Use the lines on the floor as guides; students should remain on those lines at all times during the game. In order to get to the ball they must slide on their line.

   Position the students as in the game of foosball by splitting the teams into lines based on the size of the class. For example, on one side of the court from half-court to the end line, teams should line up as follows: six from team A line up 3 feet (1 meter) back from half-court, four from team B line up 10 feet (3 meters) away on the volleyball court line, four from team A line up at the back of the volleyball court, two from team B line up halfway between the volleyball court line and the goal, and two goalies from team A line up on the end line in front of the goal. The team on the other side of the court lines up in the same formation.

Each team tries to advance the ball toward their opponent's goal using soccer kicks. Players cannot use their hands. In addition, each team tries to defend their goal. After a designated time chosen by the teacher, the team with the most points wins.

You can set up the game with any number of players, but to give you an idea, the team setup could look like this:

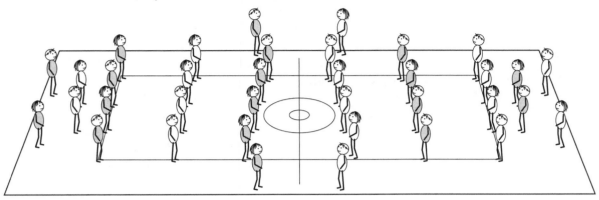

= Team A

= Team B

Modifications

• • Instead of restricting a group to a line on the floor, give them an area they must stay in.

• • The students can sit instead of standing and use a beach ball instead of a soccer ball. One row of students from each team sits along opposite walls, facing the opposing team (these are the goalies). All students must stay seated. No one can hold the ball except for the goalies, who may hold and throw the ball but also must stay seated. Start the game by throwing in the beach ball. The students hit the ball with their hands and try to get it to hit their wall for a score. No kicking of the ball is allowed.

Jump Rope Exploration

Level

II and **III**

Area

Large playing space such as a gymnasium

Equipment

Single jump rope for each student; double jump ropes; upbeat music (optional)

Objectives

Students will improve eye–foot coordination by jumping rope and demonstrate that they can follow directions while staying with the beat of the music and working together.

Setup and Description

Scatter the jump ropes throughout the playing area. As soon as students arrive, they find a jump rope that fits their body size by holding the ends of the rope with each hand and then standing on the middle of the rope and pulling the ends of the ropes up. If the rope reaches the armpits or slightly higher, it is the appropriate length. If the rope doesn't reach the armpits, students should choose a longer rope.

When the music starts (or on your signal), students jump rope in any fashion that they choose. For example, they could make shapes with the rope on the floor and practice jumping over and in the rope, or they could jump rope in the normal way by turning it over their head. They can also jump with a partner as well. This activity can last as long as you want it to. This is a great activity for assessing what the students have learned about rope skipping.

Have the students use the jump ropes to do a wide variety of jumping and rhythmic activities (e.g., Egg Beater, Double Dutch) based on the skill level of the class. Give some students single ropes and give some double ropes to use in groups of no more than six. Have the students practice basic and advanced jumping skills and encourage them to come up with their own rhythmic patterns using the jump ropes.

Modifications

- Jumping rope can be very cardiovascular and, therefore, fatiguing. If the students need to rest, have them do other activities such as keeping a rhythm by clapping or stomping feet.
- Hang posters on the side of the room or even play DVDs that demonstrate new jumping skills.
- Have students race by jumping rope in teams as safely as possible from one end of the playing space to the other and back.

Kick Back

Level
III

Area
Large playing space such as a gymnasium

Equipment

Soccer ball for every two students

Objectives

Students will become better soccer players by improving a variety of skills, including kicking, trapping, running, and dodging.

Setup and Description

Break the class into pairs using creative division methods and give each pair a soccer ball. All students with a soccer ball stand in one line and the other students stand across from their partners facing them approximately 10 to 12 feet (3-4 meters) from each other. The students stand on their nondominant foot. The partners with the ball toss the ball to their dominant foot and kick the ball right back to the other person's chest. After doing five repetitions with each foot, partners switch roles.

Modifications

After throwing to the foot, go to the thigh and foot. Then throw to the chest, thigh, and foot. Note that these modifications are extremely advanced.

Ladder Drills

Level

I, II, and **III**

Area

Large playing space such as a gymnasium

Equipment

Ladder that lies on the ground or plastic floor tape

Objectives

Students will improve eye–foot coordination, strengthen the nondominant side of the body, improve locomotor skills, and increase lower-body quickness.

Setup and Description

Place the ladder on the ground or use tape to mark off a ladder shape. Students line up single file. Specify a movement for them to perform using the ladder. The first student does the movement, and the next person in line waits until the first person is halfway down the ladder before starting so that nobody runs into each other. Movements can be simple or complex depending on class ability.

Here are some movements that you can use. The following movements should be done while facing forward:

- Step with one foot in the space enclosed between the two sides and two rungs
- Hop with two feet in each box
- Hop with two feet in two boxes, then reverse
- Hop with two feet in one box
- Hop with one foot in each box
- One foot in two boxes, then reverse and one foot in both boxes
- Two feet in the box and one foot out (diagonal)
- Hop while skipping one box every time
- Jump in every box
- Jump, skipping one or two boxes every time
- Hop to the second box and back one and repeat

The following movements are done with a designated side of the body pointing toward the line of movement and facing sideways:

- Two feet in each box
- Two feet in the box and two feet below the box
- Two feet in the box and alternate two feet below or two feet above the box

Modifications

Use jump ropes or tape to make a bigger ladder for students who can't get their feet in the ladder boxes.

Rabid Nuggets

Level
I and II

Area
Large playing space such as a gymnasium

Equipment
40 tennis balls

Objectives
Students will improve eye–foot coordination while working together to accomplish a task.

Setup and Description
Scatter the tennis balls on the floor. Students spread out in half of the basketball court and try to keep all of the balls continuously moving by kicking them with their feet. Kicks can be hard or soft and controlled. If one of the balls stops moving, yell "Rabid nugget!" The students then must locate the stopped ball within three seconds and kick it to keep it moving. If they do not locate the ball at the end of three seconds, then a point is scored. The more points scored, the more repetitions of an aerobic activity the students have to do at the end.

Modifications
- • You can reduce the playing area of the game, and you can also use larger balls so the students can better see the stopped ball.
- • Make this game competitive by having two teams kick the balls from one side of the playing area to another. Rabid nuggets that are found in one team's playing area score a point for that team.

Soccer Basics

Level
II

Area
Large playing space such as a gymnasium or outdoor field

Equipment
Foam soccer ball for every two students

Objectives
Students will learn the various soccer kicks while working on eye–foot coordination and will know where their body is in relation to a moving soccer ball, their opponents, and other teammates.

Setup and Description
Using a creative group division technique, pair the students up. Demonstrate the different kinds of soccer kicks, including the instep kick, where contact is made on the inside of the foot, and the drop kick, where you drop a ball and kick it with the top of the foot. After you have demonstrated the two kicks, have the students kick the ball back and forth to each other. First, one student uses the instep kick and the partner uses a drop kick to return the ball. Then have the partners switch so that

they get to try both kicks. Watch the students as they perform the kicks and point out any mistakes to the whole class as well as the individual student. Be sure to use constructive criticism and praise when correcting skills.

Now break the class into two teams using creative division methods. After a couple of weeks of drill progressions and lead-up activities, the students will be ready to play a soccer game. One team will go toward one goal and one team will go toward the other goal. Students will need to use the skills they have learned in previous weeks.

Modifications

●● Use other types of soccer kicks like kicking with the toe and the outside of the foot.

●● Using the instep kick, one pair at a time travels down the gym kicking the ball back and forth.

●● In groups of four, students stand in a circle and kick the ball back and forth to each other using a variety of kicks.

●● Make the field much smaller and play crab soccer with a foam soccer ball. Have the students play soccer, but they must walk around on their hands and feet in the crab position.

Soccer Slalom

Level

I and II

Area

Large playing space, preferably outdoors (the ball slows down faster on grass, creating a stronger ball-control environment)

Equipment

5 or 6 soccer balls; 20 to 30 cones, or as many as you have available

Objectives

Students will maneuver through an obstacle course with speed and control by correctly using both feet.

Setup and Description

Set up the cones a few feet apart in about five or six straight lines. Divide students into the same number of groups as lines using creative division methods. Pass out the soccer balls to the students and have them weave in and out of the cones while dribbling, kick the ball to the opposite wall or boundary, and return to the beginning using the same dribbling skills. When they return to the beginning of the line, they gently kick the ball back to the next person in line, who then performs the same drill.

Modifications

●● Shorten the distance that the students have to kick the ball, or increase the size of the soccer ball.

●● Give a ball to each student. When the first student in line is about 10 feet (3 meters) away, the next student in line begins the same task. After kicking the ball to the wall or boundary, have students wait until everyone gets there. This way, more students are involved and fewer students are standing around.

Soccer Square

Level
III

Area
Large playing space, preferably outdoors (the ball slows down faster on grass, creating a stronger ball-control environment)

Equipment
4 soccer balls; 4 cones

Objectives
Students will pass a soccer ball with both feet to other teammates in a closed environment.

Setup and Description
This drill teaches good trapping and passing skills. (Trapping refers to stopping an approaching soccer ball with the feet or the shins.) Set up the cones in the four corners of the playing area no more than 15 feet (4.5 meters) from the center of the area, creating a square. Feel free to make the playing area as large or as small as needed depending on the size and abilities of the class. Break the class into four groups using creative division methods and send one group to each corner of the playing area.

   To start the activity, kick the soccer ball lightly to the first group. The person kicking the ball can use any style of kick. Whoever is receiving the ball tries to stop or trap the ball. After receiving the ball, the student kicks it to the right and then runs to the right and joins the group that just received the ball. There will be four balls in play at all times during the activity.

Modifications
Change directions of the activity frequently and force the students to use their nondominant foot for a change.

Stock Your Closets

Level
II and III

Area
This activity can be played in a gym, multipurpose room, or outside

Equipment
6 hula hoops; soccer ball for every student; pinnies or colored shirts for half the class; 5 to 7 cones

Objectives
Students will dribble a soccer ball with control while keeping it away from a defender.

Setup and Description
Scatter three hula hoops on each side of the playing area. Divide the balls equally among the three hoops (add additional hoops if necessary). Use cones to mark off a rectangle in the center of the playing area.

Explain and demonstrate (or have two students demonstrate) the position the offense should take against a defender (turning back to defense) when dribbling. Then explain that the activity will require them to turn their back on a defender while dribbling in order to keep their ball away from the opposing team.

Break the class into two teams using creative division methods; one team wears pinnies. Students then scatter throughout the playing area in a self-space. The hula hoops on their side are their team's "closets." The object is to take balls from their opponent's closets and bring them to their closet by dribbling with their feet. No one is allowed to guard a hoop. Be sure to stress that they can take the ball away from each other so they need to keep their own ball close when dribbling!

Give them a few minutes to try to collect all the balls into their own closets. When you give the signal, they should stop. Count the balls if desired. Periodically stop play and discuss how well students are using their offensive and defensive positioning cues as well as their dribbling skills.

Modifications

•• If some children are not ready for multiple attackers, match up partners of similar skill levels and let them play one on one. Separate their playing area with cones so they can still contribute to their team's total.

•• Move each set of hoops to opposite end lines of the court rather than scattering them throughout the area. This increases the dribbling distance.

•• Have designated partners help students by dribbling and passing the ball back and forth down the floor, or by pushing children in wheelchairs as they dribble by hand.

Toe Tapping

Level
II and **III**

Area
Large playing space such as a gymnasium

Equipment
Soccer ball for each student

Objectives
Students will stay in their own personal space while controlling a soccer ball.

Setup and Description
This is a great warm-up activity for other eye–foot coordination activities. Pass out the soccer balls to the students. In their own personal space, the students jump up and gently place one foot on top of the ball. Then they jump up again and change feet, placing the other foot on top of the ball while placing the first foot on the ground. Start this activity slow and then speed it up.

> ⚠ **SAFETY NOTE**
> *Students are not to attempt to stand on the ball; they merely place their foot on the top of the ball and then quickly change feet.*

Modifications
Take this activity slow. You might want to start with smaller balls that are easier for students to use. Later add the regular-sized ball.

Chapter 7

Muscular Strength and Endurance Activities

These activities combine two parameters of physical fitness, muscular strength and endurance, to help students develop certain levels of strength or carry on activities for longer periods. Most people, including children, are usually weakest in their upper bodies, including the arms, back, and chest. Because of this, several of the activities focus on muscular strength and endurance in the upper body. Also, because cardiovascular activities demand certain amounts of muscular endurance, there are a few activities in this chapter that could fit in the chapter on cardiovascular endurance, but they have been included here because their primary focus is muscular endurance. As you will see, the number, variety, and type of activities is tremendous.

The key to appropriate activity selection is choosing activities based on the abilities of the students in the class. The levels listed for the activities in this chapter are merely recommendations; you must use discretion in choosing activities according to your students' abilities. In general, level I activities are appropriate for kindergarten and grade 1; level II activities are appropriate for grades 2 through 3; and level III activities are appropriate for grades 4, 5, and 6.

Aerobic Hoops

Level
II and III

Area
Large playing space such as a gymnasium

Equipment
Hula hoop for each student; music with a 4/4 beat (optional)

Objectives
Students will use hula hoops to strengthen the large muscle groups including the legs, arms, and shoulders.

Setup and Description
Each player gets in a hoop, places it on the floor, and faces you. The students then perform these six activities:

1. Hoop Warm-Up—Step inside the hoop and jog in place 16 steps. Then jump once in the following directions and then repeat the circuit: to the front, inside, to the back, inside, to the right of the hoop, inside, to the left of the hoop, and inside again. Jog in place in the hoop 16 steps and clap hands, then repeat the jumping pattern.

2. Hoop Hops—Hop on the right foot in and out of the hoop in a clockwise direction; then change hopping foot and direction.

3. Hoop Trunk Circles—Hold the hoop out in front and trace its shape with big movements by moving the arms and hoop in large circles just like the shape of the hoop. Change directions.

4. Hoop Pulses—Raise the hoop overhead parallel with the floor and lower it four times, bending the knees in time with the music each time. Raising and lowering the hoop, bend to the right, straighten, and then bend to the left. Repeat this sequence four times, pulsing the knees with each repetition.

⑤ Hoop Step-Kicks—Place the hoop on the floor. Step with one foot and kick with the other. Alternate this movement: Step with the right foot and kick with the left, then step with the left foot and kick with the right, and so on. Change directions.

⑥ Hoop Stretches—Hold the hoop overhead and stretch to the right, holding for 10 seconds; then stretch to the left and hold for 10 seconds. Repeat.

Modifications

Change the music tempo from slow to fast and vice versa.

Bath Time

Level
II and **III**

Area
Large playing space such as a gymnasium

Equipment
Scooters for half the class; 24 cones; rubber duck filled with sand for every fourth student; wand for every fourth student; towel for every eight students; relatively large barrel or trash can for every eight people; 2 or 3 foam balls per student; 4 hula hoops (1 for each corner); theme-appropriate music (such as "Splish Splash" by Bobby Darin, "Rubber Ducky, You're the One" from Sesame Street, or "Yellow Submarine" by the Beatles); plastic floor tape

Objectives
Students will improve their muscular strength.

Setup and Description
Set up four stations in the corners of the playing space. After demonstrating the activities, divide the students into four groups and assign them to sit at the station where they would like to begin, but make sure groups are equal in size. Allow three minutes or so at each station. The students begin the activity when the music starts and end the activity and clean up their area when the music stops. After the areas are cleaned up, allow students to move to the area of their choice as long as they haven't been there yet. The instructor should make sure groups stay the same size.

- Station 1: Scooter Swimming—Set up an oval area of cones and have the students "swim" on their abdomens on the scooters around the cones using their arms only. *Equipment needed:* Scooter for each child and 12 cones set in an oval.

- Station 2: Rubber Duck Curls—Each student should have one rubber duck and perform sets of 10 biceps curls with the rubber duck, alternating arms. *Equipment needed:* Rubber duck filled with sand for each child.

- Station 3: Row, Row, Row Your Boat—Students sit on their scooter and hold a wand. They reach out with hands on the wand and reach legs out and then pull back on the wand and heels at the same time. The heels pulling along the floor will pull the scooter forward. Continue around the tub (oval of cones) until music stops. *Equipment needed:* Scooter and wand for each student; 10 to 12 cones set in an oval.

- Station 4: Down the Drain—Holding a towel with a partner, students throw as many balls from the towel into the drain (a barrel) as they can in the three minutes. Once the ball is in the barrel it stays there. Set the throwing distance based on the skills of the students; 8 feet (2.5 meters) is a good distance for most students in grades 3 through 5. *Equipment needed:* Towel and barrel for every two students; plenty of foam balls; tape to mark the throwing line; hoops to hold unthrown balls.

Modifications

- Use your imagination to create different activities.
- Have the students navigate an obstacle course in which the challenges reinforce the theme of muscular strength and endurance.

Body Bowling

Level
I and II

Area
Large playing space such as a gymnasium

Equipment
10 plastic bowling pins per group; 2 tumbling mats per group

Objectives
Students will increase muscular endurance while rolling like logs.

Setup and Description
Break the class into several groups of six using creative division methods. Each group designates two bowlers, two pin resetters, and two guides. Set up plastic pins at the end of each mat. One by one, each bowler lies on one end of the mat across from a set of pins. Pretending to be big, colorful bowling balls, they log roll down the mat and knock over the pins at the end of the mat. Then team members exchange roles.

Modifications
Shorten the distance for students who aren't very skilled log rollers. If some student are unable to roll at all, set the pins around the students and encourage them to rock from side to side to knock the pins over.

Card Endurance

Level
III

Area
Large playing space such as a gymnasium

Equipment
Deck of cards; 4 task cards (large placards or poster boards with a picture of a card suit and an activity written below)

Objectives
Students will improve their strength and endurance.

Setup and Description
Create task cards, which should include a picture of a suit (hearts, spades, clubs, or diamonds) and an activity listed below the picture. For example,

- hearts are push-ups,
- spades are arm circles,
- clubs are jumping jacks, and
- diamonds are sit-ups.

Place one task card in each corner of the gym. Hand one playing card from the deck to each student. Once the students receive the card, they go to the designated area and perform the task. The number on the card is how many repetitions they should perform. If they receive a face card the values are as follows:

- Jacks are 11
- Queens are 12
- Kings are 13
- Aces are 14

After completing the first task, students come back to you and get another card. The process continues until the students have received five cards and completed all five tasks. Students who received lower numbers on all five cards should add their cards together. The sum is the number of laps around the play space that they should walk or jog (or any other locomotor movement you choose). Students who received higher cards take four laps using the designated locomotor movement.

Modifications
- You can give the students as many cards as you wish. You may need more than one deck if you have a large class.
- Vary the activities to fit what you have already worked on in class.
- The laps afterward can be modified; you may give them just a set number of laps to run after completing the five cards.

Centipede

Level
III

Area
Large playing space such as a gymnasium

Equipment
4 cones to mark the playing area if lines aren't marked on the floor already

Objectives
Students will work together while improving their muscular strength.

Setup and Description
Break the class into two teams, a team of girls and a team of boys. With the cones or lines that are already on the floor, mark start and finish lines about 30 feet (9 meters) apart. The teams line up single file facing the finish line. They should line up so that the first person is right behind the starting line.

    The players sit down and wrap their legs around the person in front of them to form the body of the centipede and their arms become the centipede's legs. On your signal, the players lift their bodies off of the ground with their arms and begin to push the centipede toward the finish line. If players become separated, they must try to reconnect. The winning centipede must completely cross the finish line with all its players connected.

Modifications
This activity may be a little difficult for large groups. You can make the teams smaller (a maximum of six per team) and do the same race.

Clock Stations

Level
I, II, and III

Area
Large playing space such as a gymnasium

Equipment
Enough tumbling mats to meet the needs and size of the class; cone for each station; cardboard sign with an exercise written on it for each station; whistle

Objectives
Students will increase muscular strength and endurance and cardiovascular endurance while working on the proper form of certain exercises.

Setup and Description
Make stations around the gym like the face of a clock, one for each group of five or six students. Depending on the size of the class, start with stations at 12, 3, 6, and 9 o'clock. If classes are larger, add more time slots. Put a cone at every station and place the sign with the exercise written on it on the cone. Break the class into groups of five or six using creative division methods and start each group at a different station. Everyone performs the activity at their station until the time is up and you blow the whistle. At that time, students get up from their station and go

clockwise to the next station where they perform that particular exercise. Go for 30 seconds at each station or longer depending on what you think is best for the class.

You can use a variety of activities for the stations. Some examples include the following:

- Sit-ups
- Push-ups
- Wall sits
- Tuck jumps
- Jumping jacks
- Wall jumps

Modifications

Remember to be innovative with your activities. Doing the same activities time and time again will create boredom and behavior problems. You will also have to modify the activities depending on what level you're working with.

Cooperative Fitness

Level
III

Area
Large playing space such as a gymnasium

Equipment

Tumbling mats; peppy, motivational music

Objectives

Students will work on muscular strength and endurance in a fun, innovative, and cooperative way.

Setup and Description

This activity can be used as a nice warm-up. Pair the students up according to body size and muscular strength. Demonstrate how to do a push-up and a curl-up or sit-up and then have the pairs spread out on the mats. One partner assumes a curl-up position on the mat with knees bent and feet flat, and the other partner assumes a push-up position with one hand on each of the partner's feet. As one partner curls up the other does a push-up. Have the students practice this for 30 seconds to 1 minute with periods of rest. At the end of the timed round, have the students switch places. Walk around and make sure that the students have correct form and are being safe.

After they have practiced for a while and are comfortable with this activity, put them up to the challenge of seeing how many of the exercises they can do in two minutes, switching positions after every 15 seconds. Play the music and see how well the students can perform the task. Stop the music at 15 seconds so that the students know when it is time to switch and then start it again. Finally, stop the music after the two minutes are up.

Modifications

Have the students perform the tasks together but not while touching—the students doing the push-ups do not have to have their hand on their partner's feet.

Crab Soccer

Level
III

Area
This activity can be played in a gym, multipurpose room, or outside

Equipment

2 playground balls per court or game (slightly deflated to prevent big bounces or ricocheting); 8 cones; pinnies or colored shirts for half the class

Objectives

Students will increase muscular strength and endurance in their upper back, shoulders, legs, and arms while learning to move in the crab position and working on team cooperation.

Setup and Description

Break the class into two teams using creative division methods. With four cones, set up the boundaries of the playing area; usually half of a basketball court is a good size. Set up additional cones to mark the goal areas. Have one member from each team come together and play rock, paper, scissors (see introduction) to decide which side will put on the pinnies. Goalies are chosen by team members or they can volunteer for the position.

Have the students assume the crab position, supporting the body weight on their hands and feet with the abdomen in the air and facing the ceiling. On your signal, students move around the floor in this position, passing the ball by kicking it with their feet to their teammates. The objective is to move the ball down the floor and score a goal by kicking the ball between the cones marking the goals. The goalies must also move in the crab position, but if the ball is kicked in their direction they may lower their body to the floor, catch the ball with their hands, and put it back in play by kicking or throwing it.

Make sure that the players do not crowd the goal area. Students must be aware of other players' hands when crab walking. During the game add more balls to increase the amount of activity.

SAFETY NOTE

Students fatigue quickly in this game so include plenty of rest time.

Modifications

Use a variety of balls to change the style of play, such as large cage balls that are 36 to 48 inches (91-122 centimeters) in diameter, beach balls, or smaller foam balls.

Crab Tag

Level
I, II, and III

Area
Large playing space such as a gymnasium

Equipment
None

Objectives
Students will improve muscular strength and endurance of the upper back, shoulders, arms, and legs while moving around the floor in the crab position.

Setup and Description
Choose two, three, or four students to be It. All of the students spread out and get into the crab position, supporting their body weight on their hands and feet with the abdomen in the air and facing the ceiling. When the game begins, the students move around the floor trying not get tagged by one of the It crabs. When students are tagged, the person tagged is now It and they change roles.

Regular tag rules apply. The other rule to this game is that the students cannot let their bottoms touch the floor. You are the judge and when students touch the floor, they must stand up, move to the side of the playing area, and complete five push-ups (or sit-ups or another activity). To get back into the game, another crab who isn't It must come over and tag them.

Modifications
Designate one or more students to be It and one or more students to be unfreezers. Unfreezers cannot be tagged during the game and should wear a pinnie or colored shirt. When students are tagged by an It, they should lower their bodies to the floor (to a sitting position). When an unfreezer sees them sitting, they should crab walk over and tag them to get them back in the game.

Daytona 500

Level
I, II, and III

Area
Large playing space such as a gymnasium or baseball field

Equipment
4 cones; whistle

Objectives
Students will work as a team and will learn how to stay focused and continue to work hard when they are tired.

Setup and Description
Set up a large, square playing area. Each side of the square should be at least 30 yards (27 meters) long. If you have access to a baseball field, the bases on the field would be a great place to do this activity. If not, place a cone at each corner to represent the start and finish for each group.

To begin, ask if anyone watches NASCAR. Explain to the class that the activity planned for the day is similar to that of racecar driving. The point of the activity is to catch the team or car directly in front. Break the class into four groups using creative division methods. Line up each group at one of the corners in the square.

When you blow the whistle, the first person in each line begins the race by running around the playing area counterclockwise, touching each base or cone. The goal is for students to run as fast as possible and catch the person in front of them, who also tries to catch the next person. After finishing the lap, players tag the next person in line on their team and then go to the end of the line and wait until it is their turn again. The activity continues until one student tags the person in front.

The end result should be a whole lot of running with the occasional "passing" of a car. When students catch up with another car, they tag that car. The game stops, there is a brief rest period, and then the game starts again in the opposite direction.

Modifications

Change the locomotor movement.

Exercise Bands

Level
II and **III**

Area
This activity can be played in a gym, multipurpose room, or outside

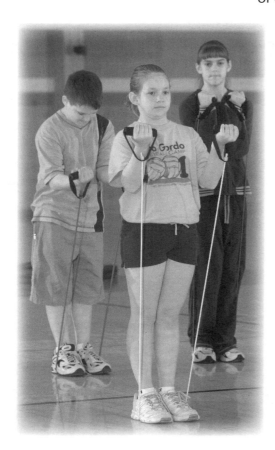

Equipment
Dyna-Band for every student or two; quick-paced music

Objectives
Students will improve muscular strength and endurance while working with unique equipment.

Setup and Description
Give every one or two students a Dyna-Band. Make sure the resistance fits the child's fitness capabilities. Here are the steps for students to follow:

First, hold one end of the band with your right hand up on your chest and punch out with the left hand, which is holding the other end of the band. Do 25 reps, then switch and punch with your right hand.

Next, put your right hand behind your back and your left hand behind your head with the elbow high. Push up to the sky with your left hand while your right hand is stationary. Do 25 reps, then switch and push up with your right hand.

Next, step on one end of the band with your left foot, and with your left palm facing downward lift upward. Do 25 reps, then switch and lift with your right hand with your right foot holding the band.

Finally, hold the middle of the band with your left hand and hold your left hand at your right shoulder. With your palm facing your shoulder, pull down with your right hand. Do 25 reps, then switch and pull down with your left hand with your right hand at your left shoulder.

Modifications

You can also do leg exercises with the bands. If students can't use their arms, then they can do exercises with their legs while everyone else is doing arm exercises (and vice versa).

SAFETY NOTE

Sometimes the bands may break or slip from a person's grip. Warn students that the bands may snap back and hit the user and it will feel like being slapped by a giant rubber band—ouch!

Fitness Cards

Level
II and III

Area
Large playing space such as a gymnasium

Equipment
Colored note card for each student (different color for each fitness activity); upbeat, motivational music

Objectives
Students will increase muscular strength and endurance.

Setup and Description

Write fitness activities on the colored note cards. You should have the same number of colors as you have number of activities. You may have 10 green cards, for example, but they must all have the first activity on them. Do the same for the red cards and the second activity, the yellow cards and the third activity, and so on.

Students come and get a note card and perform the activity on the card. Once finished, students then go and get another card in a different color. Here are just a few activity ideas:

- 10 push-ups
- 15 jumping jacks
- 20 sit-ups
- 10 V-ups
- Crab walk the length of gym
- Deep slides the length of gym
- Bear walk around the gym
- 20 squats
- Wall sits for 30 seconds

Modifications

- Vary the difficulty of the fitness activities to match class ability.
- Offer a larger number of fitness activities so the game takes longer.

Group Warm-Up

Level
I, II, and III

Area
Large playing space such as a gymnasium or outdoor field

Equipment
4 sets of 10 note cards with different exercises written on them; whistle

Objectives
Students will learn to work together to meet a goal and be physically fit in the process.

Setup and Description
This makes a great warm-up activity for other muscular strength and endurance activities, but it could also be expanded for further use. Write a different skill on 10 note cards. Students can help write the skills—examples could be sit-ups, squat thrusts, jumping jacks, and so on. Create four sets of 10 note cards, one for each group. Use creative division methods to break the class into four groups. Each group goes to their designated corner of the gym.

When teams are in their corner, one person from each group comes up and gets a card from you. When you blow the whistle, each team representative runs back to the group and everyone in the group performs the skill. When the group finishes, they choose another representative to get another card. There are a total of 10 cards for each group.

When the group has completed all of the exercises, they must sit quietly until the rest of the class has finished. The room will look completely chaotic, but the reason for the chaos is that every child in the room is being active at the same time. If the activities were done correctly, the class will be warmed up and ready to move on to the next activity.

Modifications
Use some imagination with the activities on the cards. Not only should the activities be challenging, but they should be appropriate for the age group you are teaching.

Hoop Mania

Level
I and II

Area
Large playing space such as a gymnasium

Equipment
Hula hoop for each student; note card with fitness task written on it for each hoop; aerobic music

Objectives
Students will move and recognize those movements and what muscle groups they are working.

Setup and Description

Scatter hula hoops around the playing area. Inside the hoops place fitness cards with specific activities on them. Use your imagination, but challenge the students you're working with. Here are some activity examples:

- • • Line jumps
- • • Jumping jacks
- • • Crunches
- • • Mountain climbers (students get in push-up position, alternately bring their knees to their chest, then return to the starting position)
- • • Jump over the hoop
- • • Hop on each foot

When the music starts, the students perform any locomotor movement that they want. It's their choice, but they must be moving all over the playing area.

When the music stops, the students stop, go to a hula hoop, and perform whatever task is on the note card in the hoop. Before leaving their hoop, students turn the fitness card over and again begin moving around the area with any locomotor movement. This is a nonstop activity, so be sure to include breaks.

Modifications

If you don't have hula hoops, use jump ropes or cones to form circles.

Isometric Tag

Level
I

Area
Large playing space such as a gymnasium

Equipment
Music that encourages movement

Objectives
Students will increase their muscular strength and endurance while learning to dodge and flee and work cooperatively.

Setup and Description
Designate two students to be the taggers. The rest of the class tries to avoid being tagged. If students are tagged, they must hold the push-up position until another student comes by and touches them. Make sure to change the taggers frequently.

Modifications
You can also have students hold the crab position (on the hands and feet with the abdomen facing the ceiling) and other positions that will increase strength.

Musical Push-Ups

Level
III

Area
Large playing space such as a gymnasium

Equipment
Tumbling mats, enough so that all students are on a mat; upbeat music

Objectives
Students will improve muscular endurance while following directions.

Setup and Description
Students spread out on the mats in push-up position and reach forward with their right hand while supporting themselves with their left hand. After returning their right hand to the floor, they raise their left hand while supporting themselves with their right arm. Then give them the following commands:

● ● Right hand forward, turn palm up, and return; left hand forward, turn palm up, and return.

● ● Right hand to left shoulder and return; left hand to right shoulder and return.

● ● Right hand to right ear and return; left hand to left ear and return.

● ● Right hand to left waist and return; left hand to right waist and return.

● ● Right hand to right hip and return; left hand to left hip and return.

● ● Turn to the right and repeat the steps facing the next wall

After practicing, add the music.

Modifications
● ● You can lengthen or shorten the steps to fit the abilities of the class.

● ● After the students are comfortable with the steps, they can make up their own steps. Take a break and have the class come up with steps together. Write them down on a large piece of paper so that everyone can see the steps and repeat with the new steps.

"Pop Goes the Weasel" Push-Ups

Level
III

Area
Large playing space such as a gymnasium

Equipment
"Pop Goes the Weasel" song

Objectives
Students will complete push-ups using muscles in the chest and arms in an endurance setting.

Setup and Description

Have students get in their own personal space and lie on their abdomen. When the music begins, the students raise themselves into push-up position. The music should have eight distinct counts (e.g., "Pop Goes the Weasel").

Taking the right hand, students touch the left shoulder and then they take the left hand to the right shoulder. This takes place during the first four beats. Next, the right hand taps the inside of the left elbow and the left hand taps the inside of the right elbow. Next, one hand touches the hand that is still on the floor and then the other hand touches the opposite hand on the floor. The pattern ends with an actual push-up for four counts. Repeat throughout the whole song.

Modifications

If students are unable to do full push-ups, have them use their knees as long as their back is straight.

Push-Up Hockey

Level
III

Area
Large playing space such as a gymnasium

Equipment
Tennis ball for every two students

Objectives
Students will control their behavior in a competitive situation and will develop strength and endurance.

Setup and Description

Pair up the students using creative division methods. Hand out one tennis ball to each group. The students get into push-up position. The object of the game is to get the tennis ball through the arms of the opponent. Players can use their hands and arms to roll the ball and to make sure the ball does not get past them. If the tennis ball gets past, the person who rolled the ball earns a point.

Modifications

- • Create teams instead of just pairs and have the teams compete against each other.
- • Use larger balls so that they are easier to manage. You could also slow down the pace of the game and space the children farther apart.

Push-Up Pinball

Level
II and III

Area
Large playing space such as a gymnasium

Equipment
Small foam ball for each group

Objectives
Students will use muscles in the chest and upper arms from the push-up position.

Setup and Description
Split students into groups of three or four using creative division methods and give each group a small foam ball. In each group, students form a circle and get in push-up position, facing the middle of the circle. Students create goals with their hands and pretend to be parts of a pinball machine. They try to keep the ball out of their goal and hit the ball into the other players' goals. Advance the game by putting groups together and adding more foam balls.

Modifications
If students are unable to stay in the push-up position, they can use their knees to stabilize themselves as long as their hands are still on the ground and the back is straight.

Push-Up Potpourri

Level
II and III

Area
Large playing space such as a gymnasium

Equipment
Tumbling mats; 1 tennis ball per student

Objectives
Students will improve their muscular strength by doing special types of push-ups.

Setup and Description
Sometimes performing regular push-ups can be boring. The following push-up activities should create some more excitement and provide the same benefits as traditional push-ups. In each case, students can choose to do regular push-ups (with the weight supported on the hands and feet and the body straight) or modified push-ups (with the weight supported on the hands and knees and the body between the shoulders and knees straight).

- Alphabet Push-Ups—While reciting the alphabet, students tap their shoulders, one tap per letter. On "A," they tap their left shoulder with their right hand; on "B," they tap their right shoulder with their left hand; and so on.
- Ball-Tap Push-Ups—Each student puts a tennis ball between his hands. Students gently tap the ball first with their right hand and then with their left.

Next, they tap the ball harder so it moves from side to side. Next, they touch the ball first with their right elbow and then with their left.

• • Group Goal Push-Ups—Divide the class into groups of five or six, and give each group one tennis ball. Each group forms a circle with the students facing the middle. Students try to slap the tennis ball between the hands (the goal posts) of anyone in their circle.

• • Partner Goal Push-Ups—Divide the class into pairs, and give each pair one tennis ball. Partners face each other about 4 to 5 feet (1.2-1.5 meters) apart and try to slap the tennis ball between the other person's hands (the goal posts).

Modifications

Try doing the push-ups in the crab position (moving on hands and feet with the abdomen facing the ceiling).

Push-Up Soccer

Level
II

Area
Large playing space such as a gymnasium

Equipment

Foam ball for each court; 4 cones per court to mark the boundaries

Objectives

Students will increase their muscular strength and endurance while holding the push-up position, gaining the strength to roll objects while balancing on one hand.

Setup and Description

Mark out three small courts with the four cones. The dimensions of the courts should be about 15 feet (4.5 meters) by at least 10 feet (3 meters) wide. Essentially, you'll have a small rectangle.

Break the class into six groups of five students using creative division methods. Individual games occur simultaneously so that one group of five goes against another group of five in each court. The students on one team form a line between the cones facing the other group of five in their court. The students should hold the push-up position.

Give the ball to one group in each court. The object is to hold the push-up position and roll the ball across the other team's line; they try to stop the ball with their hands while holding the push-up position. Remember that no one can move from one place to another. Everyone is stationary and holding the push-up position.

All students on the attacking team must be in the push-up position for the goal to count. Students are allowed to rest by placing knees on the floor for five seconds. Winners of one group will play the winners of the other groups.

Modifications

To allow the students to develop respect for students who are sight impaired, blindfold the students and use a ball that has a bell so that it makes a sound as it rolls. Defensive moves and blocks are now based on the sound of the approaching ball. Make sure the width of the playing area is shorter.

Scavenger Hunt

Level
II and **III**

Area
Classroom, gymnasium, or outdoor playing space with places to hide clues

Equipment
List of 20 riddles or clues made up by the students or teacher; 20 note cards with activities written on them; envelope for each note card; sticker for each group in each envelope

Objectives
Students will increase muscular strength and cardiovascular endurance while using knowledge and strategies to complete a task.

Setup and Description
Write various activities on note cards and put the note cards in envelopes along with stickers. Hide the envelopes and create a list of riddles that will lead students from envelope to envelope. Make sure the riddles are in a different order on the various papers so that all the groups aren't going to the same places every time.

Break the class into teams of three or four using creative division methods. Let them know that they will be working together as a group to figure out riddles to a scavenger hunt. Each group gets a paper with a list of riddles on it. Once they figure out the first riddle, they run to that place and find the hidden envelope. Then they pull out the note card and perform the activity written on the card. Once they have done the activity, they grab one sticker out of the envelope and place it next to the riddle. Then they can try the next riddle and continue until they have solved all the riddles.

When they are done, they come to you and show that they have all the stickers in the right spot. The first group to finish might win something or get to do something fun.

Try these sample riddles:

- ● ● There are lots of me stacked on top of me and I like to be climbed on. What am I? **Gymnastic mats**
- ● ● I am really heavy and I like to be pushed up. What am I? **Bench press**
- ● ● I'm made out of plastic and I like to be sat on. What am I? **Plastic chair**
- ● ● I'm long and wide and I like stuff to be put on me. What am I? **Table**
- ● ● I'm skinny and long and I like to be walked on. What am I? **Balance beam**
- ● ● I'm hollow inside and I like to be jumped over. What am I? **Vault**

At the stations, have the children perform various activities, such as the following:

- ● ● 20 jumping jacks
- ● ● 10 wall jumps
- ● ● Wall sits for 30 seconds
- ● ● 30 sit-ups
- ● ● 15 push-ups
- ● ● 10 tuck jumps

Modifications

- ● ● Put the stations closer together for students in wheelchairs. Make sure envelopes are within reach of students in wheelchairs.
- ● ● Designated helpers will need to help some students move to the different stations, and some students will need help pulling the note cards out of the envelopes. Students who are blind will need help getting around to the different stations as well.
- ● ● You can make the riddles very easy or hard depending on the skill level of your students.

Scooter Relays

Level
I, II, and **III**

Area
Large playing space such as a gymnasium

Equipment
Scooter for each group; cone for each group

Objectives
Students will improve upper- and lower-body muscular strength and endurance.

Setup and Description
Set up cones in a line at one end of the gym, 30 to 40 feet (9-12 meters) from the starting line. Break the class into groups of four, five, or six using creative division

SAFETY NOTE

Remind students to be careful not to run over their fingers or toes while riding and not to goof around with the scooters. Never allow students to stand on the scooters.

methods. The groups line up single file at one end of the gym. Each group gets a scooter and one at a time each student has to move on the scooter to the other end of the gym, around the cone, and back. The first group to finish wins. Students should stand when waiting to use a scooter and sit when they already have used it. This allows you to see which groups get done the quickest. Make sure you allow different students to be the first scooter rider in new relays.

Modifications

Require students to ride the scooter a certain way, such as sitting with legs crossed, lying on their abdomen, or sitting using just their legs to move the scooter.

Tug of War

Level
II and III

Area
Large playing space such as a gymnasium

Equipment

Long rope (at least 30-40 feet [9-12 meters]); handkerchief; gloves for each student (some students may want to wear gloves to prevent chafing of the hands); plastic floor tape

Objectives

Students will learn skills and sportsmanship while working toward a common goal and developing muscular strength and endurance.

Setup and Description

Break the class into two teams using creative division methods. Make a centerline using the tape and tie a handkerchief in the middle of the rope. One team moves to one side of the rope and the other team goes to the opposite side. Start with the handkerchief over the centerline. All players on both sides of the rope grasp the rope with two hands.

When you say "Go," the teams pull and try to get a player from the other team over the centerline. If one team gets the other team's players over the centerline, then they get a point. Teams have to work together. Instead of just giving the winning team a point every time, you can give the winning team the player who stepped over the line. Then that person joins the other team and the first team to get everyone on their side wins.

SAFETY NOTE

You should point out the correct way to pull on the rope so that no one gets hurt. Do not allow students to wrap the rope around their hands; when the rope is pulled from both ends, hands could be crushed. If you have gloves, give those to the students so that the rope does not burn their hands.

Modifications

●● Use a shorter rope.
●● Help students who can't hold onto the rope on their own.

Wall Sit

Level
III

Area
Space with an open wall (e.g., classroom, outer wall of a building, hallway)

Equipment
Stopwatch

Objectives
Students will build mental focus while working on the strength and endurance of several major muscle groups, specifically the quadriceps, gluteal muscles, and calf muscles.

Setup and Description
From a standing position with the feet about a foot (30 centimeters) from the wall, students lean against the wall while standing on both feet. On your command, they squat down until knees are flexed at a 90-degree angle and they hold this position for as long as they can. They should keep their arms and hands off the wall and off the knees and legs. Time the group or individuals using the stopwatch. After reaching the sitting position, students should quickly adjust their feet outward to fully support the body in a comfortable position.

Modifications
- Have the students do the wave when they're doing the wall sit. The wave consists of arms moving up and down as well as standing and sitting.
- Have the students hand a ball down the line and back as many times as they can before someone has to quit because of fatigue.

Workout Tag

Level
I, II, and III

Area
Large playing space such as a gymnasium

Equipment
4 to 6 cones to mark the playing area

Objectives
Students will increase their muscular strength and endurance.

Setup and Description
Mark off a rectangular area to be used for the game. Then have the students spread out around the area and designate two people to be It. The first time students are tagged, they have to do 10 sit-ups off to the side before returning to the game. The second time they have to do 10 jumping jacks. The third time they must do five push-ups off to the side and then they become a tagger. This game goes on as long as you want it to.

Modifications

You can modify this game for older and younger students by increasing or decreasing the number of jumping jacks, push-ups, and sit-ups. Don't forget to change the activities and the methods of moving around the playing area.

Chapter 8

Body and Space Awareness Activities

The theme of this chapter is where the body can move, including general or personal space, direction of movement, level of movement, and pathways and planes of movement. A potentially large number of activities exist for this area, and some activities cross over into other themes. For example, many of the activities involve music and could also be included in the chapter on rhythmic activities; however, due to their focus on the spatial awareness of the body, they are best suited for this chapter. As with locomotor activities, the majority of activities for body and space awareness focus on, but are not limited to, level I children.

The key to appropriate activity selection is choosing activities based on the abilities of the students in the class. The levels listed for the activities in this chapter are merely recommendations; you must use discretion in choosing activities according to your students' abilities. In general, level I activities are appropriate for kindergarten and grade 1; level II activities are appropriate for grades 2 through 3; and level III activities are appropriate for grades 4, 5, and 6.

Add-On Line Dancing

Level
II and III

Area
Large playing space such as a gymnasium

Equipment
Music with a country flair

Objectives
Students will learn to perform movements with music.

Setup and Description
Begin by letting the students vote on the music based on three or four songs you have prepared for them to vote on. After choosing a song, they find their own personal space. Play the music and let them move to the music however they want. They can do exercise movements or dance movements. After the students have gone through the song and found the beat, this time they come up with an eight-beat movement to share with the class that everyone can sequence together for a big class dance.

After designing their own movement, the students partner up and teach their part of the dance to each other so that now they know two parts of the sequence. Next, the whole class stands in a line facing the same direction. Ask a volunteer to move to the front of the line and teach her sequence to the class. Students learn the dance one part at a time without the music as each person comes forward to share his part of the dance. After the students have learned the dance, they perform it with music.

Modifications
Instead of each student coming up with a movement, break the class in groups of two or three using creative division methods to come up with one movement per group.

Alphabet Snake

Level
I

Area
Large playing space such as a gymnasium

Equipment

"My Snake" poem from the book *Something Big Has Been Here* by Jack Prelutsky; large flashcards of the snake making each letter of the alphabet (cards can be created by teachers or, even better, by students [with teacher approval])

Objectives

Students will learn body awareness and letter recognition.

Setup and Description

Students find personal space in the play area and sit down. Tell them, "We are going to hear a story about a clever creature that can make every letter of the alphabet with his body. Do you think you could make every letter of the alphabet with your body? I am going to read the story about my snake. Each time he makes a letter, I will hold up the card of that letter. I want you to try and make the same letter as he does."

The poem includes illustrations that make a wonderful visual aid for the children. Many children may be afraid of snakes, so having a picture of a friendly snake can help ease some anxiety.

Modifications

Have the students read the book as well.

At My House

Level
I

Area
Large playing space such as a gymnasium

Equipment

Hula hoop for each student

Objectives

Students will increase body and space awareness while learning to manipulate objects in their personal space.

Setup and Description

This activity requires locomotor and nonlocomotor skills. Scatter the hoops around the play space. Students each find a hoop that will be their house, or general space. Have the children get into the center of the hoop, telling them that they are now inside their house. Give the students certain movement cues that involve becoming an object they would find in the house. For example, tell them to act like a lamp and make that shape. Then they can act like a couch, a plant that grows really tall, a chair, and a table.

Next, they explore the different parts of the house, going to the basement and the attic. After that, they explore outside of their house in their backyard. They should keep one foot in the hoop while they circle around the house five times.

When they have completed this, they explore the neighborhood and walk around the gym among the other hoops, making sure that they don't step into another house. Watch to see that the children are remaining in their self-space and that they are able to stay out of other students' self-space. Ask them about their own self-space and others' and how they should respect that space.

Modifications

- • • Use larger hula hoops for children in wheelchairs.
- • • Assist students who are not able to travel through the gym on their own.

Beach Bums

Level
I, II, and III

Area
Large playing space such as a gymnasium

Equipment
Hula hoop for each student; beach decorations (e.g., beach ball, towel, sunglasses, chair, cooler, rafts); music with a beach theme (such as songs by the Beach Boys); plastic floor tape

Objectives
Students will improve body and space awareness by exploring different ways the body can move and learning about the components of personal space, levels, and directions.

Setup and Description
Students get a hula hoop and sit down inside the hoop within their own personal space in the play area. Tell the students that they are going to the ocean today and they will see lots of animals and do lots of activities. With the tape or lines on the floor, mark out the beach areas (outside the tape). Their hula hoops are boats on the ocean. Explain that you'll give them either an activity or an animal to act out when the music is playing. When you stop the music they have to yell "Shark!" and run to a boat, sit in it, and start paddling the boat away from the sharks. After everyone is inside their boat, give them a new activity or animal to act out once you turn the music back on.

Every time the music is off, the students should be running to their boats, and every time the music is on, the students get out of their boats and act out the animal or activity. The students can move anywhere in the gym as long as they maintain their personal space. Encourage the students to try to be unique in acting things out. The emphasis should be on moving in creative ways to see how the body can move.

Some of the activities will be done inside the boat and some will be done outside the boat on the beach or in the water. Here are some examples of creative movements and animals:

- Picking up seashells
- Running on the beach
- Walking like a crab
- Putting on sun block
- Swimming like a manta ray
- Swimming like a sea turtle
- Swimming like an eel
- Flying like a seagull
- Moving like waves
- Acting like the wind at the beach
- Playing volleyball on the beach with beach balls
- Surfing
- Swimming
- Jumping rope on the beach

Modifications

You might need to help students with disabilities think of creative ways to act out the animals and activities before you actually turn on the music. Students in wheelchairs and students who are blind often enjoy this activity.

Body Words

Level

I, II, and III

Area

Large playing space such as a gymnasium or outdoor field

Equipment

None

Objectives

Students will learn how to work together to make letters or words with their bodies.

Setup and Description

Break the class into groups of four using creative division methods. As a group they must work together to create numbers or capital letters or words by manipulating and maneuvering their bodies to make that particular figure. For example, you could have the groups make the letter "E," the letter "W," or the word "HI." There are endless opportunities. If the class is having fun making letters and small words, try bringing the whole class together to spell longer words, such as "ORANGE" or "YELLOW." This activity is only limited by your creativity.

Modifications

You could turn this into another cross-curricular activity that reinforces geography by having larger groups, maybe even the whole class, work together to form a state such as Oklahoma, Illinois, or Montana.

Breakfast

Level
I

Area
Large playing space such as a gymnasium

Equipment
None

Objectives
Students will learn to follow directions and perform movements in their own personal space.

Setup and Description
Tell students they are going to breakfast today. Have them get into their own space, staying close enough to hear directions. Tell them that this morning you want them to show you a piece of uncooked bacon. What does it look like? Is it standing? Lying down? Students should put their body in the shape that you request. Next, have them show you what bacon looks like when it is being cooked.

Tell them to show you an egg in the carton, then what an egg looks like when it is being cracked open, and then what it looks like being cooked. Have them get with a partner and show you a fork and a spoon.

Modifications
Use different breakfast foods and concepts. For instance, how might students interpret the crackling and popping sound of Rice Krispies?

Bubbles

Level
I

Area
Large playing space such as a gymnasium

Equipment
Mellow music

Objectives
Students will learn about body and space awareness.

Setup and Description
Students begin by standing in their own space with arms stretched out, pretending to be bubbles. When the music starts they travel around the space using any locomotor movement as long as they stay on their feet, trying not to bump into each other or the walls. You may want to have them walk to begin with and use cones around the area instead of using the walls of the gym.

If students bump or touch the wall they "pop," meaning they fall to the floor, curl into a ball, and count to five. After counting to five, the popped bubbles may travel at a low level and try to pop standing bubbles by tagging them. Make sure they are tagging gently and not trying to trip others. If a popped bubble tags a standing bubble, the standing bubble pops and the popped bubble gets to stand up and travel around the play space again.

You may want to change the size of the play space. For example, you can make the space smaller by using cones, and if a bubble travels outside of the area it pops. You could also use the lines on a basketball court as walls. Play the game for the length of a song (approximately four or five minutes).

Modifications

A faster song makes the activity more difficult.

Car and Driver

Level
II and **III**

Area
Large playing space such as a gymnasium

Equipment
Blindfolds for half the class

Objectives
Students will learn body and space awareness while following verbal directions and traveling using senses other than sight.

Setup and Description
This activity encourages trust of classmates and increases body and space awareness. It also focuses on the use of senses other than sight for movement. It works well if there are students in the class who have a visual impairment because it allows the other students to get a small idea of what it's like to have no sight. Break the class into pairs using creative division methods and give each pair a blindfold. Each pair spreads out in the open space, making sure that there is plenty of room between each group.

Tell the students that one of them is the car and the other is the driver. The car is in front and wears the blindfold and the driver is in back. The driver should place both hands on car's shoulders or waist. The cars must have their blindfold on at all times and listen to the driver's directions in order to know where they are going. The driver gives out directions such as go forward, go backward, go left, go right, faster, slower, or honk. During the activity, call out warnings such as "There's a dog in the road so everyone slam on your brakes" or "It's raining outside, turn on your windshield wipers." After a short time (to be determined by the teacher), the driver and car switch positions.

> ### ⚠ SAFETY NOTE
> *Anytime students are blindfolded in a game, there is potential for the game to become dangerous. The car is at the mercy of the driver, and safety is of utmost concern. Do not tolerate any unsafe driving. If necessary, have the bad drivers sit out. The driver is totally responsible for the safety of the car. Crashes are strictly forbidden!*

Observe the students to make sure that they are doing this activity safely. Watch to see if the cars are following their driver's directions and that the driver is giving good directions. After the activity is over, ask students how it felt to travel with no sight.

Modifications
Tailor this activity to the ability of the class by having them maneuver through obstacles.

Color Fish to the Rescue

Level
I

Area
Large playing space such as a gymnasium

Equipment
Carpet square for each student in blue, red, green, or yellow; a whistle

Objectives
Students will work on body and space awareness and teamwork.

Setup and Description
Spread the colored carpet squares out around the play area. Have students number off one to four and assign one color to each number. Instruct students to find and stand on a carpet square of that color. Ask "Do the fish want to swim today?" and encourage the children to wiggle their tails and fins in response.

Then say "Go!" and the fish swim all around the gym by walking or slowly running. Blow a whistle or use a code word and give them five seconds to find their home; they can return to any carpet square as long as it is their color. If students are not on a square in five seconds, they are thrown out of the ocean onto land and must wait until someone from their color brings them back into the game by giving them a "high fin" when play begins again.

Modifications
• • You can become a fisherperson and go out into the ocean and tag fish. When you tag fishes, they must stand in a hula hoop and wait for their team to save them by giving them a high fin.
• • Students with disabilities could move around on a scooter.

Far and Away

Level
I

Area
Large playing space such as a gymnasium

Equipment
None

Objectives
Students will move as safely as possible through general space.

Setup and Description
After introducing and practicing the concepts of finding a self-space and moving away from others in general space, tell students they will be playing a game where they will try to move as far away from each other as possible.

Choose two or three students to act as judges. The judges watch the other students as they move around general space. Call out a locomotor movement students should use while moving (e.g., walk, jog, hop, jump, skip, slide, gallop, leap).

After 20 to 40 seconds, give the freeze signal and have the judges each pick one student who is very far apart from the others. This student becomes a new judge and the old judge joins those who will be moving. Students who don't immediately freeze when you give the signal cannot be chosen as a judge even if they are far apart from others. Continue until most students have had the opportunity to be a judge.

Modifications

◦• Use music as the start and stop signal.

◦• Pick one student who is farthest away from everyone else to become the new judge. After each round, the current judge then picks a new judge.

◦• Let the judges decide which locomotor skill the group will perform.

Hokey Pokey

Level
I

Area
Large playing space such as a gymnasium

Equipment
"Hokey Pokey" by the Ram Trio

Objectives
Students will learn body parts and will move rhythmically to music.

Setup and Description

Students form circles of no more than 15 people. Demonstrate the Hokey Pokey before students perform it. When you start the music, students follow cues in the recording. Lead the activities and movements with imagination and in time with the music.

Expand the activity by having each student suggest a body part to include in the song. Discourage any inappropriate body parts.

Modifications

Most students with disabilities can perform this activity, but you may need to slow the music or sing it at a slow speed. To add difficulty, speed up the music or sing it faster.

Hoop Coop

Level
I and II

Area
Large playing space such as a gymnasium

Equipment
Hula hoop for each student

Objectives
Students will demonstrate control of an object and will develop awareness of their body.

Setup and Description
The students come up and each get a hula hoop. Then they return to their own personal space where they cannot touch anyone and place their hula hoop on the floor. Students place one body part inside of the hoop, and then two body parts, continuing until the whole body is inside the hoop. Then they work backward to remove the body parts. Keep it simple and tell the students exactly which body parts to put inside of the hoop instead of letting them decide which ones to put in.

Modifications
Have the students get into groups of two, then three, and then four. Do the same activity with multiple people around a single hoop.

Hoop Fitness

Level
I, II, and III

Area
Large playing space such as a gymnasium

Equipment
Hula hoop for each student; upbeat music

Objectives
Students will be aware of the space around them and work on physical fitness.

Setup and Description
The students come up and get a hula hoop. Then they return to their own personal space where they cannot touch anyone and place their hula hoop on the floor. They begin by holding the hoop in the right hand and, releasing their grip, spinning the hoop on the right wrist. Then they stop the hoop and spin it on the left wrist. Next they can try spinning the hoop on the right elbow and then the left elbow, and then the right ankle and left ankle. Can they balance on one foot while holding the other leg out in front of them and spin the hoop on the extended leg? Then they can spin the hoop around their waist and try to keep the hoop spinning.

Next, you can lead the students through several movements and perform a fitness routine stepping in, around, and through the hula hoop. Use your imagination!

Modifications

- • Change the tempo of the music and make the movements slower and then faster.
- • Have the students try to walk around the room while spinning the hoops on the elbows and wrists.

Look Out!

Level
I and II

Area
Large playing space such as a gymnasium

Equipment
Balloon for each student; peppy music (optional)

Objectives
Students will be aware of their own personal space and others around them.

Setup and Description

Give each student a balloon. Students then spread out into personal space and start hitting their balloon into the air with one hand of their choice. Change hands. Now they keep the balloon in the air by kicking it with one foot or the other.

After you notice that students are successfully completing this task, have them start moving around the play area, keeping their balloon in the air without touching any other students or their balloons. If they touch another student or balloon, they have to catch their balloon and, while holding it, come over to you to solve a mathematical equation or correctly spell a word. When they have accomplished the task, they can go back into the balloon activity.

When the class is over and if you don't need the balloons any more, see how many children can pop their balloon by sitting on it. After the balloons pop, students pick up the pieces and put them in the trash can.

Modifications
Have students do the same activity using other motor skills or walking backward.

Move to the Music

Level
I

Area
This activity can be played in a gym, multipurpose room, or outside

Equipment
Hula hoop for each student; music that is really slow and music that is fast and high pitched

Objectives
Students will learn about personal space and the ways their body can move.

Setup and Description

This activity simply gives students an opportunity to figure out ways that their body can move. Scatter hula hoops around the classroom. The students find a hula hoop and sit inside the hoop. They must never set foot outside of their hoop during the activity.

Play very slow music and tell the students to make themselves as big as possible and see what kind of movements they make. An example would be standing on their toes with their arms stretched out over their head. You can also add swinging or swaying arms to the activity.

Play the high-pitched chipmunk-type music when you give the command to make their body as small as they can. Crouching down into a very small body and trying to move inside the circle is a good example. How about lying down on their side and slithering like a snake? Some students will be very creative while others will struggle. It is a good idea to do the activity with the students to give them a better idea of what you want to see.

Modifications

Break the class into groups of two, three, or four using creative division methods and follow the same procedure only conducting the activity as groups.

Mulberry Hide and Seek

Level
I

Area
Large playing space such as a gymnasium

Equipment
6 to 8 folding mats; lively music

Objectives
Students will practice body and space awareness as well as listening skills.

Setup and Description

Stand the mats on their sides to create short walls randomly throughout the gym. Accordion them a bit so they don't fall over easily. Play the music and give students a locomotor movement (e.g., walking, skipping). As the music plays, students move around in one direction behind the mats without touching them. When the music stops, the children hide behind the closest mat. There may be one or more students behind a mat. Students may squat or stand but should not touch the mat. The purpose is to be quiet and hide.

Stand in the middle of the mats and sing, "All around the mulberry bush, the monkey chased the weasel. The monkey thought it was all in good fun. Pop! goes the weasel." At "Pop! goes the weasel," the children jump out sideways from behind the mats and scare you. Act totally surprised and begin the procedure again.

Modifications

Take away one, two, or three of the mats and see if the students can successfully hide in larger groups.

Musical Hoops

Level
I

Area
Large playing space such as a gymnasium

Equipment

Hula hoop for each student; enough cones to properly mark a circle or square, the size of which will depend on the size of the class; music that encourages movement

Objectives

Students will gain a better understanding of self-space and how their personal space may overlap that of other students.

Setup and Description

Make a path of hula hoops and have the students travel from hoop to hoop as music plays. When the music stops, each student freezes inside one hoop. Next, using cones or lines on the floor, designate a square or circle around which the children will travel. Place the hula hoops inside this area. As music plays, the students walk along the shape. When the music stops, the students enter the shape and find a hula hoop in which to stand, one student per hoop. Designate the hoop as each child's personal space and explain the benefits of maintaining a safe personal space.

Modifications

As the game progresses, remove one hoop at a time. Rather than eliminating children, as in musical chairs, suggest that children share their space with another student. Reduce the hoops until all children are in one or two hoops when the music stops.

Road Trip to the Zoo

Level
I and II

Area
Large playing space such as a gymnasium

Equipment

4 to 6 cones to mark the rectangular playing area; music that encourages movement

Objectives

Students will use their imagination and work on spatial awareness.

Setup and Description

Set up the cones in a rectangular area. The size of the area depends on the size of the class, so use your discretion. Tell the students they are going to go to the zoo. They must stay in their own personal space at all times, keeping their hands and movements to themselves. First, they get in their car, put on their seat belt, turn on the radio, and begin driving slowly around the cones. Have them stop at a red light every once in a while by calling out "Red light!" You could also hold up a large sign with a red circle on it. Tell them it is beginning to rain and they must turn on their windshield wipers to clear the rain. They should then move their arms back and forth as windshield wipers.

Now the rain has stopped and they are at the zoo. Tell them to park their car and come inside the cones. Then they should spread out and do animal motions as you describe them. For example, first, they see a giraffe with a long neck. Continue with other animals. The animals can have different dispositions too, for instance, a friendly bear, an angry tiger, and so on. Remind them to show you different levels and different ways to do the action than what everyone else is doing. You can also give students a snack while they are there. You could give them popcorn and pretzels and have them show you how popcorn pops or, with a partner, what a pretzel looks like.

Modifications

Let the students tell you what animals they like to see at the zoo.

Rules of the Road

Level
I

Area
Large playing space such as a gymnasium

Equipment
Hula hoop for each student; 4 cones

Objectives
Students will learn about personal space, pathways, directions, and levels, increasing body and space awareness.

Setup and Description
Set up four cones at one end of the room to create the garage. Each student gets a hula hoop that serves as a car. The students pretend they are driving around town. They are allowed to drive anywhere they want, but they must remember that they should be safe drivers and never bump into another car or driver. You are the chief of police and initiate movement. Green light means "Go" and red light means "Stop." Students try to hula until they have a green light again. You can either yell the words "Go" or "Stop" or hold up cards that have the appropriate colored circles on them.

Stress to the students that they need to drive their cars safely through the town in their own personal space and should not bump or touch any other cars. If students bump other cars, the chief of police will make them park in the garage. This serves as a time-out for students until they are ready to follow the rules of the road. When they are ready to follow the rules, they can come back onto the road.

Sample cues include the following:

• • Can you drive your vehicle in a zigzag pathway?
• • Can you drive your vehicle in a curvy pathway?

● ● Can you drive your vehicle up and down on a bumpy road?

● ● Can you drive your vehicle forward, backward, or sideways on the road?

● ● Can you turn your vehicle to the right?

● ● Can you turn your vehicle to the left?

● ● Can you drive your vehicle at a low level?

● ● Can you drive your vehicle at a high level?

Modifications

Have someone push students in wheelchairs, who can then hold the hula hoop and use it as a car. For other students with disabilities, you might need to simplify the activity so they don't get so confused that they end up not wanting to do anything. Students who are blind will need assistance moving throughout the gym.

Shape Walking

Level
I and II

Area
Large indoor playing space such as a gymnasium

Equipment

10 note cards with a different shape on each one (e.g., circles, squares, rectangles, triangles of all types)

Objectives

Students will learn how to manipulate their body in order to make a path.

Setup and Description

Create 10 note cards with shapes on them, some of which are pictures and some of which are words. Lay out the cards and tell the class that they are going to learn how to move their body to make a shape. Each student starts at a particular card, with no more than three or four students per card. After looking at the card and recognizing the shape, the students then walk out the shape that's on the card. For example, if the shape on the card is a square, they walk a large square on the floor. After a while, have the students complete the tasks again with different types of movements.

It's interesting to see students walk out the shape because some are only written. When students have walked all 10 shapes, try doing all of the shapes in a low position. This is a good activity to see if the students understand the movements their body is making.

Modifications

● ● Change the shapes to words that the students have to spell out while walking out the shape.

● ● Put mathematical equations on the cards that the students first have to figure out and then walk out the answer.

Shut Your Eyes

Level
I

Area
Large playing space such as a gymnasium

Equipment
Music (optional)

Objectives
Students will work on balance and will be aware of their body and the space around them while their eyes are closed.

Setup and Description
Students spread out in personal space. Instruct them to stand up with their arms at their sides and close their eyes. Is anyone having trouble staying balanced? Probably not. Now, with the eyes still closed, have the students lift their arms straight out to the side. Any problems yet? Now have them spin their arms in circles with the movement occurring at the shoulder like a windmill. With the eyes still closed, they put the arms back down at their sides and lift one foot off the ground. Let the students choose which foot they stand on and which foot they lift off the ground. Then they should change feet. Finally, they lift the other foot off the ground and, while the eyes are closed, reach down and hold onto that foot; then they do the opposite.

Modifications
Use your imagination with these movements. Obviously, you want to keep it safe but use challenging movements at the same time. If students are having trouble balancing, you may assist them.

Touch Your Nose

Level
I

Area
Large playing space such as a gymnasium

Equipment
None

Objectives
Students will identify the major body parts of the body.

Setup and Description
The students get into their own personal space where they cannot touch anyone else. Then ask them to identify parts of their body. Start by asking them to point to their head. Follow with the nose, ears, and eyes. Next you can do the hips, knees, and feet. Just keep the cues simple so the students can identify them.

Modifications
You could use this activity to start teaching the names of major muscles or muscle groups.

Twists and Spins

Level

I and II

Area

Large playing space such as a gymnasium

Equipment

Hula hoop for each student; "The Twist" by Chubby Checker

Objectives

Students will develop body and space awareness while learning the difference between twisting and spinning and learning rhythmic movements in their self-space.

Setup and Description

Scatter the hula hoops around the play area. Have the students pick out one of the hula hoops. Once they have chosen their spot, tell them that today they are going to learn a dance called the twist. Ask the class if they know the difference between a spin and a twist. Tell them that a twist is moving a body part around a stationary point, and demonstrate a twist by moving your wrist around. Then ask the class what other parts of the body twist. Have them demonstrate the twisting of their neck, wrists, hips, spine, and shoulders. Then ask them if they know what a spin is. Tell them that a spin is moving the body completely around one full turn. Demonstrate a spin on the ball of your foot for one full turn.

After this discussion, the class starts slowly spinning inside their hoops. They should not spin so fast as to become dizzy. Start the music and have them pick up their hoop while still standing inside and dance around the floor. When the words "Come on baby, let's do the twist" come on, they should twist. Encourage them to perform the movements in time to the music.

Make sure they use their arms while twisting. Observe to see that all of the students are able to distinguish between the twist and the spin. Also check to see that they are using rhythmic movement to the beat of the music. At the end of the class ask them what kinds of sports might use twists or spins.

Modifications

Use large hoops for children who need help and assist them in the hoops when traveling around the gym.

Chapter 9

Rhythmic and Dance Activities

Rhythmic activities frequently include music, but it's not required—contrary to popular belief, not all rhythmic activities are dances. This chapter does include a significant number of rhythmic activities that are dances, but it's not an exhaustive list. New dances are being developed all the time that stay current with recent musical hits or trends. Attend workshops and read the latest journals to keep abreast of new and developing trends.

Some activities suggest using specific songs. If you can't obtain a particular recording or simply prefer to use something different, remember to use discretion regarding quality and wholesome lyrics when playing music for your class.

Of all the themes in this book, the rhythm and dance theme seems to meet with the greatest resistance from students, particularly boys. Teachers are encouraged to make the dances fun and address the importance of good rhythm in various sport skills.

The key to appropriate activity selection is choosing activities based on the abilities of the students in the class. The levels listed for the activities in this chapter are merely recommendations; you must use discretion in choosing activities according to your students' abilities. In general, level I activities are appropriate for kindergarten and grade 1; level II activities are appropriate for grades 2 through 3; and level III activities are appropriate for grades 4, 5, and 6.

Blizzard

Level
I

Area
Large playing space such as a gymnasium

Equipment
Piece of white material (such as strips of white trash bags, sheets, or towels) for each student; winter music that may convey or sound like a snowstorm (classic songs like "Frosty the Snowman" or "Rudolph the Red-Nosed Reindeer" could also be used)

Objectives
Students will perform a dance to music using various manipulative skills.

Setup and Description
Have students perform the following activities with the piece of material, first without music and then with music:

- • Hold one corner of the material in each hand above the head and walk, run, gallop, skip, leap, jump, hop, and slide.
- • Hold the material in one hand and walk, run, gallop, skip, leap, jump, hop, and slide. Practice using both hands.
- • Hold one corner of the material in each hand and wave it up and down slowly at first and then quickly.
- • Hold the material in one hand and wave it up and down quickly and then slowly, using right and then left hands.
- • Make designs in space holding the material with both hands, then holding it with the right hand only, then with the left hand only. Make the designs in front of the body, over the head, and out to the sides. Try to make shapes, numbers, and letters.

•• Swing, shake, and twist the material.

•• Throw the material up in the air and perform different movements before it comes down, such as clapping, turning around, jumping, hopping, and so on.

After practicing these movements, play the music and let the students come up with blizzard dances using the movements.

Modifications

Use long, thin ribbons of material. Spinning and arm movements will create neat effects with the ribbons.

Dance Mix

Level
I and II

Area
Large playing space such as a gymnasium

Equipment
Music of your choice

Objectives
Students will be able to work together and use their imaginations to create one or more dance steps.

Setup and Description
Choose one song and play it as the children come into class. Break the class into groups of four, five, or six using creative division methods. Each group creates two movements to the song. Each group then demonstrates one movement and the entire class executes it. Then the next group shows its movement and the entire class executes it. Follow this pattern until each group contributes both of their movements to the dance. Then put the entire mix of dance moves together into one dance.

Modifications
You could change the tempo of the music or even require that each group put three movements into the dance, one of which must be a muscle-strengthening move (e.g., sit-ups, push-ups).

Dance Tag

Level
I, II, and III

Area
Large playing space such as a gymnasium

Equipment
"Bunny Hop" by Ray Anthony and Leonard Auletti or "Chicken Dance" by Werner Thomas; 4 cones for marking the playing area

Objectives

Students will get moving and think about dance moves previously, and they will do movements in different levels and improve their concept of self-space.

Setup and Description

Mark the boundaries of the rectangular playing area with lines or with cones; the size of the area will depend on the size of the class. Choose three students to be It; the class tries to escape the taggers. If they are tagged, they must stand there with their hand in the air. They can be untagged if a free person comes up to them and performs the chicken dance or the bunny hop. Once the free person does the dance for a minimum of 15 seconds the tagged student is free and back in the game. No one can be tagged while they are doing the chicken dance or bunny hop. Once students have been tagged three times, they become a tagger. The game goes on until you end it.

Modifications

- • • Have the students perform a harder dance routine or make up a dance routine when they get tagged. This allows the students to use their imagination.
- • • For younger children, slower music may be necessary, and you may have to add a rule to help all of the students work with each other in a cooperative sense.
- • • Have the students use different locomotor movements to move around the area, like skipping, hopping, galloping, walking, or crawling, to make the game more interesting.

Hamster Dance

Level
I and II

Area
Large playing space such as a gymnasium

Equipment

"Hamster Dance" song (see www.hamsterdance.com)

Objectives

Students will memorize a short sequence of skills and perform them in time to music while demonstrating their creativity by acting like a hamster as they perform the dance.

Setup and Description

Break the class into pairs using creative division methods. With pair members facing each other, have students form a double circle; in other words, the inside circle faces out and the outside circle faces in.

Demonstrate all of the steps to the dance and have students practice before performing to the music. Steps include the following:

1 Intro—Jump around and act like a hamster until the music says, "Here we go!"

2 Eight counts—Face your partner with your hands on your hips and give two head bobs to the right and two head bobs to the left and repeat.

3 Eight counts—Grab the hands of the person next to you and slide in the circle to the right for four counts, then slide back left for four counts.

4 Eight counts—Repeat the previous eight counts.

5 Eight counts—Slap your thighs two times, clap your hands two times, clap your partner's hands two times, and join right hands (seventh count) and then left hands (eighth count).

6 Eight counts—Leaning back with the arms straight, jump around you're until back in your original space.

7 Repeat the previous 16 counts.

Modifications

It may be difficult for young children to remember so many moves, so don't hesitate to reduce the number of moves or teach the moves in smaller, more manageable sections.

Improvisation

Level
I

Area
Large playing space such as a gymnasium

Equipment
Metronome, tambourine, or drum; timer

Objectives
Students will communicate emotion, interpret personal and group dance space, integrate personal style into expanded group expression, and gain peripheral understanding of rhythm and timing in synchronized movement.

Setup and Description
Students perform varying exercises. If you want, you can time these to keep the activity moving and to prevent a few students from dominating the activity. Here are some examples:

- Enact a verb (e.g., trembling). Enact a series of verbs. Each person can choose a verb and perform it for a specific time period.

- Enact a situation (e.g., dressing). Several small groups can each take a different situation. One person begins the pantomime and the others join and elaborate.

- March across the room next to someone else. Use the tambourine or drum to help the students keep a particular pace.

- Begin a rhythm using only hands and limbs as instruments (e.g., clapping, snapping fingers, slapping hands on limbs) and have the group join in one by one for several minutes.

● ● Do collective dance formations. Groups of approximately eight stand in a square each facing the same direction. A person from the front row chooses and begins a series of motions, which the others follow as closely as possible. That person then turns to a different direction, and everybody else turns too, creating a new front line. Another person from the new front line begins.

Modifications

Use music to help students maintain a specific beat where needed.

Lummi Stick Partner Tap

Level
I and II

Area
Large playing space such as a gymnasium

Equipment
Lummi sticks (see appendix) for each student; upbeat music (optional)

Objectives
Students will learn to tap a rhythmical pattern, to reproduce tapped sequences, and to develop their own rhythmical patterns.

Setup and Description
Students form two lines that face each other. Give a pair of Lummi sticks to each student. Stand at the end of the two rows, and with your own pair of sticks, tap out a rhythm on the floor that the students must copy. Keep the pattern simple at first, and keep tapping until everyone can match it. Then extend the pattern by adding more beats. Again, keep tapping and repeating the rhythm until everyone can match it.

After the class has mastered several different patterns, students pair off with the person directly across from them in the other line. Partners then take turns tapping out their own rhythms for each other to repeat. They should start with simple patterns of no more than four beats and move up to longer and longer rhythms.

Modifications

● ● Large groups of students could follow a rhythm of two to eight beats. Make up the rhythm for the students to follow.

● ● Break the class into pairs using creative division methods. Each pair is required to make up a routine of their own. They can do virtually anything during their routine, but they must remain seated. After approximately five minutes of creating their own rhythm, each group demonstrates the routine to the rest of the class. How many different ways (with safety in mind) can they use the sticks?

Make It Rain

Level
II and III

Area
Classroom, gymnasium, or outdoor playing space

Equipment
None

Objectives
Students will use their hands to make noises that sound like a rainstorm.

Setup and Description
Students will make the sounds of light rain, then hard rain, and then light rain again. They sit in a circle with their legs crossed and perform the following sequence of sounds:

•• The first student rubs the palms of the hands together. After three or four seconds, the second student follows and so on until everyone in the circle is rubbing their palms together. This sequence will remain the same with each of the steps. When everyone in the circle has joined in and you're back to the first student, move to the next step.

•• The next step is to snap their fingers.

•• The third step is to slap their legs.

•• The fourth step is to slap the floor.

•• After the fourth step is completed, they repeat the steps in reverse order.

When all of the students have completed the steps, the activity is finished.

Modifications
•• You can modify this activity to fit different sizes of groups. If the group is too large to make a circle, they may form lines.

•• You can really make students use their imagination in this activity. Have the students close their eyes and listen to the sound of the rain that's being made in the classroom. This makes the activity more difficult when the students can't see when they're supposed to join the rainstorm. They have to listen for their neighbor's sound to know when they should begin.

Make Your Own Sound

Level
I and II

Area
Large playing space such as a gymnasium

Equipment
Different object for each student to make noise with (such as wooden blocks with sticks, Lummi sticks, tambourines, and so on)

Objectives

Students will come up with different rhythms using different equipment.

Setup and Description

Hand out the various objects so that each student has one and have the students sit in a circle. Children will not all have the same equipment. Explain to the students that rhythms can be created by several different objects. Have the students experiment with their equipment. Then one at a time the students share their rhythm. The meter is two beats—one-two, one-two, one-two—in a consistent underlying pulse. Each student makes their rhythm last for two beats.

After all students have shared their two beats, combine them and go around the circle several times to see if all the students keep the same pulse at the same tempo. After the first continuous rhythm, the students pass the equipment to the person next to them in a clockwise motion so that they get to use other objects.

Modifications

Have the students create their own noisemakers. They can put rocks inside tin cans and tape them closed, for example, or, taking 12 sticks that are 8 inches (20 centimeters) long, they can tape the sticks together at one end and, while holding onto the taped end, slap the other end into their open hand to make a noise.

March to the Beat

Level
I

Area
Large playing space such as a gymnasium

Equipment
Drum

Objectives

Students will march to the beat of a drum and demonstrate that they can stay with the beat.

Setup and Description

This activity is fairly easy; however, some students might need help. Make sure demonstrations are clear and instructions are easy. Break the class into four lines using creative division methods and have the lines spread out. Emphasize personal space so that students are not touching anyone. Begin beating the drum and then tell the students to begin marching to the beat. With all the students moving at the same time, they walk forward five steps and backward five steps to the beat. Then you can add turns to the side.

Modifications

- Use your imagination by changing the locomotor movement or combining several movements.
- Divide the students into groups no larger than five and have them make up their own routines to the beat. Then have them demonstrate their activity to the class.

Memory Circle

Level
II

Area
Large playing space such as a gymnasium

Equipment
None

Objectives
Students will repeat sequenced rhythmic actions and remember patterns of rhythm while performing various rhythmic actions.

Setup and Description
Students sit on the ground in a circle so that everyone has a clear view of each other. On your signal, the first student performs some kind of simple action to a four-beat count: clapping her hands, slapping her knees, knocking on the floor with her hands or knuckles, stomping her feet, snapping her fingers, gently tapping the top of her head, nodding her head from side to side, flapping her elbows up and down like a chicken, and so on.

Next, the student seated to her left repeats that action and adds a new one of his own. Continue around the circle, with each student repeating all previous actions and adding a new one at the end of the sequence. Remind the children that each action should follow a four-beat count.

Once the class has gone around the whole circle and returned to the first student, the activity ends.

Ideally, the idea is for the entire class to do this together, but some children (adults too!) could get confused with the large number of activities to remember. If this is the case, divide the class into groups of six to eight members. Then have each of the groups do the task. This way each person only has to remember six to eight movements.

Modifications
If the class has trouble remembering so many movements, break the class down into smaller groups of four, five, or six.

Men in Black Dance

Level
II and III

Area
Large playing space such as a gymnasium

Equipment
Men in Black movie theme song

Objectives
Students will learn to perform the *Men in Black* dance with accuracy and consistency while keeping in rhythm with the music.

Setup and Description

Using creative division methods, break the class into groups of no more than five and have them line up in squads. All students should face the front of the room so they can see you. Break down and demonstrate the dance for the students as follows:

Step 1

• • Starting with the right foot, walk four steps forward (four counts).

• • Kick with the left foot four times (four counts).

• • Step backward four, starting with the left (four counts).

Step 2

• • Do eight knee bounces (eight counts).

• • Step with the right foot to the right and then pull the left foot toward the right (slide right together), do the opposite (slide left together), slide right together, and slide left together (eight counts).

Step 3

• • Do eight head bobs (eight counts).

• • Do four arm waves over the head, two counts to each side (eight counts).

Modifications

Depending on the students' level, you can combine or break down any of these steps. If the students are having difficulty, it's best to teach one step at a time and once they have learned a step, add on the next.

Move to the Beat

Level
I

Area
Large playing space such as a gymnasium

Equipment
Music with a peppy beat

Objectives

Students will pick out the beat of the music and practice a large variety of locomotor skills.

Setup and Description

Students spread out over the playing area, making sure they don't run into each other. Tell them a locomotor skill they are to perform, such as running, walking, hopping, skipping, crawling, slithering, rolling, and so on. Once the music starts, count out the beat and have the students perform the locomotor movement to the beat. When the music stops, the children freeze in position.

Modifications

Change the pace of the music. Use some slow music in order to challenge the students to control their movements in slow motion.

The Old Brass Wagon

Level
I

Area
Large playing space such as a gymnasium

Equipment

Hula hoop for every four students; "The Old Brass Wagon" song (if you can't find this song, one of your choosing is fine)

Objectives

Students will learn directional control by going left and right while also learning to move rhythmically in different directions.

Setup and Description

Have the students gather around the center of the play space. Tell them that they are going to do a song called "The Old Brass Wagon," but first they must practice. Ask the students to close their eyes and raise their right hand without looking at each other. Then they should raise their left hand. Look for students who have difficulty distinguishing between left and right and put an *R* on their right hand and an *L* on their left.

Using creative division methods, break the class into groups of no more than four people and distribute one hula hoop to each group. Each group circles around the hoop, holding it parallel with the ground.

1. Students circle left the old brass wagon by turning sideways, grasping the hoop with their right hand, and circling to the left in a clockwise motion.
2. The students then hold the hula hoop with their left hand and circle counter-clockwise.
3. Then they circle right the old brass wagon. This time using their right hand, they move clockwise.
4. Tell everyone to get inside the old brass wagon by pulling the hula hoop over their heads so that they are all inside the hoop.
5. Signal everybody to get out of the old brass wagon. The students then move from under the hoop and hold the hoop to the outside of their bodies.

Play the song so they can listen to the timing of the music while you give the directions. Repeat until the class can do the movements smoothly and correctly.

Modifications

Change the locomotor pattern to skipping, hopping, jumping, and so on. You could also place the hula hoop on the floor and the students could move around the hoop as they circle. This would give the students a specific pattern to move around.

The Raccoon's Tree

Level
I

Area
Large playing space such as a gymnasium

Equipment

Hula hoop for each student; upbeat music

Objectives

Students will learn to be creative with movement and raise their heart rate for cardiovascular health.

Setup and Description

Hand out the hula hoops and have students place them on the floor in front of them. The hula hoop represents the tree and the student is the raccoon. Before you start the music, explain the four movements that the students will be performing. Each move is four counts:

1. During the first four counts, make raccoon ears, placing your hands on your head with your fingers extended to represent the ears.
2. During the second set of four counts, make raccoon whiskers by placing your hands to the sides of your mouth so that the fingers extend outward like whiskers.
3. During the third set of four, make a raccoon mask by placing your hands over your eyes like a mask.
4. During the last four counts, jog around your hula hoop once.

After explaining and demonstrating the dance, ask if there are any questions. Then start the music. The music should have an obvious beat so the students can catch on easily. After completing the dance once, have the students come up with their own movements and repeat the process. You can use this dance to see what movements the students come up with for each body part used in the dance. The students can be very creative.

Modifications

Use different animals such as a bear, lion, raccoon, horse, elephant, and so on. Use your imagination and make it fun for the students.

Ribbon Motion

Level
III

Area
Large playing space such as a gymnasium

Equipment
Rhythmic gymnastics ribbon (see appendix) for each student; lively music

Objectives
Students will practice various locomotor skills and experiment with moving to music.

Setup and Description
Put on some lively music and allow children to express the rhythms through dance and the ribbons. Students should be free to express what the music is sharing with them. They can use a variety of locomotor activities like jumping, running, skipping, galloping, hopping, and walking, and they can move the ribbons above their head, below their knees, or out to the sides of their body while they move around the gym.

Modifications
Change the tone and tempo of the music. If the first music was fast and peppy, make the next music slow and methodical.

Santa Claus Is Coming to Town

Level
I and II

Area
Large playing space such as a gymnasium

Equipment
"Santa Claus Is Coming to Town" song

Objectives
Students will move to the rhythm of the music while keeping time with the steps in the dance.

Setup and Description
Teach students the steps to the dance:

1. During the intro sway the upper body to the right and left while reaching out with the arms at the same time.
2. When the jingling starts, shake the right hand (eight counts), then the left hand (eight counts), and then both hands for eight counts.
3. When the singing starts, take four steps up and four steps back. Repeat for a total of 16 counts.
4. Take four steps to the right and four steps to the left, which will take you back to the starting point. Repeat for a total of 16 counts.

⑤ On the last "Santa Claus is coming to town," shake arms up and down and bend at the waist.

⑥ For a total of 16 counts, jump forward eight times with arms crossed, then jump backward eight times with arms crossed.

⑦ On the last "Santa Claus is coming to town," shake arms up and down and bend at the waist.

⑧ Grapevine to the right four counts and then grapevine to the left for four counts. Repeat for a total of 16 counts.

⑨ On the line "He knows when you've been bad or good," hold up the right hand and then the left with palms up like a scale weighing something. On "So be good for goodness sake," shake a finger.

⑩ Repeat the dance from the beginning.

⑪ At the very end, shake the arms up and down and bend at the waist.

Modifications

If the grapevine steps are too difficult, use side steps instead.

Seven Jumps

Level
I and II

Area
Large playing space such as a gymnasium

Equipment

"Seven Jumps" song from the *International Folk Dances* album (sometimes also called *All-Purpose Folk Dances*) by the Michael Herman Folk Dance Orchestra (RCA Victor); 4 cones to mark the rectangular playing area

Objectives

Students will move to the rhythm of the music while keeping time with the steps in the dance.

Setup and Description

Students find their self-space in the activity area. During the first stanza of "Seven Jumps," they skip throughout the room without running into each other. Remind them to use all the space.

After the upbeat stanza of music, they freeze in a balanced position of their choice when they hear the tone. They hold that balance until the end of that tone and then begin skipping again when they hear the upbeat stanza of music.

They continue this throughout the song. The number of tones increases incrementally (i.e., two, three, four, and so on up to eight tones) with each upbeat stanza. The students change their balance position after each tone; for example, on the last tone section of the song there are eight breaks in the tone, so the students to do eight static balances in their self-space.

Insist on good balance and praise the students who are doing interesting static balances during the tone phase of the song.

Modifications

- • • Use another song with a faster tempo or, if you are able, use the same song and increase the speed.

- • • Change the locomotor patterns from skipping to other options like hopping, jumping, walking, and so on.

Shadow Dancing

Level

I, II, and **III**

Area

Large playing space such as a gymnasium

Equipment

Upbeat music

Objectives

Students will express themselves through dance, and they will learn how to be a leader and how to mimic the leader.

Setup and Description

Students stand in a circle and you stand in the center of the circle. Tell the students that shadow dancing is simply mimicking exactly what the person in the middle is doing and give an example. For instance, slowly lift your left arm up over your head and touch your right shoulder followed by standing on your left foot and lifting your right foot off the ground. Then return to the starting position. Leaders should challenge the ability levels of the class.

Play music during the dance and designate someone to be the leader. When the music stops, it is time for a new leader. The leader picks someone else in the circle and that person becomes the new leader. Students should not be forced to lead if they don't want to. Most students choose to lead after they see all of their classmates lead anyway. Encourage the students to do dance moves that haven't already been done. If students are having problems coming up with a move, assist them. This game is a great way to teach students how to be a leader; all they need is the initiative.

Modifications

The modifications for this activity are limitless. Any combination of body movements that challenges the group would be effective. You can also change the tone or the mood of the music. Some music might be slow and pensive and other music might be fast and spirited.

Shakers

Level
I

Area
Large playing space such as a gymnasium

Equipment
Shaker for each student; music in various tempos

Objectives
Students will use shakers in manipulative activities involving rhythm and dance.

Setup and Description
Shakers are containers that are half full of beads or rocks. You can make them or purchase them. Whatever you choose, they must produce some noise when they're shaken. Give each student a shaker. They can play with the shakers for a while at the beginning of class and get familiar with the noise it makes and how to make the loudest and softest noise. Then have students follow you as you teach them some different rhythms with the shakers. Next let the students create their own rhythms. One at a time they come to the front of the class and present the rhythm to their classmates and then everyone repeats the rhythm.

Modifications
Break the class into groups of two or more using creative division methods and have them develop a shaker routine together. It's fine for them to gently toss the shakers back and forth during this task.

Simon Says "Move"

Level
I and II

Area
Large playing space such as a gymnasium

Equipment
Drum

Objectives
Students will march to the beat of a drum and follow directions.

Setup and Description

Break the class into four lines using creative division methods and have them spread out while staying in straight lines. Start beating on the drum while all the students march forward to the beat, staying in their lines. Then add commands to the activity. Students should do the command if it begins with "Simon says." However, if a command does not begin with "Simon says" and the students do the command, they are eliminated. They move to the side of the play area, perform 10 sit-ups or push-ups or jump rope 25 times, and then rejoin the game.

The commands are endless, so use your imagination. Here are some examples:

- • "Simon says, 'Move your right arm above your head and hold it there.'"
- • "Simon says, 'Move your left arm above your head and hold it there.'"
- • "Drop both your arms to your side."
- • "Simon says, 'Place your right hand on your head.'"
- • "Place your left hand on your hip."

Some students may have trouble following the commands, so speak loudly. Demonstrations and simple instructions are vital.

Modifications

Instead of walking at the beginning of the activity, have students do another locomotor activity.

Snap

Level

I, II, and **III**

Area

Large playing space such as a gymnasium

Equipment

None

Objectives

Students will learn to maintain a rhythm while concentrating on a number.

Setup and Description

This game involves a three-count rhythm, which students should practice so the game can be successful. The rhythm goes like this:

- • On count 1, slap your knees.
- • On count 2, clap your hands.
- • On count 3, snap your fingers.

Students sit in a circle and number off so that each person has a different number. Beginning the rhythm slowly, call out a number on the third count, the snapping. The player whose number was called must then call another number the next time the group gets to the third count. Players are not eliminated for making an error; correct them and try again.

Following are types of errors that students must avoid:

- • • Breaking the rhythm
- • • Not calling another number after theirs has been called
- • • Calling a number when their number has not been called
- • • Calling the number of a player who has already been called

Modifications

- • • You can develop a variety of sequences to challenge the group.
- • • Start with smaller groups if students are having trouble with the skills. Smaller groups would be less intimidating.

Stayin' Alive Dance

Level
II and **III**

Area
Large playing space such as a gymnasium

Equipment
"Stayin' Alive" song by the Bee Gees

Objectives
Students will enhance rhythmic ability and cardiovascular endurance by moving in unison to the beat of a fast-moving song.

Setup and Description
This dance, performed to "Stayin' Alive," is fast moving with lots of activity. Break the class into groups of no more than five using creative division methods, or have them simply spread out around the play space.

It usually is best to demonstrate the steps first, have the students follow you, and then put the steps to music. Here are the steps to the dance:

1 Take four steps forward (four counts).

2 Take four steps backward (four counts).

3 Grapevine to the right (four counts).

4 Grapevine to the left (four counts).

5 Point with your right index finger to the ceiling (one count).

6 Point with your right index finger to your left toe (one count).

7 Point with your right index finger to the ceiling (one count).

8 Point with your right index finger to your left toe (one count).

9 Flap your arms with your hands under your arms and click your heels (four counts).

10 Tap your right toe forward twice (two count).

11 Tap your right toe to the back twice (two counts).

12 Tap your right toe forward (one count).

13 Tap your right toe to the back (one count).

⑭ Tap your right toe to the side (one count).

⑮ Bring your right knee up and pivot in a one-quarter turn to the left (one count).

⑯ Repeat the sequence.

Modifications

• • Beginning students find it less confusing if they do not turn the dance by pivoting. Instead they could just bring their leg up and hold for one count or do a hop without changing the direction they are facing.

• • If the students find the grapevine too difficult, use side steps instead.

• • After learning the dance, students could create their own disco dance by using the steps and putting them into a different sequence.

Stomp

Level
I, II, and **III**

Area
Large playing space such as a gymnasium

Equipment
Large variety of everyday objects from which sound can be produced (e.g., cups, spoons, basketballs, beanbags); music in a variety of tempos

Objectives
Students will understand different types of beats and tempos and realize that rhythm is all around them.

Setup and Description
Tell the students that there are different types of beats and tempos all around them in all types of sports, actions, and routines. Then give students one item each that they can use to make noise. Students can be spaced randomly around the area or in a circle; teachers may use their discretion. Starting with a central steady beat, one by one each student creates another portion of rhythm with a different beat, experimenting with slow tempos, fast tempos, and syncopations. Each student demonstrates a rhythm, and then all students follow that rhythm.

Modifications
Have students play their instruments to different types of music from different countries, which will teach some diversity of sounds and instruments. Some great examples are the differences among Latin, German, Chinese, Russian, and American music.

Swim to the Beat

Level
I

Area
Large playing space such as a gymnasium

Equipment
Music in 4/4 time

Objectives
Students will perform steps in time with music.

Setup and Description

Students spread out in their own personal space with everyone facing the same direction. Play part of the music to familiarize the students with it. Next, teach some of the steps and have the students perform them first without music and then with music. Continue teaching the steps while building on what the students have already learned until they have learned all the steps.

Here are the steps for the measures in the song:

1. 1 through 4—Sit on the floor and lean back on the forearms. Flutter kick, alternating legs on the beat.

2. 5 through 8—Turn over onto the abdomen, spin around so you're facing the teacher, and lie in a prone position. Flutter kick the legs, alternating legs on the beat.

3. 9 through 12—Stand and do the arm stroke of the backstroke while jumping in place, one jump per beat.

4. 13 through 16—Repeat the steps for measures 9 through 12.

5. 17 through 18—Do the arm stroke of the front crawl (freestyle) while hopping and stepping to the left. Do one arm stoke for each hop on the left foot and each step on the right foot.

6. 19 through 20—Repeat the last sequence while moving to the right (hopping in place). Alternating feet should hit the floor each beat.

7. 21 through 22—Repeat the steps for measures 17 and 18.

8. 23 through 24—Repeat the steps for measures 19 and 20.

9. 25 through 28—Do the arm stroke for the breaststroke while running in place. Alternating feet should hit the floor on each beat.

10. 29 through 32—Do the arm stroke for the butterfly while jumping forward. Jump once on each beat.

11. 33 through 40—Pretend to dry off with a towel while doing the twist.

Repeat as many times as desired.

Modifications

You can use different sport skills and create the same type of dance.

Texas Star Square Dance

Level
III

Area
Large playing space such as a gymnasium

Equipment
Square-dance music; microphone and public address system (optional)

Objectives
Students will follow directions while staying with the music and working together to accomplish a task.

Setup and Description
This is a level III activity, and it's assumed that you have already taught the students many of the basic square-dancing skills. Students should already be able to perform steps like do-si-do, squares, grapevine, forming a star, swinging your partner, promenade, and others.

Using creative division methods, break the class into groups with four couples in each group so that eight people make up one square with four gents and four ladies. Walk through the dance slowly at first. You want to make sure that everyone understands the basic movements and can complete them. After walking through the movements two or three times, introduce the music, still watching to make sure everyone understands and is demonstrating the dance correctly. Because the gents will leave with a new lady after the first set is done, the dance needs to be repeated three more times so they can get back to their original partner.

Calls
- Ladies to the center and back to the bar.
- Gents to the center and form a star.
- Right hand cross to the center.
- Back with the left and don't get lost.
- Meet your pretty girl, pass her by.
- Hook the next gal on the fly (star promenade).
- The gents swing out, ladies swing in, and form that Texas Star again.
- Break that star and everybody swing.
- Promenade home with the new little thing (gents have new partners).

Repeat three times until students are back with their original partners.

Modifications
If students are having a difficult time with this, you could show a video or DVD to demonstrate the correct way to perform these skills and how they go together.

Tinikling

Level
II and III

Area
Large playing space such as a gymnasium

Equipment

2 PVC pipes that are 8 feet (2.5 meters) long for every six students; 2 blocks of wood that are 2 by 4 by 24 inches (5 by 10 by 61 centimeters) for every six students

Objectives

Students will improve their rhythm by keeping time with pipes and jumping to the rhythm of the pipes.

Setup and Description

Break the class into groups of no more than six using creative division methods. One student sits cross-legged on the ground at each end of the two pipes. They each hold the ends of the two pipes with the fingertips. The pipes should rest on top of the blocks of wood.

The students holding the pipes practice making the tinikling rhythm, which involves hitting the pipes together at the same time twice. Then, spreading the pipes apart by at least 16 inches (40 centimeters), they hit the pipes on the blocks at the same time twice.

Once the pipe holders have the rhythm down, two people stand to the side of the pipes. After studying the rhythm, they begin jumping. While the holders are hitting the pipes on the wood, the jumpers should jump twice in the middle. When the pipes are being hit together, the jumpers should jump to the outside of the pipes for a count of two.

One of three techniques can be used here.

• • First, the jumpers may start with both feet on one side of the pipes. When the pipes are hitting each other, the players jump twice on the outside of the pipes. When the pipes are tapping the boards, the players jump twice in between the pipes.

• • Second, the jumpers may begin by straddling the two pipes. When the pipes are together, the players jump twice, and when they're separated and hitting the boards, the players jump up and land both feet between the pipes for two counts and then return to a straddle.

• • Third, jumpers may start on the outside of the pipes with both feet on the same side, and when the sticks are open, they move into the separated sticks, stepping one foot in at a time and then out the other side using a step-together-step-pause rhythm. Keeping the appropriate pace, the jumpers move back through to the original side.

The students can make up any combination of jumps they wish as long as they

SAFETY NOTE

Warn the students not to fully grasp the pipes because they could hit their fingers, and they should not stick their thumb or fingers in the end of the pipe. In addition, the pipe handlers must focus on their task and try not to hit the jumper's legs or feet with the pipes.

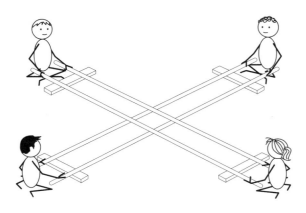

maintain the same rhythm. They can work on jumping on one foot, adding half turns, and so on.

Change pipe handlers frequently so everyone gets a chance to jump. When everyone gets pretty good at jumping, add more than one jumper at the same time.

Modifications

- • • Add two more pipes to form a cross pattern (see figure). All pipe handlers use the exact same rhythm. This modification is called the Eggbeater.

- • • Add music. Although this is a rhythmic activity in itself, adding music helps the students maintain the rhythm.

Tony Chestnut

Level
I

Area
Large playing space such as a gymnasium

Equipment
"Tony Chestnut" song

Objectives
Students will memorize a short sequence of skills and perform them in time to music while also demonstrating knowledge of body parts.

Setup and Description
Students stand in their own personal space where they can see you. They perform movements when specific words are spoken in the music. Words associated with actions are as follows:

- • • Tony—Touch toes then knees.
- • • Neal—Kneel onto one knee.
- • • Chest—Touch chest.
- • • Pat—Pat knee.
- • • Nut—Touch head.
- • • Bob—Bounce up and down.
- • • Knows—Touch head.
- • • Russell—Hit sides of thighs.
- • • I—Touch eye.
- • • Skip—Skip four times in circle.
- • • Love—Cross hands over heart.
- • • Silly—Shake head back and forth.
- • • You—Point.

    • • Hip—Hands on hips and swing hips.

    • • Eileen—Touch eye, then lean.

    • • End—Turn around and pat bottom.

Modifications

Children of this age may have difficulty remembering 15 different commands and movements, so break them down into groups of five or even three if necessary.

Chapter 10

Team-Building Activities

Team-building activities are designed to help students go beyond their perceived boundaries to reach personal and team goals. Noncompetitive games and group problem-solving activities are the methods used to help students reach these goals. The emphasis of these activities is "play hard, play fair; nobody wins, nobody loses" (Fluegelman 1976). Through teamwork, students can improve self-esteem, learn decision-making strategies, and learn to respect differences within a group.

Many of the team-building activities in this chapter are an excellent way to get children of all ages to start defining goals and refining decision-making skills. These activities will help young people define their relationships with others, develop the confidence to take risks, and learn about themselves. Students will learn the value of working both independently and together.

While these goals are probably part of every physical education curriculum, sometimes instructors get so caught up in teaching skills that we forget about the child. While the connection between these activities and decision making might seem vague, after participating in a few of the activities yourself, you will begin to feel the effects of increased self-confidence, mutual support, and the joy of movement and discover for yourself how these elements help students become better decision makers. It's hard to make a negative life decision when you are feeling so positive about your life (Rohnke 1984).

As with any activity program, you must pay special attention to safety. Due to the nature of some team-building activities, it's especially important for everyone to practice effective safety procedures in order to prevent injuries.

The key to appropriate activity selection is choosing activities based on the abilities of the students in the class. The levels listed for the activities in this chapter are merely recommendations; you must use discretion in choosing activities according to your students' abilities. In general, level I activities are appropriate for kindergarten and grade 1; level II activities are appropriate for grades 2 through 3; and level III activities are appropriate for grades 4, 5, and 6.

Abandon Ship

Level
II and III

Area
Large playing space such as a gymnasium

Equipment
4 hula hoops; 2 stacks of tumbling mats (a stack should be no higher than 3 mats)

Objectives
Students will learn how to work as a team and how to use critical thinking to achieve a task.

Setup and Description
Break the class into two groups using creative division methods. Each group must pretend that they are in a boat that is sinking. They need to figure out how to get everyone off the boat and onto rescue platforms and safely back to shore as quickly as possible.

Designate an area of the floor as the shore and start each group on a stack of mats that represents the sinking ship. Hand each group two hula hoops that represent the rescue platforms. The rescue platforms cannot move with people inside them, but the team members can move from platform to platform to get to shore. Groups need to figure out the easiest way to get to shore by moving the rescue platforms from place to place. Once each member of the group has made it to shore that team is finished. The first team to get all members on land wins the race.

Modifications

Increase the number of groups playing the game and the areas of land to which they can rescue their groups. You can decrease the numbers of team members so there are fewer people to move or you could increase the number of hoops (rescue platforms) for each group.

Breakdown

Level
II and **III**

Area
Large playing space such as a gymnasium

Equipment
Tumbling mats

Objectives
Students will interact with their classmates while improving muscular strength and trusting in their partner.

Setup and Description

Break the class into pairs using creative division methods. Partners get into push-up position facing each other with their heads about 6 inches (15 centimeters) from each other. Using one hand, they attempt to push each other off balance by pushing on shoulders only. Students may not push on the head, face, or arms. There should also be no butting heads or pulling someone's hands out from under them.

Modifications

If students are unable to stay in push-up position, they can try the modified position of resting on the knees. This will make it harder for their partner to push them over, but they'll still be able to participate.

⚠ SAFETY NOTE

Tumbling mats should be used to make this activity safer. Remind students that there should be no pushing of heads or faces and they can't pull or push their partner's arms. They also may not butt heads or pull their partner's hands out from under them.

Chin to Chin

Level
III

Area
Large playing space such as a gymnasium

Equipment
4 tennis balls

Objectives
Students will work together to accomplish a goal.

Setup and Description
Split the students into four groups using creative division methods. Two groups should include all girls and two groups should include all boys. The groups line up across the gym in single-file lines spaced about 4 feet (1.25 meters) apart.

The first group to transport the tennis ball to the other end of the playing area without letting the ball touch the ground wins. However, every team member has to gain possession of the ball. In addition, students are not allowed to touch the ball with their hands; they can only hold the ball between their chin and neck. If the ball touches the ground, then the group has to start over. After passing the ball to the next person, students quickly run to the end of the line to wait the arrival of the ball.

Modifications
For obvious reasons, it is crucial that groups consist of all boys and all girls. However, there is no problem with having more than four teams. This would simply allow the students more opportunities to play.

Circle Chair Sit

Level
III

Area
Large playing space such as a gymnasium

Equipment
Chair for each student

Objectives
Students will improve their quickness, ability to look ahead, and ability to work together to accomplish a common goal.

Setup and Description
In this fast-moving game, the students form a circle of chairs with everyone sitting in a chair and facing the center of the circle. Choose one person to be It and stand in the center of the circle, leaving an open chair. The person who is It must try to sit in an open chair. At the same time, the other students try to prevent the person who is It from sitting in the open chair by moving to that chair before It arrives.

This movement leaves other chairs open, which in turn need to be filled by students moving from one chair to another while keeping the person who is It out of an open chair. Chairs may be filled by the person sitting next to the empty chair or by someone willing to come over from across the circle. If the person who is It manages to sit in the open chair, choose someone else to be It.

Modifications

•• If the game is not moving fast enough or you have too many people in the circle, encourage more people to move or break up the larger circle into smaller circles of no less than 10 per circle.

•• Make the game more challenging by having students call out their own name as they move from one chair to the open chair.

SAFETY NOTE

⚠️ *In this fast-moving game, students cannot grab or push each other or pull chairs out from under other people. They also cannot sit on another person's lap.*

Circle Sit

Level
III

Area
Large playing space such as a gymnasium

Equipment
None

Objectives
Students will work together in order to accomplish a task.

Setup and Description
The group stands in a tight circle facing the center. At your command, students turn to the right so their left shoulder is facing the center of the circle. Each student must take steps into the center of the circle until the circle is relatively close. At your command, the students hold onto the shoulders of the person in front of them and slowly sit on the knees of the person behind them. If done properly, the students will be sitting in a circle on the knees of the person behind them. At your command, all students should stand back up at the same time.

SAFETY NOTE

⚠️ *This activity must be done slowly. Any student who misses the knees will create a domino effect and all students will fall on each other.*

Modifications
It may difficult for some groups to sit simultaneously. If this is the case, have smaller groups try it, and after successful attempts make the groups larger and larger.

Circle Trust

Level
III

Area
Large playing space such as a gymnasium

Equipment
None

Objectives
Students will learn to trust their peers and work together as a team to accomplish a task.

Setup and Description
You must have an even number of students to make this work. If you have an odd number, you may participate. Students stand in a large circle. Students number off into ones and twos.

Everybody in the circle holds hands. On your count, ones slowly lean in while the twos lean out. This must be done gradually! Students must balance and counter-balance each other to keep from falling. Then on your count, they switch roles so that the twos go in and the ones go out.

Modifications
If students are having difficulty completing the task, see if they can do the activity in smaller groups. Try two in and two out and then gradually make the groups larger. This activity should be done with older, more mature students.

Cross the Beam

Level
II and III

Area
Large playing space such as a gymnasium

Equipment
Low-sitting balance beam (no higher than 10 inches [25 centimeters] off the ground) for every 8 or 10 students

Objectives
Students will work together to cross a balance beam.

Setup and Description
Break the class into groups of four or five using creative division methods. Teams line up single file, one team at each end of each balance beam, or log. Each team holds hands. The first person from each side starts walking from opposite ends of the beam toward each other and the rest of the team walks with them. Once the first two students meet each other in the middle, the strategy begins. The teams need to cross to the other end of the beam without falling off or touching the floor.

There are multiple ways this can be accomplished, but here are some examples:

- • One team can kneel down very low and the other team can slowly step over the kneeling team. Each team will slowly inch forward to the opposite end.
- • The teams can pass side by side, facing each other, or back to back. This method is more difficult when holding hands.

Each person is very important to the team's success. Once a person in the link has reached the end of the beam they may let go of that hand.

Modifications

If you have more than one beam, you may want to separate the boys and girls. Some students may feel uncomfortable with the opposite sex in such tight quarters.

Detective Valentine

Level
II and III

Area
Large playing space such as a gymnasium or outdoor blacktop area

Equipment

Pencil and puzzle for each group; 26 cones; 26 note cards; chalk or 26 paper hearts; mats, jump ropes, and any other equipment you deem necessary for the specific fitness activities you choose

Objectives

Students will improve fitness and work together to solve a Valentine's Day puzzle.

Setup and Description

Create valentine puzzles in advance using valentine terms (e.g., heart, cupid, sweetheart). The puzzles have blanks representing each term and under each blank is a number that corresponds to a letter. Create a key for yourself where each letter of the alphabet is represented with a number (a = 1, b = 2, and so on). Number each puzzle in the corner for organization.

❸				
8	5	1	18	20

On the activity area, use the chalk to draw 26 hearts and write a number in each one (1-26), or use paper hearts if the play space is indoors. Be sure to spread these out randomly so students have to move around a lot. Next to the hearts, place a tall cone. Underneath the cone, place a note card with the letter of the alphabet that corresponds to the number in the heart and a fitness activity (e.g., 20 push-ups, jump rope).

When class begins, break the class into groups of four or five using creative division methods. Explain to the students that they are going to be valentine detectives. They are going to try and solve a puzzle by moving all around the area looking for evidence. When students receive their puzzles, they start with the first number under the blank. They need to search for the heart that has the number in it. The person in their group who finds the heart gives the signal (thumbs up) so the rest of the group can find them. When the entire group arrives at the heart, they lift up the cone and read the clue. All students in the group must complete the fitness activity before writing the letter on their puzzle.

When everyone in the group is finished, they move on to the next number. Stress that you are going to be watching for teamwork (students waiting for each other to finish before moving on), being good sports (cheering each other on, slowing down in an activity for others), and participation (finishing the entire activity at each station, not fooling around). When students finish the puzzle, they come back to a designated area, sit down, and hold up the puzzle (this way you won't have students running up to turn in the puzzle).

Modifications

To avoid having too many students at a particular area, give each group of students a different puzzle.

Field of Obstacles

Level
II and III

Area
This activity can be played in a gym, multipurpose room, or outside

Equipment
50 to 100 tennis balls; blindfolds for half the class; 4 cones to mark the square playing area

Objectives
Students will develop trust in their classmates.

Setup and Description

Scatter 50 to 100 tennis balls across the floor. Use lines on the court or use cones to mark out the playing area of approximately 40 by 40 feet (12 by 12 meters). Break the class into pairs using creative division methods and have one partner put on a blindfold. Both students stand at the starting line with the nonblindfolded partner staying behind the line.

On your command of "Go," the partner who can see verbally leads the blindfolded partner through the area safely so they don't touch any of the tennis balls.

If students touch an object, they have to start over from the beginning. After one partner makes it through the area, the other partner is blindfolded and they exchange roles.

Modifications

- • • The blindfolded students can crawl on their hands and knees while being verbally guided through the maze of balls.
- • • Challenge the class by requiring the verbal commands to be non-English in nature. The commands can be words from a foreign language or sounds (e.g., clapping, whistling, snapping of fingers).

Find Your Partner

Level
II and III

Area
Large playing space such as a gymnasium

Equipment
Peppy music that encourages movement (optional)

Objectives
Students will work their memory in developing word relationships while increasing camaraderie.

Setup and Description

This game works well as a warm-up or cool-down activity. Break the class into partners using creative division methods. Then lead students through the following steps.

1. Shake hands with your partner and remember that this is your shake-hands partner.
2. Find a new partner by the count of six and give this partner a high five. This is your high-five partner.
3. Stand back to back with a new partner by the count of six. Now, stand side by side with this new partner and bumps-a-daisy (gently bump your hips together) with your partner. This is your bumps-a-daisy partner.
4. Find your shake-hands partner and shake hands.
5. Find your high-five partner and give a high-five again.
6. By the count of six, stand face to face with a new partner. Join right hands and thumb wrestle with your new partner. This is your thumb-wrestling partner.
7. Stand side by side with a new partner. Shake right hands and join left hands underneath while standing side by side. This is your skating partner. Move through the general space with your skating partner.
8. Find your high-five partner and give a high-five again.
9. Find your shake-hands partner and shake hands again.
10. Find a new partner and stand in a face-to-face position. This is your shadow partner. Play shadow as your partner leads you through self-space movement. Switch roles so that you are the leader.

⑪ Find your bumps-a-daisy partner and do the appropriate activity.

⑫ Find your thumb-wrestling partner and do the appropriate activity.

⑬ Find your shake-hands partner and do the appropriate activity.

⑭ Find your high-five partner and do the appropriate activity.

⑮ Find your skating partner and do the appropriate activity.

⑯ Find your shake-hands partner and do the appropriate activity.

⑰ Find your shadow partner and do the appropriate activity.

The fun really begins when the tasks are performed with music and the commands are performed quickly. Laughter and enjoyment are guaranteed.

Modifications

Obviously, the combinations are limited only by your imagination. You could also change the locomotor movement as the children move from one location to another.

Four-Goal Soccer

Level
III

Area
Large playing space such as a gymnasium or outdoor field

Equipment

Foam soccer ball; 12 cones to mark the square playing area and four goals

Objectives

Students will stay moving and thinking about the best way to score.

Setup and Description

Divide the play space into a square with a soccer goal (defined by the cones) on each side of the square for a total of four goals. Break the class into two teams using creative division methods. Each team has two goals into which they may score. The goals will be opposite each other. At any time students may score in either of their two goals. The team with the most points wins.

Modifications

•• Add more than one soccer ball to increase activity and awareness.

•• Make this game much more difficult by playing four-goal crab soccer. Each player gets in the crab position (body weight supported by hands and feet with the abdomen facing the sky) and plays the game in this position.

Hand Squeeze

Level
II and III

Area
Large playing space such as a gymnasium

Equipment
None

Objectives
Students will work together to send an impulse around a circle as fast as possible.

Setup and Description
Sit together with the students in a circle. Students hold hands with the person on each side. Squeeze the hand of one of the people next to you. That person squeezes the hand of the next person and so on. The idea is to get the hand squeezes around the circle as fast as possible and back to you. The activity ends when you feel the returning squeeze.

Modifications
- Start with smaller groups and gradually move up to larger groups.
- Have the students do the task with their eyes closed.
- Time the task as the group tries to improve its time and do it faster and faster.

Hoop Twister

Level
I

Area
Large playing space such as a gymnasium

Equipment
As many different colored hula hoops as needed to cover the size of the class; spinner with the same colors as the hoops (optional); music of your choice

Objectives
Students will understand how the body moves.

Setup and Description
Scatter many different colored hula hoops throughout the play space. Separate the children into groups of five or six using creative division methods. Each group stands in single file at one end of the play space.

When the music begins, the first student in each line chooses a locomotor movement and performs it while traveling around the hula hoops, with the group shadowing the leader. When the music stops, the teacher either calls out specific directions, such as "Put your right hand in a green hula hoop" or "Stand with your left foot in a blue hula hoop," or spins the color-coded spinner and then has the students place the spoken body part (e.g., hand, foot, elbow, knee) in the correct colored hoop. The leader then goes to the end of the line and the next person becomes the leader.

Modifications

- • • Encourage the leaders to change the locomotor activity frequently.
- • • Challenge the students' ability levels with a large variety of movements using both sides of the body.

Hot Chocolate River

Level
II and **III**

Area
Large playing space such as a gymnasium

Equipment
At least 7 wooden 2-by-4s (5 by 10 centimeters) that are 2 feet (60 centimeters) long, pieces of foam rubber, or poly spots for each team of eight or more (these pieces will be the marshmallows); 8 to 10 ropes or cones for marking the river, which should be 30 feet (9 meters) wide

Objectives
The students must work together with their minds and bodies to accomplish this challenging task; without complete cooperation from each person in the group, success will be difficult.

Setup and Description
Mark off an area (the size is your choice) with the cones or ropes that will be called the Hot Chocolate River. Break the class into groups of 8, 9, or 10 using creative division methods. Give each group seven props, or marshmallows. These marshmallows will float and support a person in the river.

The groups must decide how they are going to use the marshmallows to get their members across the Hot Chocolate River without anyone falling in. The only way to get across is to use the props. When standing on a marshmallow, people are safe from the burning heat of the river. Any part of the body can be touching the marshmallow as long as no parts of the body touch the ground.

Modifications
Make the river narrower or give the groups more marshmallows. If you want to make it more challenging, do just the opposite: Make the river wider and give the children fewer marshmallows.

Human Bowling

Level
I and II

Area
Large playing space such as a gymnasium

Equipment
Soft foam ball; floor tape or 10 poly spots or place mats

Objectives
Students will learn about a pivot foot and use bowling skills in a new game.

Setup and Description
Set tape or 10 place mats or poly spots on the floor in the formation of bowling pins. With 10 students, have each student place one foot on a marker. The foot that is on the marker is the pivot foot. They must keep this foot on the ground at all times. The rest of the students are bowlers. One student rolls the foam ball at the group of students. If the ball hits any of the students, they are out for the rest of the game. The bowler gets 10 attempts, one for each pin.

If needed, you could create smaller groups to make game go faster. This will allow more students to stay active in the game.

Modifications
Students can roll the ball with their nondominant hand. In other words, if they are right-handed, they should roll the ball with the left hand.

Human Pretzel

Level
III

Area
Large playing space such as a gymnasium

Equipment
None

Objectives
Students will work together to get into and out of a twisted pretzel.

Setup and Description
Break the class into groups of no more than eight. The number in each group should be even (six or eight). Each group forms a circle and then walks forward into the circle until everyone is very close to each other. Once this happens, they find someone directly across from them and join their right hand with the other person's right hand. They cannot join hands with the person next to them. When the right hand is joined, they find someone else and hold that person's left hand with their left hand. The group is now in a human pretzel.

The strategy then begins. The group must get out of the pretzel by moving in and out and around their classmates to untangle their arms. Hands cannot be dropped. Some students may have to climb through other students' arms or legs. It should be possible to get out of the pretzel almost every time.

Modifications

If students don't want to hold hands with each other, have some scarves or short pieces of rope available. The students can hold on to each end instead of hands.

Human Pyramid

Level
III

Area
Large playing space such as a gymnasium

Equipment
Tumbling mats

Objectives

Students will work together to produce a human pyramid.

Setup and Description

Break the class into groups of 12, 13, 14, or 15 students. Tell students how to make the pyramid. If there are 12 students in a group, for example, there should be four students on the bottom, three on the second row, two on the third row, and one on the fourth and final row. The remaining students will be spotters.

The students need to figure out who will be on each row. Usually, the largest are on the bottom and the smallest and lightest student is on the top. The base students get on their hands and knees on the mats with their shoulders touching the shoulders of each person next to them. The students in the second row get on their hands and knees on top of the bottom row, and so on. Gradually build the pyramid to the top.

This is not a race. You do not want to get any one hurt in this process. Having spotters in front and back of the pyramid is a must. Their job is to help students up and to help slow down falls if anybody in the pyramid loses their balance. Take a picture of the final product. The students will get a kick out of seeing themselves as such an important part of something.

⚠ SAFETY NOTE

This activity can be dangerous because people can fall on others or off the pyramid. Remember to have mats on the floor and to designate spotters. Discuss with the students what spotters do and what their responsibilities are.

Modifications

- • You might want to have all-girl pyramids and all-boy pyramids.
- • Start with smaller groups like three (two on the bottom and one on the top) and gradually move up to larger groups.

Hunters and Gatherers

Level
I

Area
Large playing space such as a gymnasium

Equipment
None

Objectives
Students will learn what their ancestors had to do to survive.

Setup and Description
Discuss with the students what the Pilgrims and Indians had to do to survive (they had to hunt for their food and gather food). Ask them to use their imagination to create bows and arrows, fishing rods, and so on to bring food home for supper. There are no props; the children just use their imagination to pretend they're hunting various animals. For example, they hunt in pairs or groups of four, stalk the animals, and go through the motions of nocking the arrow, pulling the bow back, and releasing the arrow. When a "kill" is made, they prepare the meat and carry it back to the community for cooking.

Also have the children work together to plant a garden, hoe the land, pick weeds, and harvest vegetables.

Modifications
Change the environmental situations while the children are out hunting. What would they do if they were caught in a rainstorm or a snowstorm or if they got caught out after dark? What would they do if they got lost?

Invent a Game

Level
II and III

Area
Large playing space such as a gymnasium

Equipment
1 or 2 items for each student (all different types and sizes of balls and unique equipment such as hoops, scooters, wands, Lummi sticks, ropes, cones, bats, rackets, and so on)

Objectives
Students will learn to work with each other and compromise.

Setup and Description
Put all the different types of equipment and balls in a pile. Split the class into teams of no more than six people using creative division methods. One person in each group comes and gets one or two items from the pile, and then the next person in each group gets one or two more items, and so on until everyone in the group has picked up one to two items (or until you run out of items).

After the teams have picked up the equipment, give them the challenge. Their job is to take the equipment and work together to invent a game that uses every piece of equipment they picked. The game must involve two or more facets of motor development (eye–hand coordination, eye–foot coordination, balance, rhythmic activities) or physical fitness (cardiovascular endurance, muscular strength and endurance, flexibility). Emphasize that they need to work together to come up with the game.

Give each group no more than 10 minutes to come up with a game. When the time is up, each group comes up with a name for their activity and then presents it to the class and demonstrates how to play it. You will get some really good games and some not-so-good games.

At the end of the class, be sure to discuss the process of how they came up with their games. What procedures did they use to arrive at mutual decisions? Address each game in the discussion. After the discussion, you might find a game that, with a few modifications, would be a really great game to play with all your classes.

Modifications

A neat idea is to test each of the games after the teams present them. This gives the class a hands-on evaluation of the success of the game.

Learn and Line

Level
II and **III**

Area
Large playing space such as a gymnasium

Equipment
None

Objectives
Students will learn about each other and use teamwork to accomplish a goal.

Setup and Description
This game helps students learn about the people around them. Students form one line. Then tell them that they have a certain amount of time to get in alphabetical order of first names.

Here are some other ideas for line order:

- Age
- Shoe size
- Height
- Hair color (darkest to lightest)

Modifications
Have the students complete some of the tasks without speaking to anyone.

Merry-Go-Round

Level
II and III

Area
Large playing space such as a gymnasium

Equipment
Stopwatch

Objectives
Students will work together to accomplish a challenging task.

Setup and Description

This seemingly simple task can be quite challenging. It takes the well-known pastime of Ring Around the Rosie a bit further. The students circle up, hold hands, and pretend they're on a merry-go-round. Start the stopwatch as the group tries to move 360 degrees clockwise and then return 360 degrees counterclockwise as quickly as possible. If any students break their grip, stop the time and the group must start over.

Here are a couple of hints: In establishing a time goal, use one second for each person in the group. Also, you can use a cone to indicate the starting place (representing 12 o'clock).

Modifications

●● To increase the difficulty, the group can start from a sitting position.

●● If you are having trouble getting the entire group to cooperate, start with smaller groups. If some students just don't want to cooperate, have them sit out.

Monster Walk

Level
III

Area
Large playing space such as a gymnasium

Equipment
Enough cones to effectively mark the playing area (2 cones per group)

Objectives
Students will use teamwork along with strategy to accomplish an increasingly difficult activity.

Setup and Description

Set cones parallel with the starting line and finish line about 10 feet (3 meters) away from each other. Split class into groups of four or five students using creative division methods. Each group must figure out how to get across the line while using only half their total number of feet. For example, in a group of five students, only five feet can touch the ground at one time.

After they accomplish the task, decrease the number of feet they can use to move the group. Remind students that this is not a race against the other teams; the winning team develops the best way to carry the group with the fewest number of feet touching the ground.

Modifications

Larger groups require more communication and a greater ability to critically think together in order to be successful. To make the game more interesting, use larger groups and have them choose some other challenges that require students to use some critical thinking skills.

Mummy Wrap

Level

II and **III**

Area

Large playing space such as a gymnasium

Equipment

Several rolls of toilet paper for each group

Objectives

Students will use their creativity while working together as a team in a fun holiday activity.

Setup and Description

Although there are no physical fitness benefits of this game, it makes an enjoyable holiday activity around the time of Halloween and requires teamwork. Break the class into teams of no more than four using creative division methods. Give each team several rolls of toilet paper.

Each team chooses one person to be the mummy. The remaining team members wrap up their mummy in toilet paper, trying not to tear the paper. Ideally, no part of the mummy should be left exposed. However, if the mummy has a problem with his nose, eyes, and mouth being covered, it's OK to leave the face uncovered. Each team must work together and involve everyone on the team. An impartial judge inspects each mummy for exposed body areas. You can be the judge, or the class can choose a few students to be the judges.

Modifications

Take pictures of the mummies and the members of each group. Blow the pictures up and post them on the bulletin boards around the school.

Name Toss

Level
I, II, and III

Area
Large playing space such as a gymnasium

Equipment
Foam soccer ball

Objectives
Students will learn information about classmates while passing and catching an object.

Setup and Description
Form a large circle with the students. Begin the activity by handing a foam soccer ball to the student on your left. While handing the ball, shout out your name and something unique about yourself. The person who receives the ball must repeat your name and unique fact about you and then tell her own name and something unique about her. This process continues until the ball returns to the beginning of the circle.

Start the activity again, only this time tossing the ball to anyone in the circle instead of to the person to the left. Repeat this process until everyone has had a turn.

Modifications
Put more than one ball in play at once. Start with two, then add a third, and so on. This gets very exciting and demands that students pay very close attention to the activity.

Over-Under Relay Rally

Level
I, II, and III

Area
Large playing space such as a gymnasium

Equipment
5 or 6 volleyballs; 5 or 6 beanbags; 1 balloon for every two students

Objectives
Students will work together to accomplish a task.

Setup and Description
Split the class into five or six groups using creative division methods. Try the following relays:

Each group lines up single file. Give the first person in each group a volleyball, and when you say "Go," each group alternates passing the ball over their head and between their legs until the ball gets to the last person in each group. The last person then runs to the front and the process starts all over again. The relay continues until the first person is at the beginning of the line again.

For the next game, have everyone lie on their back, head to toe. Start the ball in the first person's feet. That person must transport the ball to the next person's feet. Once students give the ball away, they get up and run to the end of the line and lie down again. The relay continues until one group passes the finish line.

The third game is a partner game that uses balloons. Each group pairs off and only one pair in each group goes at time. Each group of two has to put their heads together, place a balloon on their heads, and balance it without touching it with their shoulders or hands. They have to balance the balloon on their heads all the way to the finish line and then all the way back to their group without dropping it. If they drop the balloon, they have to start over again. After they successfully carry the balloon to the line and back, they hand off the balloon to the next two people in their group. The first team to get all members to the line and back successfully wins.

Modifications

Set up various obstacles (with mats, chairs, tables, and so on) and have the students do the over and under relay using these obstacles.

Partner Hop Race

Level
III

Area
Large playing space such as a gymnasium

Equipment
Tumbling mats

Objectives

Students will work cooperatively with each other while improving their balance.

Setup and Description

In this activity, students hop on one leg across the gym while their partner holds the other leg. Set out the tumbling mats for the students to hop on. Break the class into partners of the same size. Start by having the students practice hopping on one leg. Then have the partners hold one bent leg while the other partner hops down the floor. The students hop together to one end of the gym and back, then switch legs and repeat. Have a race to see who can finish first.

SAFETY NOTE

This is a difficult task. It's hard enough to hop on one foot, but when someone else holds the other leg while you hop, it's even more difficult. Make sure students who are holding their partner's leg are not pushing the hopping student down the floor but merely assisting by holding the leg. If the hopping partner starts to fall, the person holding the leg must let go of it.

Modifications

If students cannot maintain balance with the other person holding their leg, they can just hop on one leg while holding their partner's leg. If students still have trouble, have them hop with both legs while holding their partner's leg.

Partner Spinning

Level
II and III

Area
Large playing space such as a gymnasium

Equipment
Tumbling mats

Objectives
Students will work cooperatively while trusting each other.

Setup and Description
The object of this activity is for students to trust one another by spinning each other around. Pair up the students according to size and strength. The students face each other, grasp hands tightly, and, with arms extended, slowly lean back to balance each other. Make sure each person's feet are close together and partners' toes are almost touching. Then the groups spin around quickly, making sure that the partners hold on to each other's hands tightly throughout the activity.

⚠ **SAFETY NOTE**

This activity can be a bit precarious as partners will be spinning quickly and the centrifugal force will attempt to separate the partners' hands. Encourage the students to hold on tight and go only as fast as they feel comfortable with.

Modifications
Incorporate more people into the circle.
Instead of having two people spinning, change it to three, then four. Make sure group members are roughly the same size.

Partner Towel Volleyball

Level
III

Area
Large playing space such as a gymnasium

Equipment
Volleyball or beach ball; volleyball net; towel for every two players

Objectives
Students will work cooperatively with each other while learning to catch and throw in a unique way.

Setup and Description
In this game, students play a game of volleyball, but instead of hitting the ball with their hands, they partner up and catch the ball in a towel and then toss it over the net.

Break the class in half using creative division methods, and then have each team partner up. Give each pair a towel and teach them how to catch and throw using only the towel. Let them practice that skill, and when they have the idea, begin the game. The game is played the same as a normal volleyball game: three hits (catches and tosses) per side are allowed, and points are scored when teams cannot catch or return a ball properly.

Modifications

You can use larger towels or sheets if the students are having trouble catching the ball. If certain students are having trouble, assist them; you could just have them catch the ball and then you can throw it over the net for them.

Partner Trust Fall

Level
II and **III**

Area
Large playing space such as a gymnasium

Equipment
Tumbling mats; stack of mats, table, or balance beam

Objectives
Students will work cooperatively while learning to trust each other.

Setup and Description

Divide students into pairs according to strength and size. Students form two lines where the partners are facing each other. Choose one person to be the faller. If he agrees to do so, he stands up on a stack of mats, balance beam, or table so he is above the rest of the students, who are standing on the floor. The catchers, who are facing each other in the two rows, extend their arms toward their partner with opposite arms interchanged. The faller stands on the stack of mats with his back to the catchers and puts his arms across his chest, keeping them there through the entire fall.

The Faller must say "Falling!" and the catchers must reply "Catching!" before the fall. After the catchers' response, the faller stays straight and firm with arms across the chest and falls backward into the waiting arms of the catchers. Catchers should bend their knees slightly to absorb the shock of the catch.

⚠ SAFETY NOTE

Trusting people to catch you when you fall can be quite daunting. Do not force students to be fallers if they do not want to do so. This activity requires a mature group of students. Don't allow people to touch inappropriate parts of the body.

Modifications

Instead of falling from heights, have the catchers kneel and the faller fall from a standing position on the floor.

Pass It Back

Level
III

Area
Large playing space such as a gymnasium

Equipment

Hula hoop for each group of five or six students; small foam balls and other small items of various sizes and shapes (e.g., yarn balls, beanbags); large coffee can or other can (e.g., large cans from school cafeteria) for each group

Objectives

Students will work together to accomplish a common goal.

Setup and Description

Explain to students that they will need to work together to accomplish this activity. In addition, they will need to use positive, supportive language when working with their teammates (discuss and review examples if necessary). You will not be looking for teams who finish first, but for teams who help each other out and work together.

Split the students into groups of four or five using creative division methods. Use one group to demonstrate the general idea of the activity. The students lie down on their backs head to toe in a line. At the foot of the first student is a hula hoop with a number of various objects inside, and at the head of the last student in line is a can. This first person must lift an object from the hoop using his feet and pass it over his head to the next person in line, all while still lying down! The next person then grasps the object with her feet and passes it to the next person down the line.

Hands cannot be used, except for balance. Along the way, students should use positive verbal affirmations such as "Do you have it?," "Yes, let go," "No, let me get a better grip," and "Okay, I'm letting go now!" to help each other out. When the object reaches the last person in line, that person attempts to drop the object into the can while using his feet. If he succeeds, he removes the object from the can with his hands and walks to the front of the line. Everyone scoots down one place and the process begins again.

When everyone has had the opportunity to put the first object in the can, the team may move on to a different item from the hoop. Ultimately, the goal is to get all items in the can and empty the hoop before students change positions. As students participate in the activity, reinforce teams for using positive words and comments. If necessary, stop the activity and discuss strategies or positive talk that different teams may be using.

Modifications

If students are having difficulty, use larger objects like beach balls or large soccer balls. Towels are nice to use as well because they're easy to pick up and pass from one person to another. You can speed this up a little bit by having a race.

Ping-Pong Golf

Level
III

Area
Large playing space such as a gymnasium

Equipment

9 large note cards or pieces of paper with the numbers one through nine marked on them; table-tennis ball for each group; plastic floor tape

Objectives

Students will create a sense of team unity while working together to accomplish a difficult task.

Setup and Description

Construct nine holes of golf on pieces of paper or note cards, and fold and tape them on the floor. This is the hole as it would be taped on the floor, looking through the hole (upper figure). You should write the hole number on the hole along with an arrow to indicate the direction in which the ball should travel (lower figure).

Arrange the holes randomly around the playing area so that some holes are short and some are long. Break the class into teams of four or five using creative division methods. Give each team a ping-pong ball and have them begin their golf game at a certain hole. Be sure you don't start a team on each hole; try to have one hole between each team to begin with. In other words, one team will start on the first hole, another team on the third hole, another on the fifth hole, and so on.

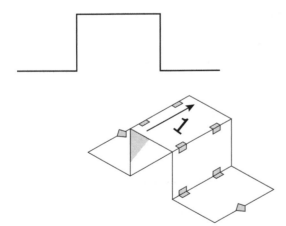

Each team blows the ball sequentially through each of the nine holes. If a team starts on hole 9, when they blow the ball through hole 9, they must move to hole 1. If a team starts on hole 3, they move to 4, then 5, and so on. No one is allowed to touch the ball with any body part, and no one is allowed to impede the movement of another team's ball in any way. When a team has completed a full nine holes in proper sequence, the game is over.

Modifications

If you have a really large group, create an 18-hole golf course. Some students may have problems crawling around on the hard floor on their knees. If this is the case, designate them as a hole spotter who finds the location of the next hole.

Pipeline

Level
III

Area
Large playing space such as a gymnasium

Equipment

15 pieces of PVC pipe 2 inches (5 centimeters) wide cut in half lengthwise in varied lengths from 1 to 3 feet (30-90 centimeters); 3 to 5 golf balls

Objectives

Students will work together to move a golf ball from one end of the floor to the other.

Setup and Description

Break the class into teams of no more than four people using creative division methods. Give each team four pieces of halved PVC pipe and a golf ball; each team member will have a piece of pipe. Each team lines up single file about 30 feet (9 meters) away from one end of the playing area.

On your command, the first person in each group places the golf ball on the PVC pipe and rolls it down the pipe to the next person in line, who is also holding a pipe. When the pass is successfully received, the first person quickly runs to the end of the line. This process continues until groups reach the end of the play space. They then turn around and return to the beginning using the same technique.

The ball must never stop, it must never roll backward, and it must never be touched by anyone's hand. If any of these infractions occur, the group must return to the beginning of the race.

Modifications

Use balls of different sizes (marbles, tennis balls, and so on) to make the game more exciting. You could even add more than one ball if you want to make the groups larger.

Planet Pass

Level
III

Area
Large playing space such as a gymnasium

Equipment
Earth ball (see appendix)

Objectives

Students will use many parts of the body and work together to move a large ball around a circle without dropping it.

Setup and Description

Students form a circle and lie down on their back with their head toward the center of the circle. Then they raise their hands into the air toward the ceiling. Gently place the Earth ball on one of the student's hands. Slowly, the students start passing the Earth ball around the circle from one person to the other. To keep the ball moving along, the students may also want to raise their feet to help control the ball.

Remind students that this ball is very large and this activity is not a race. It should be done slowly.

Modifications

If students are having trouble passing the ball while lying down, they can sit up facing the center of the circle and roll the ball around the circle while it's still on the floor. As they gain confidence, have them push the ball around the circle with it slightly off the floor, then progress to lying down.

Quicksand Alley

Level
II

Area
Large playing space such as a gymnasium

Equipment
As many as 20 hula hoops (use your discretion if you want more or less); 8 bean-bags per rescue person; 4 cones to mark off the playing area

Objectives
Students will use teamwork while practicing throwing and catching skills.

Setup and Description
Using cones, set up a rectangular space approximately 20 by 30 feet (6 by 9 meters) depending on equipment availability. Fill in the rectangle with hula hoops, leaving some space between the hoops. This area is the quicksand alley; the hoops represent areas of quicksand.

Break the class into pairs using creative division methods. One partner is the traveling expert and the other partner is the rescue expert. The travel expert starts at one end of the area and the rescue expert stands around the sides of the rectangle area with eight beanbags. On your signal, all the travel experts attempt to cross quicksand alley (to the other end) by leaping over the hoops.

If travelers land in or on any of the hoops, they are stuck in the quicksand. The only way they can continue their journey is to successfully catch a beanbag, which their partner, the rescue expert, tosses to them underhanded. If travel experts fail to catch a beanbag, they may toss it back to the rescue expert and try again. Once the traveler has proceeded through quicksand alley, the partners switch places.

Modifications
- Allow throwers to move around the quicksand alley to get closer to their traveler.
- Vary the size of the hoops.
- If the floor is slippery, use jump ropes in place of hoops.

Radioactive River

Level
I, II, and III

Area
Large playing space such as a gymnasium

Equipment
Scooter for each group of three students; 2 small carpet samples for each group of three students; plastic floor tape

Objectives
Students will understand how to work as a team and how to use critical thinking to achieve a task.

Setup and Description
Make two radioactive rivers outlined with tape on the floor. The two rivers should be 20 yards (18 meters) wide to cross and the two rivers should be 5 yards (5

meters) apart. Split the class into groups of three using creative division methods. The goal is to get across the river using two carpet samples and one scooter without touching the gym floor, or water, and without going out of bounds. Every group should go once.

Cooperative activities require every person in a group to participate in order to reach one central goal. If one or two people don't do their part, then no one will succeed. This particular activity makes the team work as a whole to come up with a plan for getting across unscathed. Be sure to leave plenty of room in between rivers, and go over scooter safety (watch out for those fingers and wheels!) before the activity. When the activity is over, ask the class what worked best. Some students will find out that they made the activity way too hard, and others will find that their method was easier than other teams' methods.

Modifications

If the activity is too easy, make larger groups and limit the amount of time they have to get across the river. If groups are struggling, give tips on how to do the activity successfully, such as moving the carpet squares to appropriate places to assist in moving people faster.

Roll the Bod

Level
III

Area
Large playing space such as a gymnasium

Equipment
Tumbling mats

Objectives
Students will learn to work cooperatively while trusting other students and controlling their emotions.

Setup and Description

Break the class into two groups so that one group is all girls and the other group is all boys. The students should sit very close together in a circle with their legs straight out in front of them. Tell them that there will be one person in the middle who will trust everyone in the circle to keep her from falling. The students in the circle hold their hands out and up and, working with each person next to them, catch and then pass (or roll) the person when she falls in their direction. Catches should be made above the waist. Students in the middle must stay straight and cross their arms across their chest. Switch students in the middle regularly.

> ## SAFETY NOTE
> *Trusting people to catch you when you fall can be quite daunting. Do not force students to be in the middle if they do not want to do so. This activity requires a mature group of students. Don't allow people to touch inappropriate parts of the body.*

Modifications
Instead of passing the student around the circle, toss him back and forth, being careful not to hurt him.

Rolling Raft

Level
III

Area
Large playing space such as a gymnasium, preferably with a wood or tile floor

Equipment
2 sticks with rubber tips that are 4 feet (1.25 meters) long for each group; plywood piece that's 4 feet (1.25 meters) long and 2 feet (.5 meter) wide for each group; 20 to 30 tennis balls for each group

Objectives
Students will work together to develop and implement strategies to move their raft across the floor without it touching the floor.

Setup and Description
Break the class into groups of no more than four using creative division methods. Place 20 to 30 tennis balls close together on the floor and then place the plywood raft on top of the balls. Two of the students in each group kneel or sit on the plywood raft. The people on the raft are *not* allowed to stand on the plywood raft.

The balls act as the water. The two students row themselves across the balls by pushing off the floor with the sticks that have the rubber tips on them. (The rubber tips prevent damage to the floor. As they begin to push themselves down the floor, the raft will roll on top of the balls. As the raft is rolling down the floor, the other two students must continually pick up the balls that come out the back of the raft and run to place them on the floor in front of the raft. When the raft has reached a designated distance of 12 to 18 feet (4 to 5.5 meters), the team members switch positions and return to the starting line.

Modifications
- • Only one student at a time could be on the raft. The size of the plywood raft can then be decreased.
- • Have students move the raft backward instead of forward.

Ropes Course

Level
II and III

Area
Large playing space such as a gymnasium

Equipment
Tumbling mats; 15 to 20 long jump ropes; yarn (a lot will be needed to make the spiderweb); plastic floor tape

Objectives
Students will move through the ropes without touching them.

Setup and Description

Set up a ropes course by laying down mats in the activity area. Lay the ropes down on the floor to mark the pathway through the course. Tape the yarn to the wall or other sturdy objects to create a kind of spiderweb. Break the class into groups of three or four using creative division methods. Each group travels through the course together. Students may need to crawl or step over the rope, but the goal is to get all members of the team through the course without touching the yarn. If you only have one course, then each group needs to enter the course the same way.

Modifications

Set up similar courses next to each other and have the students race through the course. Or, you could time each group and see who is the fastest.

Scaling the Wall

Level
II and **III**

Area
Large playing space, preferably outdoors

Equipment
2 stacks of mats that are 6 feet (2 meters) high; tumbling mats for padding

Objectives
Students will work as a team and use critical thinking to achieve a task.

Setup and Description

Ideally, it would be great to have one wall in the middle of a field that stood about 6 feet (2 meters) high and was surrounded by grass, but unfortunately not many of us have access to this kind of setup. For most, a stack of mats about 6 feet high (2 meters) is the best option.

Choose four students (for each group if you have multiple groups) as spotters and two others as stabilizers of the wall (mats). Teach the spotters that their responsibility is to assist the climbers when needed and to try to prevent unsafe movements.

The object of this game is to get every member of the group up and over the wall. It is up to them to find a solution to the problem. The hardest part of this activity is figuring out how to get the first person and the last person over.

Here are some possible solutions:

- Students can climb up the sides of the mats with their fingers and toes (edges of shoes) on the edges of the mats. These people can then assist others to the top and down the other side.

- Students can boost one or more people to the top of the wall. These people can then assist others to the top and down the other side.

⚠️ SAFETY NOTE

As you can imagine, climbing over a 6-foot (2-meter) wall could create some safety issues. Make sure each group has spotters and they have been properly instructed. Set up the wall on a platform of mats in case students fall as they're going over or coming down from the wall.

●● One or more students can get on their hands and knees and students can use them as steps to get closer to the top.

●● One strong person can stand in a straddle position with hands braced on the wall. Another smaller person or two can climb up the person to the top.

Overall, this activity is fairly simple, but it requires a lot of safety precautions. Throwing people over the wall is not allowed, and neither is jumping down from the top of the wall. Make sure that the ground around the wall is well padded in case there are any miscues. There is no way for one person to do this activity alone; it requires help from everyone on the team. That is what makes this activity worthwhile.

Modifications

●● Use multiple stacks of mats and smaller groups.

●● Use taller or shorter walls. Walls should be no higher than 8 feet (2.5 meters) and no lower than 4 feet (1.25 meters).

Shepherds and Sheep

Level
III

Area
Large playing space such as a gymnasium

Equipment
8 headphones; blindfolds for all students except eight; variety of equipment that could be used as obstacles (cones, poly spots, balls, ropes, and so on—you will need about 40 or 50 items)

Objectives
Students will learn how to use senses that they don't normally depend on when doing physical activity, and they will learn that it is sometimes impossible to complete a task without working together.

Setup and Description
This activity forces students to work as a team because they don't have use of all their senses. Discuss what cooperative activities consist of (see chapter introduction) and then split the class into four groups using creative division methods. In each group there are two shepherds and the rest are sheep. The shepherds will not be able to hear or speak. The sheep will not be able to see. The shepherds will have headphones on so they can't hear anything and the sheep will have blindfolds on.

Assign two groups to each half of the play space. One group on each side uses items to construct an obstacle course. They have five minutes to put it together while the other group sits facing away from the course trying to figure out how they are going to get through the course without the use of all five senses. When the five minutes are up, the shepherds have two minutes to figure out the layout of the course.

The shepherds and the sheep can come together for a short time to discuss nonverbal signals that can be used to guide the sheep through the course. The shepherds walk the sheep to the starting line. Emphasize that there is no running and that the shepherds cannot touch the sheep, but they can communicate with the predetermined signals. Have the other team make sure that everyone who is blindfolded stays safe throughout the activity.

When they are done, the groups switch roles and the same process is done again. When the activity is over, discuss why there was no way that they could have done the activity on their own and why they all needed to work together in order to finish the games.

Modifications

If this activity is too difficult, have one shepherd for every sheep. Again, they can use some type of nonverbal communication to help guide the sheep through the maze.

Shoes Together

Level
III

Area
Large playing space such as a gymnasium

Equipment
None

Objectives

Students will work together to accomplish a goal.

Setup and Description

Break the class into teams of six or seven using creative division methods. Designate a specific distance to complete the task; usually 20 feet (6 meters) is sufficient. Choose a judge from each team who will be the judge for another.

Excluding the judges, each team lines up next to each other on a starting line. They then try to move their entire group the designated distance with the requirement that all teammates' shoes must be touching the shoe of the student next to them in their team. The members on each end will only be connected to one person's shoe. Tying shoestrings together is not permitted. If students' shoes come apart from each other, the group must go back to the start. The judges must watch carefully and make the team begin again if shoes come apart.

There are lots of ways to accomplish this goal, but the most common is to take the shoes off, hold them in their hands, touch the shoes to the shoes next to them, and walk over to the other side. You'll probably have multiple groups trying to accomplish the same thing, and it's common for them to watch each other for ideas. This is OK, but teams should not duplicate the methods of another team. Encourage them to be original.

Modifications

Set a specific amount of time in which to complete the task.

Smiley

Level
II and III

Area
Large playing space such as a gymnasium

Equipment
None

Objectives
Students will be creative in trying to make people smile or laugh without touching them.

Setup and Objectives
This game works well as a warm-up or cool-down activity. Split the class into two teams using creative division methods. Students on each team line up single file facing the same direction. The teams should be spaced about 10 feet (3 meters) apart.

On your signal of "Go," the first person in each line crosses over to the other team's line, faces it, and walks slowly down the line while students in the line do anything they can to make that person laugh or smile; the only rule is that there's no touching. Stand at the end of the line watching each player for smiles or laughs. When they get to the end of the line, note whether they smiled or not. When you say "Go" again after the first two students reach the end of the line, the next two begin. This process continues until all the students have had a chance to go.

Modifications
Have the people who are standing in line use nonverbal methods to get the other team's person to laugh. They can use only actions.

Space Portal

Level
III

Area
Large playing space such as a gymnasium

Equipment
Hula hoop for each team; tumbling mats

Objectives
Students will build team unity and cooperate in class.

Setup and Description
Break the class into two or three groups using creative division methods. Each team gets one hula hoop. The hoops are portals to space, and the students must find a way to get through their hoop without touching it. If they touch the hoop, they're sent back down to Earth (meaning they return to the beginning).

You can hold the hoops or suspend them in the air using string, but they should start about 3 feet (1 meter) off the ground and then you can move them up depending on the students' skill level. Have teams race one another. Make sure students do not dive through the hoops. Teams will have to work together so everyone can get through the hoop without touching it.

Modifications

- •• Make the groups smaller and have more teams and hoops so that fewer people are standing around.
- •• Give students different objects (like stools, buckets, chairs) and see if the object can help them in any way. This can get creative, but make sure students are being safe!

Spiderweb

Level
II and **III**

Area
Large playing space such as a gymnasium

Equipment
Tumbling mats; yarn; 2 vertical poles 8 to 9 feet (3 meters) tall with stands; plastic floor tape

Objectives
Students will come up with a strategy to get the entire class through the spiderweb without anyone hitting the web with any part of their body.

Setup and Description
Although you can purchase spiderwebs, you can also make them right in the classroom. Take the two poles and wind the yarn back and forth around each of the poles and in between each of the strings, creating a maze of holes, or a spiderweb. Use the tape to attach the yarn to the poles where necessary. The holes should be big enough for a person to go through either squatting or lying flat as the students lift and hand various people through the holes. The web should have some large holes and some smaller holes that would be very difficult to get through. For safety, put the mats on the floor under the spiderweb.

Again, the goal is to get the entire class from one side of the spider web to the other by going through the various holes. This task can be completed at a lower level, where students have to crawl or stay low to get through the web, or it can be completed at a higher level where students can walk through it.

There are various options or requirements you can use in this game. For example, you could make a rule that if someone hits the web, the whole class starts over, or you could say that the class gets three touches and then has to start over. Challenge the group to accomplish the task within certain limitations.

Modifications

- •• In order to move the class more efficiently, you could make more than one spiderweb.
- •• You can substitute other pieces of equipment for the poles. For example, many schools have physical education classes in a multipurpose room where lunch is also served. In the room there are usually collapsible lunch tables. When these are folded up, you could tie the strings on their edges.

Split-Second Jumps

Level
I, II, and III

Area
Large playing space such as a gymnasium

Equipment
Long rope approximately 20 feet (6 meters) or longer; beanbag

Objectives
Students will jump over a rope while developing timing abilities and eye–foot coordination.

Setup and Description
All the students form a circle. Stand in the middle and, after tying the beanbag on one end of the rope for weight, begin turning the rope in a circle. Try to keep the beanbag and rope on the floor, but it can lift a few inches off the ground. You need to turn the rope relatively quickly, but it is possible to slow it down significantly. It also helps to bend over and to pass the rope behind your back as it turns.

The students must jump over the rope as it spins past them and not get hit by it. If the students get hit, they must step out of the circle, perform a prescribed number of exercises or laps around the gym, and then reenter the activity.

SAFETY NOTE

The rope may get wrapped around the children's legs and feet if they don't jump quickly enough. Their feet may be taken out from under them and they could fall. Encourage them to jump quickly.

Modifications
Depending upon the skill level of the students, turn the rope slowly, especially at the beginning. This will help all students to jump over the rope.

Tunnel Relay

Level
III

Area
Large playing space such as a gymnasium

Equipment
10 note cards with a different city written on each one; black felt-tipped markers

Objectives
Students will work together to move their group by building bridges.

Setup and Description
With the markers, write the names of different cities (e.g., Chicago, Denver, Portland) on note cards and place the cards on the floor in different parts of the playing area. It doesn't matter which cities you use, but you should place them on the floor in correct geographic locations.

Break the class into teams of five, six, or seven students using creative division methods. Each of the teams must give a time estimate on how long they think it will take their team to go from city A to city C through city B. In order to travel, the team members must make bridges with their bodies. Holding their weight on their hands and feet, all students line up and arch their back with their stomach facing the floor, essentially forming a tunnel. The last person in the line crawls to the front of the team through the tunnel and then forms a bridge and becomes part of the tunnel. The new last person in line does the same. This continues until a team has reached all locations.

Modifications

Instead of everyone in the group making a bridge, one person makes a bridge, the next person a "log" (lying on the floor on the abdomen), the next a bridge, and so on. The last person goes under the bridge and over the log and under the bridge and so on toward the destination.

Under the Bridges

Level
I and II

Area
Large playing space such as a gymnasium

Equipment
Music that promotes and encourages movement (optional)

Objectives
Students will build teamwork and improve their skills of strength, muscular endurance, creativity of body positions, various locomotor movements, and balance.

Setup and Description

Break the class into two groups using creative division methods. The members of one group find their own self-space in the playing area. Then they make their body into a bridge by putting their weight on their hands and feet and arching their body. Their abdomens should be facing the ground.

On your signal, the other group tries to go under as many of these body bridges as possible in the time limit, which may be two to three minutes, or the length of a song. Challenge the children to change the levels and shapes of their bridges. Have the traveling children perform different locomotor movements. Reverse roles as often as you want.

> **SAFETY NOTE**
> *T*ell the students they are not to touch or hit the bridges as they move under them and are not to jump or step on the stones (see modifications) as they go over them.

Modifications

- Students form their bodies into tight shapes (i.e., stones) and then the rest of the students step or crawl over the stones. Do not let students jump over the stones, and make sure you stress that the stones need to stay in a tight shape at all times, especially as others are going over them.
- Students can't go under the same bridge or over the same stone twice in a row. They must visit another stone or bridge before coming back to the previous one.

What Am I?

Level
I

Area
Large playing space such as a gymnasium

Equipment

Note card for each student; plastic floor tape; music that encourages movement

Objectives

Students will act out various animals while working cooperatively with each other.

Setup and Description

Write an animal (e.g., frog, elephant, deer, rabbit, bird, snake, fish, kangaroo) on each note card so that you have one note card for each student. Tape one note card on each student's back without letting them know what it is.

Students travel around the room and find someone to act out what their card on their back says. They then have one guess as to what animal it is. If they do not answer correctly, they must move on to another student. Continue until everyone has discovered what animal they are. Make sure they do not look at their own note cards or have the other students tell them what they are.

Modifications

- • You can also do this activity with different objects or people.
- • If some students need help, give them clues or sounds that will help them discover what their card says.

Chapter 11

Academic Activities

The academic activities in this chapter are movement oriented, but they are also related to what is commonly referred to as the three Rs—reading, 'riting, and 'rithmetic. Each activity focuses on one or more of the fitness or motor-development parameters discussed earlier in the book. In these activities, students must frequently work on another academic area (science, math, drama, and so on) in order to successfully complete the task at hand.

Academic activities are a great opportunity for physical educators to develop positive relations with other educators in the school system. This chapter encourages you to make contact with the classroom teachers to see what they are currently teaching in other subjects. Playing a variety of academic games not only provides wonderful activity, it reinforces what the classroom teacher is teaching at the same time.

The key to appropriate activity selection is choosing activities based on the abilities of the students in the class. The levels listed for the activities in this chapter are merely recommendations; you must use discretion in choosing activities according to your students' abilities. In general, level I activities are appropriate for kindergarten and grade 1; level II activities are appropriate for grades 2 through 3; and level III activities are appropriate for grades 4, 5, and 6.

Academic Blob

Level
I, II, and **III**

Area
Large playing space such as a gymnasium

Equipment
None

Objectives
Students will answer academic questions while playing a game of tag.

Setup and Description
Designate two students to be the taggers, or the blob. The blob must always be holding hands as they tag people. If they let go of each others' hand, then the person they tagged is not out. The other students line up at one end of the gym and you or the students think of an academic question to ask the blob. Letting the students make up the questions allows for some creativity and lets you see what the students know.

Once the blob says the correct answer, the students try to run to the other side of the gym without being tagged by the blob. Students who are tagged become part of the blob. The game goes on until there are two students left. Then they become the new blob and a new game starts.

Modifications
•• You could create a list of questions to ask the blob before class begins.

•• You also could have the students form little blobs of two or more people instead of one huge blob.

Academic Relay

Level
I, II, and III

Area
Large playing space such as a gymnasium

Equipment
Dry-erase board, eraser, and marker for each team; 40 to 50 note cards with academic questions written on them (7 questions from each academic area)

Objectives
Students will increase knowledge in geography, history, spelling, math, art, and science while learning how to work as a team.

Setup and Description
Before class, write questions on note cards that deal with geography, history, math, spelling, art, or science, such as "Spell this word as shown in the picture," "What state does the picture show?," "What is 300 × 4?," or "What is the official name of your knee bone?"

Break the class into two, three, or four teams using creative division methods. Each team has a dry-erase board, eraser, and marker that are 20 to 40 yards (6-12 meters) away from them. Spread the note cards facedown around each dry-erase board. The first person in each group runs to pick up a note card and read what it says on it. Then each student writes down the answer on the dry-erase board and shows it to you. Students have to keep guessing until they get the answer right. Each team can help their teammate figure out the answer. The first team to answer all the questions correctly and sit down wins.

Modifications
- • For younger children you can do colors; shapes; and short words like cat, dog, and hat.
- • Have the rest of the players do some form of exercise while they're waiting their turn.

Academic Tag

Level
II and III

Area
Large playing space such as a gymnasium

Equipment
None

Objectives
Students will answer questions pertaining to other subject areas while competing in a physical activity.

Setup and Description

Pick one or two students to be It. The rest of the students start at one end of the play space. They huddle together and, with your guidance, pick an academic subject (history, science, math, spelling, and so on) and a question related to that subject. Then you ask the students who are It that question. When they get the right answer to the question, everyone tries to run to the other end of the play space without being tagged. Students who are tagged must immediately stop with their feet frozen, but they can move their upper body to try to tag other people. The game ends when all of the players have been tagged. The last player tagged will be It in the next game.

Be sure to frequently change the academic subject. Also, make sure that the questions are challenging enough to meet the skills of the children.

Modifications

Instead of running, have the students perform a different locomotor movement.

Air Play With Feathers

Level
III

Area
Large playing space such as a gymnasium

Equipment
2 paper plates for each student; small feather for each student

Objectives

Students will work together to try to accomplish a goal while gaining a better understanding of the science of wind currents.

Setup and Description

Give students each a feather and tell them to keep the feather in the air by blowing at it. Then give students a paper plate and ask them to see how high they can get the feather by flapping the plates. How the students decide to move the plates is up to them.

Next, break the class into groups of two, three, or four using creative division methods to find out how high the feather can go in the air. Finally, come together as one big group and see if the group can get the feather to touch the ceiling. Be sure to discuss how the children believe the air currents are moving and how they can move the plates more efficiently to make the feather go higher.

Modifications

Have the children move toward a wall and, while facing the wall, move their plates so the feather moves up the wall.

Alphabet Relay

Level
I

Area
Large playing space such as a gymnasium

Equipment
1 set of alphabet flash cards per team

Objectives
Students will be able to quickly and efficiently recognize the alphabet while competing in a relay.

Setup and Description
Break the class into two or more teams using creative division methods. Place shuffled alphabet cards in a pile in front of each team about 15 feet (4.5 meters) in front of the starting line.

On your command of "Go," the first player runs to the pile of cards, finds the letter *A*, places the card above the pile, runs back to the team, and tags the next player. This player runs to the pile, finds *B*, and places it next to *A* in the correct order. The game continues with each player placing the next letter in the correct order. The first team to finish the alphabet is the winner.

Modifications
- If the students are working on other languages in the classroom, you could do this relay with different alphabets.
- Do the relay with numbers.

Alphabet Search

Level
I

Area
Large playing space such as a gymnasium

Equipment
Large cut-out letters of the alphabet plus some duplicates

Objectives
Students will exercise their knowledge of the alphabet while refining locomotor skills.

Setup and Description
Scatter the letters around the floor of the play area. Give clues that describe a letter, such as "Find the letter that zebra starts with," and the students all find the letter and stand next to it. Call out different clues to have the student go to different letters.

Modifications
- Use cards with words or pictures on them and have students spell words out.
- Change the movement pattern to the letters.

- • Place pieces of paper with a large variety of letters on them on the wall and on the floor. With tennis balls, have the children spell their name by hitting each letter with the ball.
- • Use numbers instead of letters and have the children solve math problems.
- • Hand out sheets with questions in different academic subjects and physical activities next to the questions. For example, to answer "12 × 2 = ?" a student would jump rope 24 times, to answer "How many states are in the continental United States?" a student would volley a ball 48 times, and so on.

Animal Environment

Level
I

Area
Large playing space such as a gymnasium

Equipment
20 foam balls; 2 folding, tumbling mats; 10 to 15 handkerchiefs

Objectives
Students will learn how humans can affect an animal's environment.

Setup and Description
Begin with the whole class pretending to be the same kind of animal—for example, everyone in class might be a lion. Two tumbling mats on the floor are the animals' homes. The animals start roaming in the area. After a few minutes, tell them that the hunters are coming and they have to race back to their homes. Then decrease the size of one of the homes by folding an edge or two and tell a story about why the size of the home was reduced. For example, perhaps there was a forest fire that destroyed some homes, or there was a rock slide that covered the entrance to a cave, or pollution in a river made the water bad. After telling the story, send the animals back out to roam the land.

Now when you say that the hunters are coming, they all race to their homes, but some cannot get into the home because it has been reduced, so they die because they have no shelter. Then roll some foam balls out for food and everyone tries to grab one. Students who did not get a ball die because they did not eat. This would be a great place to talk about humans' effects on animals and their food sources.

The handkerchiefs are for wounded animals. You can say that some animals hurt their eye and must tie a handkerchief around one eye and still attempt to survive in the wild. Again, this would be a great teaching opportunity to address how improper human behavior can cause injury to animals. The game continues like this, showing how animals are affected by everything we do.

Modifications
- • Tell the story of a pond and let the class be fish. Instead of running, the fish need to swim in the water to safety or food.
- • Allow students to be all different animals and show them how the food chain works.

Around the World Knowledge

Level
II and III

Area
Large playing space such as a gymnasium

Equipment
2 basketballs per group; several basketball goals (if available)

Objectives
Students will combine the shooting skills of basketball with their knowledge of geography.

Setup and Description
This game is similar to the familiar basketball game called Around the World. However, an educational twist is added to this simple game of taking turns to make baskets and move around the world: Before students can shoot the ball, they must correctly answer a geography question. You can start the game by asking a question such as, "What is one country where the Nile River is located?" Anyone who answers the question correctly gets to shoot the ball. The first one to score baskets all the way around the court wins the game. Divide the class into groups as needed so there are not too many people standing around.

Modifications
If you don't have enough baskets, students who are waiting could participate in other activities like jumping rope, using Dyna-Bands, or performing other strengthening activities.

Body Part Match-Up

Level
I, II, and III

Area
Large playing space such as a gymnasium

Equipment
Music that encourages movement

Objectives
Students will learn how to work with a partner and increase knowledge of anatomy while participating in a variety of movement patterns.

Setup and Description
Using creative division methods, pair up classmates. When the music starts, the students skip around the gym away from their partner. When the music stops, call out two body parts for the pairs to put together between them:

- • For level I, yell out the same body parts (hand to hand).
- • For level II, yell out opposing body parts (ear to chin).

●● For level III, students can match up bones or muscles; for example, cranium to patella or gastrocnemius to biceps brachii. If the teacher calls hand to hand, partners should touch hands together. If the teacher calls cranium to patella, partners should put their head on their partner's kneecap.

You can make the vocabulary as hard or as easy as you want. After giving each command, be sure to demonstrate to the class what you want to see. (Not all students will know what you're looking for, and some will not know their anatomy as well as others.) When all students achieve the match-up, start the music again, possibly changing the locomotor movement.

If done correctly, teammates will help each other figure out what they need to match up when the music stops. Try to get the pairs as far away as possible when the music stops so it takes the students awhile to find each other.

Modifications

You could eliminate partners from the game by having the last pair to finish move over to the side of the play area and complete a designated task, such as jumping rope around the perimeter of the play area, before returning to the activity. Reward the last remaining pair at end of game.

Calcium Blowup

Level
II and **III**

Area
Large playing space such as a gymnasium

Equipment
Balloon for each student; diagram of human skeleton (optional)

Objectives
Students will come up with creative ways to keep a balloon in the air with specific body parts while learning or reinforcing knowledge of the major bones and muscles of the body.

Setup and Description
Before playing this game, it is assumed that the students know the major bones of the body through their "bone or muscle of the week" work earlier in the unit. (Many elementary schools by mandate of state departments of education are teaching this material in physical education classes.) Students each blow up a balloon to any size they want and tie the balloon. Next, call out a bone. Students have to use that bone and only that bone to keep the balloon in the air. For example, if you said "Use your patella," students have to keep the balloon in the air with their kneecap and try not to let the balloon fall to the ground.

Keep switching it up by calling out other bones. Then have the children pick a bone that hasn't been used and have them yell it out while they are using that particular bone to keep their balloon up. One person can also pick a bone and then everyone in the class has to try it.

Here are some examples of bones to use in this activity:

- Patella (kneecap)
- Scapula (shoulder blade)
- Clavicle (collarbone)
- Humerus (upper-arm bone)
- Radius (inner bone of the forearm)
- Ulna (outer bone of the forearm)
- Tibia (front bone of the lower leg)
- Fibula (outer bone of the lower leg)
- Femur (upper-leg bone)

Modifications

If you have used all the major bones, continue with major muscles.

Colors

Level
I

Area
Smaller playing space with many different colors

Equipment
Color flash cards

Objectives
Students will identify colors in the environment.

Setup and Description

The students should sit facing you. Then flash a card with a color on it. The students run around the play area and touch three things with that color on it and then return to their seats. It helps to have a smaller playing area so the students have a good idea of where to look.

You can also turn this activity into a relay. Break the class into groups of no more than five using creative division methods and have the teams line up at the end of the playing area. The first person in each line views the card, touches the required number of colored items, and returns to their squad. The second person in line then views the second card and completes the task. The activity continues until all students have participated.

Modifications

Have the students only touch one color and return to their seats.

Fire

Level
II and III

Area
Large playing space such as a gymnasium

Equipment
Beanbag for every 2 students

Objectives
Students will think, react, and speak more efficiently while participating in a very active game.

Setup and Description
Break the class into two teams using creative division methods. Teams should line up facing each other. Choose a player to throw the beanbag to any member of the opposite team. When throwing the object, the student says "Earth," "Air," "Water," or "Fire" and counts to 10. The student who caught the object must answer before the other person finishes counting to 10. If earth is called, the student must name a four-legged animal found on earth. If water was called, the student must name a fish. If air was called, the student must name a bird. However, should fire be called, the person catching the beanbag must remain perfectly still until they are identified by the teacher. They can get back into the activity after completing a predefined activity.

When players catching the object give a wrong answer or speak when they should remain silent, they must leave the game to perform a designated activity and then return to the game. In the meantime, choose someone else to throw to the opposite side and the game goes on as before. The side whose players answer correctly or stand still the longest wins the game.

Modifications
- Tosses and catches must be made with the nondominant hand only.
- The person catching the beanbag must start with their back turned. When the tosser says "Go," the catcher turns to catch while the tosser throws the beanbag.

Fishing for Food

Level
I and II

Area
Large playing space such as a gymnasium

Equipment
Hula hoop for every three students; at least 40 pictures of healthy foods plus paper clip for each cutout; stick that's 3 to 4 feet (1 meter) in length, 3 to 4 feet (1 meter) of string tied to each stick, and magnet for every three students; blank food guide pyramid handout for each student; tape (optional)

Objectives
Students will learn about nutrition while participating in physical activity.

Setup and Description

You must complete several tasks before the class begins:

- Cut out food items in the newspaper from grocery store ads.
- Place a paper clip on each cutout.
- Tie a string to the end of a stick and tie a magnet on the end of the string.
- Depending on the size of your class, lay out a number of hula hoops in the gym.
- Place the cutout food items face down inside each hula hoop so that the children cannot see the pictures.

Break the class into groups of no more than three using creative division methods. Each group gets a stick with a string and magnet hanging from it, and every student gets a paper with a blank food guide pyramid on it. Give the students a locomotor skill they have to do to get to a minipond (hula hoop) to fish for food. You can change the specific locomotor skill throughout the activity. Then the students fish with their pole for food. They catch the food by picking it up with the magnet on their stick.

After students catch a piece of food, they return to their group using the same locomotor movement and hand the stick to the next person. They then put the food in the correct area on the pyramid. You may want to use some tape, but it's not necessary. When fishing, the students don't know what food they are getting because it is facedown, so, for example, they might end up with a lot of fruits but not much meat.

When they have caught all the food, have students tell the class what food they caught and what they didn't catch that they needed to make a balanced diet. This helps them know what is healthy and what food items they need to eat more or less of to keep a healthy body.

Modifications

If needed, you could give the students clues as to where they can fish to get the right foods of the food pyramid.

Foreign Exercise

Level
III

Area
Large playing space such as a gymnasium

Equipment
Worksheet and pencil for every three students; cones, jump ropes, or other equipment necessary for your chosen physical activities

Objectives
Students will learn or reinforce foreign language skills while performing designated exercises.

Setup and Description
This activity is designed to reinforce the classroom teacher's foreign language lessons while incorporating physical activity. To do this activity, develop three kinds

of worksheets before the class. One set of worksheets should require English to Spanish (or another foreign language) translation of physical activities, another set should require Spanish to English translation of physical activities, and the final set should include some translation helpers.

Using creative division methods, break the class into groups of no more than three or four. Give each group one of the worksheets with sentences that need to be translated (either English-to-Spanish or Spanish-to-English) as well as a worksheet with some translation helpers. Every word that the students will need to know should be on the worksheet.

Once the students convert each sentence into English, they perform the task described by that sentence. For example, the students might need to jump rope from one end of the play area and back five times. Once they complete the task, they come back and do the next sentence, and so on. The first group to finish and sit down wins.

Modifications

Start the translators with single words or small phrases if students struggle with this task.

Geography Ropes

Level
II and **III**

Area
Large playing space such as a gymnasium

Equipment
40 to 50 jump ropes (or any number that works for your space)

Objectives
Students will work together and learn about states and countries.

Setup and Description

This activity reinforces geography that students are already learning in the classroom. After the students arrive, give them a state or country and five minutes to take the jump ropes from the box and make the state or country by laying the ropes on the ground to form the shape. They can use the entire area and they must use all of the ropes in the box, but they must all work together to accomplish the task.

When they are done, they should all stand where the capital of the state or country should be. If the students don't finish in five minutes, they have to start again with a new state. Upon completion, discuss how well they cooperated during the activity.

Modifications

The state or country can serve as the space for warm-up activities.

Human Checkers

Level
II and III

Area
Large playing space such as a gymnasium

Equipment
11 or more poly spots for each group

Objectives
Students will work together to develop strategies to accomplish this difficult and challenging task.

Setup and Description
Break the class into groups of five using creative division methods. One team of five sits on the poly spots single file facing the same direction. The next team sits on poly spots in single file facing the first group. There should be an open space between the two groups. The groups are not competing against each other; they are working with each other to complete a common task.

The object is to get the students who are facing one direction to trade places with members of the other group so they are facing the other direction, essentially ending up in the opposite spots on the floor from where they started. However, they must follow very specific guidelines. This is done by moving only one person at a time. Students can jump over or go around only one person at a time, whether that person is on their own team or the opposing team. The game is over when the objective is accomplished.

Modifications
Have groups compete against each other to see who can get done first. You could also have the groups count how many moves it takes to complete the challenge or time the groups for speed.

Island Hopping

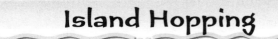

Level
II and III

Area
Large playing space such as a gymnasium

Equipment
40 to 50 different colored beanbags, poly spots, balls, or other objects; 5 poly spots, 1 tumbling mat, or 1 carpet square per person for the raft parts; cones or plastic floor tape to mark off the island; dry-erase board and marker

Objectives
Students will learn to use cooperation, communication, problem-solving skills, and math skills.

Setup and Description

Scatter the colored beanbags around the floor (ocean). Each colored object has a numerical value. For example:

- Green beanbags = $100
- Blue beanbags = $25
- Yellow beanbags = $10
- Pink beanbags = $5
- Red beanbags = $1

Using cones or plastic floor tape, mark off an "island" at one end of the play space. Break the class into small groups of 4 to 6 people using creative division methods and have them go to the island.

Write a math problem on the board. Each group discusses how to solve the problem. Once they know the answer, they must use the pieces of their raft to transport every member of the group out into the ocean to collect the correct number of valuables—the correct number is the answer to the math problem. Make sure you have enough objects for each team to collect the correct number. Transportation of team members is accomplished by putting down the pieces, picking up the pieces from behind them, and moving the pieces to the front so they can keep moving around the ocean. If a member of the group falls off the raft, the group must return to the island and begin again.

Once the students return to their island, discuss the problem and check the answers of each group.

Modifications

Have fewer parts for the raft so that students have to work harder to move the group.

Lemonade

Level
II and **III**

Area
Large playing space such as a gymnasium

Equipment
None

Objectives

Students will work on their acting skills while participating in an active game.

Setup and Description

This activity involves running, dodging, and pantomiming. Break the class into two groups using creative division methods and designate one team to be It first. This group huddles with you and decides what occupation they will act out. Then they approach the other group, which is waiting at the other end of the playing area.

1 As they approach, they call out "Here we come!"

2 The waiting group responds, "Where are you from?"

3 The first group names a city or area of the country that is famous for the occupation they have chosen. For example, if the group has chosen to be blacksmiths, they may say they're from Arizona or Montana, where there are many blacksmiths. Students are encouraged to choose occupations that can be described by these parameters.

4 The waiting group says, "What's your trade?"

5 The first group says, "Lemonade!" Lemonade is a filler word because they can't say their trade.

6 The waiting group ends by saying, "Show us something if you're not afraid!"

At this point, the first group should now be standing in front of the other group and should pantomime the occupation they have chosen. If students on the waiting team have a guess, they must raise their hand and wait for you to call on them. If their guess is incorrect, the original team simply continues to pantomime the chosen activity. If their guess is correct, however, the waiting team chases the first team back to their end line, trying to tag as many of them as possible in the process. All team members who have been tagged must trade teams. The game continues by switching team roles.

Modifications

Change the chasing locomotor movement. For example, students can chase people by skipping, hopping, or jumping.

Math Fitness Bingo

Level
II and **III**

Area
Large playing space such as a gymnasium

Equipment

Math bingo sheet for each student; bingo markers

Objectives

Students will perform fitness skills after they answer a math problem.

Setup and Description

Create bingo sheets with as many boxes as you would like to have on them. Typical bingo sheets have 25 boxes in five rows of five. Increase or decrease the number of boxes as you see fit. In each box there should be a fitness activity and a math problem. The answer to the math problem is the number of times students must do the fitness activity. Of course, you should make the problems easier or more difficult to fit the abilities of the class. Here are some sample math problems you can use. (Obviously, the answers would not be included on the sheet.)

Level I (grades K-1)

$3 + 5 = 8$	Push-ups
$12 - 3 = 9$	Sit-ups
$1 + 3 + 5 = 9$	Squat thrusts
$12 - 3 - 4 = 5$	Jumping jacks
$10 - 2 + 3 - 5 = 6$	Crunches

Level II (grades 2-3)

$12 + 13 - 11 + 5 = 19$	Half-squats onto a chair
$4 \times 3 - 3 + 4 = 13$	Seconds in a flexed arm hang
$(12 - 8) \times 3 = 12$	Seconds in a sit-and-reach flexibility position
$12 \div 3 \times 2 + 5 = 13$	Sit-ups
$15 \div 5 \times 6 + 2 = 20$	Seconds of ankle stretch off the edge of a step

Level III (grades 4-6)

$(20 \div 10 + 15 - 10) \times 3 \div 7 = 3$	Jogging laps around the gymnasium
$21 \div 3 \times 4 + 2 = 30$	Seconds in the "iron chair" (back against the wall with knees flexed at 90 degrees with arms across your chest)
$(13 + 13 + 4) \div 5 \times 3 = 18$	Biceps curls with a light dumbbell with each arm
$20 \div 5 \times 3 + 13 - 5 = 20$	Squeezes on the "stress ball" with each hand
$(10 - 5) \times 4 \div 2 \times 3 - 15 = 15$	Defensive slides between cones set 10 feet (3 meters) apart

Break the class into partners using creative division methods. Once a group of two has completed the selected activity, they can fill in their box on the sheet with their marker. The first group to get bingo (completing one row or column of five boxes) wins.

Modifications

Math is not the only subject you can use in this game. For example, you could use geography pictures to complete questions.

Math Jumping Jacks

Level
I, II, and **III**

Area
Large playing space such as a gymnasium

Equipment
Deck of playing cards; note cards with math problems written on them

Objectives
Students will improve their math skills while participating in a physical activity and working cooperatively.

Setup and Description

Break the class into groups of four, five, or six using creative division methods. Groups gather at one end of the play area while you place playing cards facedown at the other end. Then hold up a note card with a math problem on it. The type of problems depends on the class level, such as simple addition or subtraction problems for level I and more complex equations for level III. Communicating with the classroom teacher to find out what types of math the students are working on is a good idea.

Each group decides what the answer is and sends one person to the other end of the space to try to find a card with the same number as the answer or a combination of cards with numbers that add up to the answer. For example, if the answer is 9, they would find a 9 card or a 5 and a 4. Face cards, jokers, and aces are 10.

The students each flip over one card. If it is one of the numbers they need in their answer, they run back with the card. If it is not one of the numbers, they perform that many jumping jacks and flip the card facedown and return to the group. The next person then goes down and tries to find the next number. When the group finds the answer, they call out "We have the answer" and state the answer out loud.

Modifications

If students are unable to perform jumping jacks, have them do another type of activity.

Math Problem Relays

Level
I, II, and **III**

Area
Large playing space such as a gymnasium

Equipment
Worksheet and pencil for each student; 6 cones

Objectives
Students will combine math and physical education in a relay race.

Setup and Description

You will need to develop worksheets with math problems before class. Be sure you make the worksheets challenging enough to meet the needs of the class. You could talk to the classroom teacher to see what they are covering. Before class begins, place three cones at each end of the play area. When students arrive, use creative division methods to break the class into three teams.

Each team gets the same worksheet and must figure out the correct answer to each problem without the use of a calculator. Once a team has finished a problem, the entire team runs to the cone and back the same number of times as the answer to the problem. For example, if the answer to the problem was nine, then the team must run to the other cone and back nine times. The first team finished and sitting down wins the relay.

Modifications

● ● You can use any subject in this game.

● ● You can use any locomotor skill as well. For example, have the team skip, hop, jump, or slither.

Math Team-Ups

Level
II and III

Area
Large playing space such as a gymnasium

Equipment
Playing card for each student (no face cards, aces, or jokers)

Objectives
Students will improve their math skills while learning to look to others for help and learning how to include all classmates in a game.

Setup and Description
In order to do this game every student needs to know basic addition and subtraction. Students sit down for a short introduction to this activity. Go over some sample addition and subtraction problems and then explain the game.

Give everyone a number card (all face cards, including aces and jokers, should be removed from the deck). Then shout out a number. Students have to join other people in the class in order to end up with the number you called. For example, if you yelled out "Nine," three people with a three card could get together because $3 + 3 + 3 = 9$. Students should try to include everyone in the game. Emphasize working as a class to get everyone into the addition and subtraction.

Modifications
Change the activity to have the students form equations or answer equations.

Molecule Mania

Level
I and II

Area
Large playing space such as a gymnasium

Equipment
Pinnies for one-third of the class

Objectives
Students will learn about molecules and what elements make up water while participating in an active game.

Setup and Description
Ask the students what kind of forms water can be found in. Explain that water comes in gas, liquid, and solid forms and ask them for examples of each. Tell the

students that when a substance like water is in gas form, the molecules are spaced wide apart and move rapidly. When it is in a liquid form, the molecules are closer together and move a little slower. When it is in a solid form, the molecules are almost touching and they move slowly.

After this introduction, tell the students that they are going to pretend to be water in different phases. Tell the students what phase they are in and have them move about the play space by walking. Move them through the gas, liquid, and solid stages. After walking, change the movement to jogging and then to running. If they're a gas, the students are far apart from each other in their movement. If they're a liquid, they're closer to each other, and as a solid, they're very close together.

Next, tell the class how water is made of H_2O and then tell them that now they are going to play molecule tag. Have one-third of the class put on pinnies and be oxygen; the rest of the students are hydrogen. Oxygen molecules have to tag two hydrogens to form H_2O. If an oxygen tags a hydrogen, they have to join hands and try to tag another hydrogen. When all or most of the oxygens get their two hydrogens, the game can start over.

Modifications

Use different compounds depending on the grade level, such as salt (NaCl). Communication with the classroom teacher would help you add to the compound list.

Opposite Relay

Level
I and II

Area
Large playing space such as a gymnasium

Equipment
40 note cards with words written on them; 40 note cards with the opposite words written on them

Objectives
Students will learn about opposites while participating in an active game.

Setup and Description
Prepare a set of 40 note cards by writing a different word on each card. Then prepare another set of 40 note cards by writing the opposites of the words in the first set, such as hot and cold or high and low.

Spread the note cards all around the gym. Break the class into four teams using creative division methods and have them all line up behind a designated starting point. When you say "Go," the first student in each line runs and picks up one card and then runs around to find the opposite card, pick it up, and take the cards back to the line. Then the next person goes. The first team to get all of the players through the race and sit down wins the game. No contact is allowed, and students cannot hide words from other teams.

Modifications
Use harder words or easier words based on the students' level. You can also have the students skip, hop, or gallop to find the note cards.

Physical Phonics

Level
I

Area
Large playing space such as a gymnasium

Equipment
26 paper plates or more (at least 1 for each student); markers

Objectives
Students will reinforce their familiarity with the alphabet and spelling while incorporating locomotor skills with the alphabet.

Setup and Description
Create the alphabet by writing a different letter on paper plates. Scatter the plates throughout the play area. You are not limited to just 26 plates; you can also place duplicates of letters on the floor if necessary so that there is at least one plate for each student. Give the students a letter that you want them to find and a locomotor movement to perform while looking for the letter (e.g., skip, jog, walk, gallop). All students will not get the same letter.

Next, have the students move through the entire alphabet from A to Z. More advanced students can look for an entire word or small sentence and move from letter to letter spelling the word or sentence.

Modifications
In addition to moving from plate to plate with various locomotor skills, the students could throw beanbags at the appropriate letters. They move to pick up the beanbags with one or more locomotor patterns and then move outside of the play area to start over.

State Capitals Toss

Level
I, II, and III

Area
Large playing space such as a gymnasium

Equipment
Foam soccer ball for each group

Objectives
Students will identify state capitals while working cooperatively.

Setup and Description
This activity reinforces state geography that the classroom teacher is teaching the students. Break the class into groups of no more than five using creative division methods. Each group then forms a circle and sits down. Give each group a soccer ball. The student who has the ball calls out a state and then throws the ball to another person in the group. The person who catches the ball then has to name

that state's capital. Students who get the answer right then pick a state and throw the ball to someone else. Those who get the answer wrong have to do five sit-ups. Continue until all the states have been used.

Modifications

• • Have level I and early level II students say a state and throw the ball to someone else, who then has to say a different state. If students don't know all the states yet, have them partner up so they can help each other. For higher-level students (upper level II and level III), have the students perform the tasks faster and recite the state capitals within a certain time limit.

• • Assign a state to every player in the first group and a capital to every player in the second group. A student in the state group throws a beanbag up into the air as high as possible while calling out the state. The player in the opposite line who has the name of that state's capital runs forward to catch the beanbag. If the catch is missed, the two players leave the game. If they complete the catch, they pass the bag to another player in the state group and the game continues.

Vocrab

Level
II

Area
Large playing space such as a gymnasium

Equipment
None

Objectives
Students will practice spelling while participating in a physical activity.

Setup and Description
Break the class into two teams using creative division methods and have teams number off. If each team has 10 members, for example, then the numbers will range from 1 to 10. Give each team a word and then call out a number. The student from each team with that number begins to walk like a crab toward the center of the playing area (moving on hands and feet with the abdomen facing the ceiling). Whoever makes it to the center first earns a letter to spell their word with. The first team to earn all the letters in their word wins the game.

Modifications
If some students cannot participate, have them write down the letters of each team to keep track of which letters they have and how many more they need.

Woodland Animals

Level
I

Area
Large playing space such as a gymnasium

Equipment
None

Objectives
Students will recognize various animals and how they move.

Setup and Description
Have the children sit in a large circle. Discuss how different woodland animals move. For example, birds fly, rabbits hop, squirrels scamper, and snakes crawl. Let the children each pick an animal they would like to be and then move around the circle pretending to be that animal. You can also have a parade of animals.

Modifications
Add appropriate music to the activity. For example, "Baby Elephant Walk" by Henry Mancini would be a neat choice.

World Search

Level
II and III

Area
Large playing space such as a gymnasium

Equipment
World ball (a very large beach ball)

Objectives
Students will cooperate and improve their geography skills while participating in a vigorous activity.

Setup and Description
Break the class in half using creative division methods. Designate one team as the search team and the other team as the standing team. Throw the world ball to a random area of the play space and call out a location on the world ball (e.g., island, country, city, lake). The search team chases after the ball and finds the requested information.

One person in the standing team runs laps around the standing group while the other team tries to locate the predetermined spot on the beach ball globe or the map. When the search team finds the location, they yell "Found it!" or "Stop!" and the runner must stop. For the next round, the standing team becomes the search team and vice versa. The team with the most laps at the end of the game wins.

Modifications
Students on the standing team can perform sit-ups or push-ups or any other type of physical activity while the laps are being run around them.

Chapter 12

Parachute Activities

The parachute is one of the most popular activities among children. Its uniqueness creates excitement, and it has a positive effect on a number of fitness and motor-development parameters. Through many of the games in this chapter, students will improve upper-body strength, cooperation skills, eye–hand coordination, and cardiovascular fitness.

Make sure students realize that the parachute is a team activity and everyone has to work together. Many children love to be under or inside the parachute; consequently, don't punish them for getting under the parachute, but create activities where they are allowed to go under it.

Parachutes may be purchased in a variety of sizes to accommodate various class sizes. Most parachutes are made of multiple colors, have a number of handles on the edges, and have a hole in the middle. These colors, handles, and holes can be used for some of the activities. Many of the activities are highly active and should be supervised with safety in mind.

The key to appropriate activity selection is choosing activities based on the abilities of the students in the class. The levels listed for the activities in this chapter are merely recommendations; you must use discretion in choosing activities according to your students' abilities. In general, level I activities are appropriate for kindergarten and grade 1; level II activities are appropriate for grades 2 through 3; and level III activities are appropriate for grades 4, 5, and 6.

Introduction to the Parachute

Level
I and II

Area
Large playing space such as a gymnasium

Equipment
Parachute

Objectives
Students will be introduced to the parachute and will become comfortable with the parachute and its movements.

Setup and Description
There are many introductory parachute movements that students should learn and practice before beginning any advanced games or skills. These beginning activities are described in the following list. In each of the activities, the students should stand on the outside of the circle, grasping the parachute with their hands by using the handles provided or by rolling up the parachute a little to create a better handle with the edge of the parachute.

- Ripples—From a standing position, the students hold the parachute with both hands and make small waves by moving the parachute up and down with their hands and arms, creating ripples across the surface of the parachute.

- Waves—Students can create larger ripples by moving their arms in larger motions. Students grab the parachute with both hands and take one big step back so that the parachute is pulled fairly tight. Instruct the students that a storm is blowing in and the waves are small at first (ripples). Then the storm is getting worse and the waves are getting bigger so their arm motions are getting bigger.

• • Whirlpool or Tornado—In this activity students create a wave that forms a bubble that circulates under the parachute. This is done by students' raising and lowering the chute one at a time around the circle. This would be similar to the wave performed by spectators at a sporting event.

• • Cloud—With all students facing the center, they raise the parachute above their head and hold it up. The parachute will billow above them.

• • Mountain—In this movement, students pull a large "cloud" down to the ground without walking under it and capture air under the parachute.

• • Inside the Mountain, Making a Tent, or Making a Cave—This activity is a lot of fun, especially for younger children. Students stand around the outside of the parachute, pick up the edge of the parachute, lift it over their head, walk to the center of the circle and, as the parachute rises above them (mountain), bring the parachute down behind them and sit on it. Make sure there aren't any holes where air can get out. While sitting in the tent, you can talk to the students about a game they're going to play or you can just sit in there for a few minutes. Tents can be small or large. Since students love to play games under the parachute, be ready to give the rules to the next activity while they're under the canopy.

• • Mushroom—Students make a cloud and walk slowly to the center (three to five steps). The parachute will billow up above them. Then they walk back out.

• • Merry-Go-Round—While holding on to the parachute with one or both hands, students circle around with the parachute using different locomotor skills.

• • Freeze the Lake—Students pull the parachute tight.

After completing some of the basics, you can combine them into more complex movements. The combination of these movements is limited only by your imagination. Here is a simple example:

1. Students gather around the parachute and take hold of it with the right hand.

2. Students travel in a circle walking clockwise.

3. On your command, they switch to the left hand and move counterclockwise.

4. After you're done with the circles, the students stop, face the center, grasp the parachute with both hands, raise the parachute above their head, and walk to the center of the circle. The parachute will rise above them in what looks like a cloud.

5. At your command, they let go and watch the parachute fall to the ground on and around them.

6. After regrasping the parachute, students raise it like before, only this time they walk back out and pull it down to the ground.

7. After they are comfortable with that movement, they can create a cave

SAFETY NOTE

Parachute handles are notorious for tearing away from the parachute. Depending on the activity, this can sometimes be dangerous. Sometimes the best handle is simply rolling up the edge of the parachute a little and grasping the roll.

by raising the parachute, walking to the center, pulling the parachute down behind them, and sitting on the inside of the cave with the parachute billowing above and around them.

8 From there you can begin various games inside the tent.

Modifications

Use your imagination with the combinations you create with the basics.

- • • You can create effective warm-ups with the basics as the students prepare for more advanced skills.
- • • Have students choose three or four basic skills and their progression.

Bears in the Cave

Level
II and III

Area
Large playing space such as a gymnasium

Equipment
Parachute

Objectives
Students will follow directions while trying to get away from the bears without running into other players.

Setup and Description
Pick two or three students to be the bears. The rest of the students raise the parachute above their head, step under the parachute, and bring it down and sit on the inside, creating a cave. You should join the students in making the cave. Once they have made and secured the cave, the bears try to get in by lifting up the edges of the parachute.

Once the bears find a way in, you say "Bears in the cave!" and all the students try to get out and run to closest of the four walls in the play space. If a bear tags them before they touch the wall, then they too become a bear. If the students make it to the wall, then they are safe and will rejoin the other students to create another cave. Bears can tag as many people as possible, so the second round you will likely have more bears and fewer people in the cave.

⚠ SAFETY NOTE

This can be an exciting game. The bears must not trample on the top of the parachute while attempting to get in and people in the cave must not hit the bears as they try to lift up the edges of the cave.

Modifications

- ○ ● The number of bears that you start with is up to you and should be based on the class size.
- ○ ● You can use different safe zones instead of the four walls. You can also reduce the number of safe zones to make it harder to escape the bears.

Chuting Baskets

Level
I, II, and III

Area
Large playing space such as a gymnasium

Equipment
Parachute with 12-inch (30-centimeter) hole in the middle; 25 foam balls

Objectives
Students will throw a ball through the center of the parachute as their classmates try to keep the ball from going through the center.

Setup and Description
This game is great because it can be played by all students. The students face the center of the parachute and hold it with an overhand grip. Then they number off from one to four. All of the ones are on the same team and so on. All of the ones drop their grip on the parachute while the other numbers maintain their grip. Give two balls to every student who is a one and give them one minute to throw as many balls as possible through the hole in the center of the parachute. Once students throw their balls, they can go get another one and attempt to throw it through the center of the chute. When the minute is up, the next team gets a chance and so on. The team who throws the most balls through the center of the chute wins.

Modifications
You can use balls of different sizes and increase the time that each team has to throw the balls through the center of the parachute.

Circular Dribble

Level
III

Area
Large playing space such as a gymnasium

Equipment
Parachute; basketball for each student

Objectives
Students will combine multiple motor skills to complete this activity.

Setup and Description

Students hold onto the parachute with the left hand and start dribbling with the right hand, and then on your signal they start to walk and then run or even jog counterclockwise in a circle while dribbling the ball. Reverse directions as needed. If students lose control of their ball, they must let go of the parachute, recover the ball, and try to grab the parachute at the original spot.

Modifications

This is a challenging task. If students are having difficulty, they can practice dribbling to the side first without holding onto the parachute.

Climbing the Mountain

Level

II and **III**

Area

Large playing space such as a gymnasium

Equipment

Parachute

Objectives

Students will learn that some things are not as solid as they first appear.

Setup and Description

Spread the parachute out across the floor and have the students stand around it. The students then lift the parachute up and bring it down and kneel on its edge, creating a large bubble. Next, pick some characteristics and students with those characteristics move over the parachute. For example, you might say something like "Climb over the mountain if you're wearing shorts." In response, the students who are wearing shorts walk up the bubble. At first, the bubble looks like it will support the weight of the people crossing, but the bubble quickly deflates. Students crossing the bubble should take a vacated place on the opposite side of the parachute. The last student to get to a spot calls out the next characteristic.

Every characteristic should start with the words, "Climb over the mountain if you . . . ." Monitor what students are saying to make sure that the characteristics are appropriate and to help those students who cannot come up with something to say. Here are some other examples:

- Climb over the mountain if you have green eyes.
- Climb over the mountain if you have a birthday in March or June.
- Climb over the mountain if you have a brother.

Modifications

If you do not want the students to come up with their own characteristics, before starting give each student two or three questions to keep with them and read when it's their turn.

Gone Fishing

Level
II and III

Area
Large playing space such as a gymnasium

Equipment
Parachute; 25 or more foam or plastic fish; 7 hula hoops

Objectives
Students will use basic movements with the parachute and will also learn new ways to move objects while engaging in physical activity.

Setup and Description
Have the students perform various movements with the parachute. First, they can make small ripples in the water and then make bigger waves. Next, throw on the fish and students make the fish jump around the water (parachute). Then they can make the fish jump as high as possible.

Last, tell the class that they are going to go fishing. Place several hula hoops around the parachute. The object is to move the fish around the parachute and then get the fish to land in the hula hoops outside the parachute.

Modifications
Break the class into two teams using creative division methods. Assign the yellow and red hoops to one team and the blue and green hoops to the other team. The team who gets the most fish in their hoops in a certain amount of time wins.

Jingle Bell Parachute

Level
II and III

Area
Large playing space such as a gymnasium

Equipment
Parachute; "Jingle Bells" song

Objectives
Students will coordinate their movements and work together to successfully complete a parachute routine.

Setup and Description
The classic song "Jingle Bells" can be used in the winter holiday season with students of any cultural origin or religion. First, play and sing the song so students can focus on the words. Then they sit around the parachute, waiting for instructions before they pick it up. Tell them that the activity will require them to perform a pattern to the beats of the music.

Have students grip the parachute overhand with thumbs on bottom and fingers on top (as if playing the piano) and come to a standing position. Introduce the movement patterns without the music, demonstrating each one by singing or saying the words while performing the movement. Once students have learned them all, put them together and add the music.

- Chorus line 1: "Jingle bells, jingle bells, jingle all the way ..."
- Movement line 1: Lift the parachute slowly up, slowly drop it down, slowly lift it up, and slowly drop it down.
- Chorus line 2: "Oh what fun it is to ride in a one-horse open sleigh, hey!"
- Movement line 2: Fast shakes!
- Verse 1: "Dashing through the snow, in a one-horse open sleigh, over the fields we go, laughing all the way, ha ha ha!"
- Movement verse 1: Slide to the right
- Verse 2: "Bells on bobtails ring, making spirits bright, what fun it is to ride and sing a sleighing song tonight!"
- Movement verse 2: Slide to the left.

Repeat the sequence a number of times. After the activity, ask students to identify how the activity relates to mathematics or music. Did they find any patterns? This is a great time to make the connection between patterns in math and music, which are closely related. It also helps students realize that dancing is as simple as repeating a basic pattern.

Modifications

- Other songs can be used. One example is "American Patriot" by Lee Greenwood.
- You can change the movements as appropriate depending upon the skill level of the class. For example, instead of sliding to the right or left, students move four steps into the middle, move backward four steps, and repeat.

Keep the Balls On

Level
II and III

Area
Large playing space such as a gymnasium

Equipment
Parachute; 10 to 12 foam sport balls

Objectives
Students will improve muscular strength and endurance in their upper body while working together to complete a task.

Setup and Description
Place as many as 10 to 12 foam balls on the parachute and have students each take a place around the parachute. When you instruct them to do so, they raise the parachute and bounce the balls on it, creating as many ripples as they can, but also maneuvering the parachute so that no balls bounce off. If balls do bounce off, the student closest to the ball should drop the parachute, pick up the ball, throw it back on, and regrasp the chute.

Modifications

Create two teams and have one team try to get the balls off and the other team try to get the balls to stay on.

Knock the Balls Off

Level

I and II

Area

Large playing space such as a gymnasium

Equipment

Parachute; 2 different colored beach balls or 4 red and blue small foam balls

Objectives

Students will accomplish a goal by working together, and they will develop upper-body strength.

Setup and Description

Using creative division methods, break the class into two groups. Team 1 grabs one side of the parachute and team 2 grabs the other side of the parachute. Throw two different colored beach balls onto the parachute and assign one to each team. Team 1 tries to knock their ball off the parachute and team two tries to knock their ball off the parachute. The first group to knock off their ball wins.

Another way to approach this game is to designate one team as the hot team and the other as the cold team. Using red and blue small foam balls, the hot team tries to get the blue foam balls off the top of the parachute and the cold team tries to get the red foam balls off. Using teamwork skills, each half must work together to keep their color on and get the other color off.

Modifications

You can create teams using the colors of the parachute. For example, those on red and green are on the hot team and those on blue and yellow are on the cold team.

Lifeguard! Lifeguard!

Level

I, II, and III

Area

Large playing space such as a gymnasium

Equipment

Parachute

Objectives

Students will exercise their arms and make a wave using a parachute.

Setup and Description

Students sit around the parachute with the parachute covering their legs. They should not cross their legs under the parachute but should stretch them out straight. Then tell the class to pick up the parachute and hold it at their chest. Tell the class how to create waves with the parachute by shaking it slightly. Once they can perform this skill, explain the object of the game.

Choose three people to be sharks and two people to be lifeguards. Everyone else is a person sitting on the beach with their feet in the water, their legs straight, and the parachute pulled tight and held around chest height. People holding the parachute should not look under the parachute to find the location of the sharks. Note that if the class is larger or smaller, you can appoint more or fewer sharks and lifeguards.

Both sharks go under the parachute and crawl on their hands and knees while the class starts making gentle waves. The waves hide the location of the sharks. While the sharks are under the parachute, the lifeguards are walking behind the people sitting on the beach.

At their discretion, the sharks grab students' ankles and gently try to pull them under the parachute. When students sitting on the beach sense that they may be pulled under or are actually being pulled under, they call for help by yelling "Lifeguard, lifeguard!" The lifeguards run around the parachute and pull that student by the arm from under the parachute. Lifeguards *must never run over the top of the parachute* to help someone. If they can't get there in time, the person is pulled under the parachute and becomes another shark. Students who are pulled to safety resume their position and the game continues.

As you can imagine, the sharks will quickly outnumber the lifeguards and the game will end with all or most people under the parachute.

Modifications

Appoint more lifeguards and have the swimmers standing up so the lifeguards aren't outnumbered by the sharks from the beginning.

Number Chase

Level
I, II, and **III**

Area
Large playing space such as a gymnasium

Equipment
Parachute

Objectives
Students will improve cardiovascular fitness and upper-body strength.

Setup and Description
All students grab onto the parachute and number off by fours. Holding the parachute with one hand, they jog in a clockwise or counterclockwise circle as directed by you. Call out a number. All of the students with that number drop the parachute, run around the outside of the parachute, and take the place of the first person in front of them with the same number. Be sure to call all the numbers to make sure everyone gets a turn.

Modifications
If students are having difficulty with running, start out with walking and progress to running.

Parachute Aerobics

Level
II and III

Area
Large playing space such as a gymnasium

Equipment
Parachute; upbeat music with a strong beat

Objectives
Students will combine multiple motor skills and work on multiple physical fitness parameters.

Setup and Description
Students spread out evenly around the parachute. With the accompaniment of any upbeat music with a strong beat, they hold on to the parachute with one hand and move clockwise or counterclockwise while performing various locomotor skills that you have chosen (e.g., walk, run, gallop, skip). Then, facing the center with both hands on the chute, they slide in one direction and then the other, and then jump in toward the center and back out again.

Next, everyone raises the parachute at the same time and follows your lead in performing aerobic movements. Here are some examples:

- Straddle jumps
- Stride jumps
- Jogging in place
- High knee lifts
- Skier squats

The children should continue to do the movement as the parachute falls and begin a new movement when the parachute rises again.

Modifications
Once they have the idea, go around the circle and allow each student to lead the new aerobic movement. By the time it gets back to the first person, everyone will have had a great workout.

Parachute Ball

Level
II and III

Area
Large playing space such as a gymnasium

Equipment
Parachute with 12-inch (30-centimeter) hole in the middle; 2 different colored volleyballs

Objectives
Students will work together to accomplish a goal while improving upper-body strength in a cooperative and competitive activity.

Setup and Description

Break the class into two teams using creative division methods and have them stand opposite of each other around the parachute. As the teams start making waves, throw two different colored balls onto the parachute, assigning one ball to each team. The object is for the teams to maneuver the parachute to get their ball through the hole of the parachute, thus scoring a point. Play to 5 points, and when one team wins, start the activity again.

Modifications

Students may play sitting down or on their knees if it would help those students with disabilities.

Parachute Fitness

Level

II and **III**

Area

Large playing space such as a gymnasium

Equipment

Parachute; music that encourages movement

Objectives

Students will elevate their heart rate for cardiovascular health while learning the basics of using the parachute.

Setup and Description

Have the students space themselves evenly along the parachute and grasp it. There are many different activities to do with a parachute; these are just a few

examples that will help elevate the students' heart rate. Try doing each of the activities in time with the music.

- Jog while holding the parachute in the left hand.
- Shake the parachute.
- Slide while holding the parachute in both hands.
- Perform sit-ups while holding on to the parachute. (People pulling on the parachute from the opposite direction can actually help students up!)
- Skip while holding the parachute in the right hand.
- Move into push-up position while holding the parachute with one hand and shake the parachute.
- Shake the parachute and jump in place.
- While sitting down, let go of the parachute with one hand and spin in a circle, switching hands when necessary.

Modifications

Use your imagination to create your own movements according to the abilities of the class.

Parachute Pull-Down

Level
I, II, and III

Area
Large playing space such as a gymnasium

Equipment
Parachute

Objectives

Students will demonstrate proper use of the parachute while developing strength and endurance in the upper body.

Setup and Description

Parachutes are usually made of numerous colors that are sequentially organized. If the parachute you have is only one color, the children can choose their own personal space on the parachute. Otherwise, they all grab one color of the parachute. This is their area and no one else's.

Students start in a squat while holding on to the parachute. On your command, they slowly stand up while pulling up on the parachute as hard as they can until it floats up in the air. Then they pull down on the parachute as hard as they can. Tell the students to go slow and stay in control when doing the activity.

Modifications

Repeat the activity by having the students release the parachute with the right hand while still holding on with the left hand; then do the activity again with the other hand.

Parachute Turtle

Level
I

Area
Large playing space such as a gymnasium

Equipment
Parachute

Objectives
Students will gain an understanding of why turtles go inside their shell and will practice responding to specific directions.

Setup and Description
This activity is a great way to introduce the parachute to small students. All students sit with one of the parachute handles in their hands. Ask them, "What does a turtle have on its back?" and "Why does a turtle hide in its shell?" After the discussion, the children pull the parachute so only their heads are sticking out. Then, build onto the image of the turtle. Use a visual description like, "The turtle is in the woods and sees a bear. What should you do?" Most of them will say, "Hide in the shell" (the parachute). Use the word "Boo!" to let students know that they have been frightened as little turtles and need to get in the shell. The students then meet you under the parachute to briefly discuss why they're inside the shell.

Modifications
You can use the same activity to address how other animals react to danger. How about an ostrich, a chipmunk, a prairie dog, or others?

Parachute Volleyball

Level
III

Area
Large playing space such as a gymnasium

Equipment
2 parachutes; volleyball; volleyball net

Objectives
Students will increase their upper-body strength while working together as a team.

Setup and Description
Break the class into two teams using creative division methods. One team circles around and holds onto one parachute and the other team does the same around the other parachute. Each team is on opposite sides of the net just like in the game of volleyball.

Throw a volleyball onto one of the parachutes. Students vigorously flap the parachute in attempt to force the ball off the parachute and over the net. The other team works together to catch the volleyball as it comes over the net. The game continues until one team misses the ball, in which case the other team earns 1 point. Play until one team scores 5 points.

Modifications

You may want to try different weighted balls to determine which ball is easier to throw, or you could even lower the net to make the tosses easier. Try two balls to increase the challenge.

Popcorn

Level

I, II, and III

Area

Large playing space such as a gymnasium

Equipment

Parachute; 25 to 30 balls in a variety of shapes and sizes

Objectives

Students will learn various parachute movements while working cooperatively.

Setup and Description

As a warm-up, have the students perform various basic movements with the parachute. Next ask the students how popcorn looks before being popped, while it's being popped, and after it's been popped. Put the balls on the parachute. Have the students make little ripples that represent the beginning of making the popcorn. Then they start to increase the height of the kernels by progressing from ripples to waves. After they have successfully completed this task, have the students try to get all the popcorn out of the pan by making the largest waves possible, launching the balls off the parachute. Challenge the students to make the balls touch the ceiling.

Modifications

Create different games using the balls. For example, Clear the Table is a cooperative game that is similar to Popcorn. Choose one, two, or three people to "clear the table" by getting under the parachute and knocking all the balls off. All other students are standing and holding on to the parachute with one hand. When balls are knocked off the parachute in their direction, they try to hit them back onto the chute with their free hand before the ball hits the ground.

Sit Down

Level

III

Area

Large playing space such as a gymnasium

Equipment

Parachute

Objectives

Students will try to sit down and stand up using the parachute.

Setup and Description

Students sit down around the parachute with their feet under the parachute. When you instruct them to do so, they pull the parachute tight and try to pull themselves up off the ground from a sitting position to a standing position. They will all be pulling on the parachute at the same time. Some students will make it to a standing position while others will not.

After trying this a couple of times, the students stand up holding on to the parachute and try to sit down while pulling the parachute toward them. Some students will fall right to the ground and some will pull on the parachute. They should try to sit down as slowly as possible and not just plop down to the ground. Remind students not to sit on the parachute when they go down.

Modifications

Have every other student do the opposite thing. For example, if one is standing, the next one sits, then the next one stands, and so on.

Snake Shake

Level
II and III

Area
Large playing space such as a gymnasium

Equipment
Parachute; 10 to 15 jump ropes

Objectives

Students will work together to accomplish a task while improving their upper-body strength.

Setup and Description

Break the class into two teams using creative division methods. Place the jump ropes on the parachute. Students shake the parachute and try to make the ropes (representing snakes) hit the players on the other team. Whenever a rope touches a student, that person's team has a point scored against it. The team with the lowest score is the winner.

Modifications

To increase the physical activity, if students get touched by a rope they must drop their grip, move to the side of the floor, do a prescribed exercise, and get back in the game.

Switching Places

Level
I, II, and III

Area
Large playing space such as a gymnasium

Equipment
Parachute

Objectives

Students will develop upper-body strength while having fun with the parachute.

Setup and Description

Students circle around the parachute and number off from one to three. Then they lift the parachute as high as they can. At this time, call out a number (one, two, or three) and those students whose number was called let go of the parachute and run underneath it. They have to find an open space where another student has just left. As the students are running under the parachute, count out loud to three or four seconds. The other students pull the parachute down after three or four seconds, and if the students don't find a spot during this time, they get trapped underneath.

Modifications

• • Instead of numbering off, use the colors of the parachute or types of fruits to choose students.

• • The students can incorporate any kind of locomotor pattern that they choose when crossing to the other side, such as skipping, hopping, galloping, and so on.

The Wave

Level
I, II, and III

Area
Large playing space such as a gymnasium

Equipment
Parachute; 12-inch (30-centimeter) playground ball

Objectives
Students will work as a team in order to get a desired result.

Setup and Description

Students each take a place in a circle around the parachute. Tell them that the object of this game is to transport the ball around the parachute numerous times without the ball stopping or flying off the side. Start by asking all students to stand up and hold the parachute tight at about hip level. Then they practice making the wave. This is similar to when spectators at a sporting contest rise from their seats, lift their hands above their heads, and then pull their arms back down and sit down. The only difference is that the students will not sit down and then stand up; instead they will do the wave from a standing position.

After the students have successfully performed the wave, place a ball on the parachute. To get the ball moving, students must either lift up or pull down the parachute. After a while the class will figure how to make the ball move around by using the wave. If they're having trouble getting the job done, offer suggestions and have them try again. This activity requires a tremendous amount of cooperation from everyone.

Modifications

If the class gets really good with one ball, try adding another ball or switching directions of the wave.

Appendix

Specialized Equipment

Many activities in this book use pieces of equipment, often identified by a specific brand name, that aren't commonly available in most elementary schools. These items are described briefly here along with information about where they can be purchased. Note that the vendors listed aren't the only possible sources of equipment; they're just a good starting point.

Cage Balls

The giant balls help develop coordination and cooperative play. Sizes range from 24 to 72 inches (61-183 centimeters) in diameter. This is a big ball for a big crowd! They're perfect for large group activities, with a high-quality, multicolored nylon cover over an almost indestructible vinyl bladder.

Reprinted, by permission, from Gopher Sport.

Dyna-Bands

Lightweight Dyna-Bands, or resistance bands, are an ideal resistance material for any age. They provide progressive resistance and strengthen all the major muscle groups for upper-body, abdominal, and lower-body conditioning. If you are unable to buy bands, latex comes in 6-inch (15-centimeter) widths of 50-yard (46-meter) and 25-yard (23-meter) rolls, with four thicknesses allowing progressively more challenging workouts. You can cut the rolls to any length you desire.

Reprinted, by permission, from Gopher Sport.

Earth Balls

An earth ball is a very large ball measuring from 36 to 52 inches (91 to 132 centimeters) in diameter and made of durable vinyl or canvas. It is also a globe, with the various continents, countries, islands, oceans, and seas of the world printed on it. A variety of academic games can be played with this innovative object.

Frisbees

Frisbees are hard, plastic, durable disks that range in size from 8.5 to 13.5 inches (22-34 centimeters) in diameter and 5 to 7 ounces (130-200 grams) in weight. These versatile flying discs can be used for a variety of eye–hand coordination activities, from simple tossing and catching skills to the highly active games of ultimate Frisbee and Frisbee golf. Some companies even make flying discs of high-density foam that eliminate injuries when a person fails to catch the disc and it hits the body.

Lummi Sticks

These colorful rhythm sticks are 12 inches (30 centimeters) long and can be purchased from a variety of sources. Many come in a variety of colors and with a musical CD that describes a variety of activities. Lummi sticks are usually used in rhythmic activities.

Rhythmic Gymnastics Ribbons

These ribbons are used for a variety of rhythmic activities. Attach a 3- to 6-foot (1- to 2-meter) ribbon to the end of a stick such as the aforementioned Lummi sticks (or longer sticks). When the stick is moved through the air, the ribbon trails through the air in the direction of the movement. For older students the ribbons can be as long as 9 feet (3 meters).

Scooters

Scooters are classic pieces of equipment that come in a variety of shapes and sizes with wheels on the bottom of a flat board. The most common shapes are circles or squares. Circular scooters can range up to 24 inches (61 centimeters) in diameter that can hold up to three children at once, and square scooters range from 12 to 16 inches (30-40 centimeters). The platforms are usually made of hard plastic or wood and come with and without handles. Scooters can be used for a large variety of games and relays.

Speed Stacks Sport Stacking Cups

Speed Stacks are the official cups of the WSSA (World Sport Stacking Association). The Speed Stacks Sport Pack is a class set of sport stacking equipment and includes everything you need to get started. Speed Stacks, Inc., offers written instructions and step-by-step instructional videos about sport stacking.
© Speed Stacks, Inc.

Wobble or Balance Boards

Balance in everyday life is taken for granted, but it can be enhanced with a variety of balance activities. Some of the activities in this book suggest the use of a balance or wobble board. Although there are different names for this apparatus, it comes in a variety of lengths, shapes, and sizes and helps improve balance and coordination of the balance senses.

Z-Balls

These unusual rubberized balls help improve eye–hand coordination. These balls have a 3- to 5-inch (8- to 13-centimeter) diameter and are designed with five to seven knobs that create unpredictable bounces when the ball hits a hard surface. The unpredictability of the bounces demands greater attention along with improved movement and reaction time when catching the ball.

Equipment Sources

Champion Sports
P.O. Box 2030
Bethania, NC 27010
800-662-6048
Fax: 800-592-1443
www.ChampionCatalog.com

GameTime
Cunningham Associates
P.O. Box 240981
Charlotte, NC 28224
800-438-2780
Fax: 704-525-7356
www.gametime.com

Gopher Sport
220 24th Ave. NW
P.O. Box 998
Owatonna, MN 55060-0998
800-533-0446
Fax: 800-451-4855
International fax: 507-451-4755
www.gophersport.com

Jaypro Sports
976 Hartford Tpke
Waterford, CT 06385
800-243-0533
Fax: 800-988-3363
www.jaypro.com

Project Adventure
Corporate Office
701 Cabot St.
Beverly, MA 01915
978-524-4500
Fax: 978-524-4501
www.pa.org

Speed Stacks, Inc.
14 Inverness Dr. East, Suite D-100
Englewood, CO 80112
303-663-8083
Fax: 303-663-8580
www.speedstacks.com

Sportime
P.O. Box 922668
Norcross, GA 30010-2668
800-444-5700
Fax: 800-845-1535
International fax: 770-510-7290
www.sportime.com

Wolverine Sports
745 State Circle
P.O. Box 1941
Ann Arbor, MI 48106
800-521-2832
Fax: 800-654-4321
www.wolverinesports.com

Bibliography

Clements, Rhonda L. "How to Begin Play." Hempstead, NY: Hofstra University, n.d.

Fahey, Thomas D., Paul M. Insel, and Walton T. Roth. *Fit and Well: Core Concepts and Labs in Physical Fitness and Wellness.* 7th edition. Boston: McGraw-Hill Higher Education, 2006.

Fluegelman, Andrew. *The New Games Book.* Garden City, NY: Dolphin Books/Doubleday, 1976.

Fluegelman, Andrew. *More New Games!* Garden City, NY: Dolphin Books/Doubleday, 1981.

Gabbard, Carl P., Elizabeth LeBlanc, and Susan Lowy. *Game, Dance and Gymnastic Activities for Children.* Englewood Cliffs, NJ: Prentice Hall, 1989.

Gilbert, Anne Green. *Teaching the Three R's Through Movement Experiences.* Minneapolis: National Dance Education Organization, 2002.

Gregson, Bob. *The Outrageous Outdoor Games Book.* Belmont, CA: Pitman Learning, 1984.

Grineski, Steve. *Cooperative Learning in Physical Education.* Champaign, IL: Human Kinetics, 1996.

Hodes, Stuart. "Transforming Dance History: The Lost History of Rehearsals." *Design for Arts in Education* 91, no. 2 (1989): 10-17.

Kirchner, Glen. *Physical Education for Elementary School Children.* Dubuque, IA: Brown, 1988.

Lieberman, Lauren J., and Cathy Houston-Wilson. *Strategies for Inclusion: A Handbook for Physical Educators.* Champaign, IL: Human Kinetics, 2002.

Martens, Rainer, Francine V. Rivkin, and Linda A. Bump. "A Field Study of Traditional and Nontraditional Children's Baseball." *Research Quarterly for Exercise and Sport* 55 (1984): 351-355.

Mollenhoef, Clark. "Teachers." *Des Moines Register.* Taken from *Molder of Dreams,* Focus on the Family, Colorado Springs, CO, 1990.

Morris, G.S. Don. *How to Change the Games Children Play.* 2nd edition. Minneapolis: Burgess, 1980.

Nichols, Beverly. *Moving and Learning: The Elementary School Physical Education Experience.* 3rd edition. St. Louis: Times Mirror/Mosby College, 1999.

Pangrazi, Robert P. *Dynamic Physical Education for Elementary School Children.* 14th edition. San Francisco: Pearson/Benjamin Cummings, 2004.

Prelutsky, Jack. *Something Big Has Been Here.* New York: Greenwillow Books, 1990.

Rohnke, Karl. *Silver Bullets: A Guide to Initiative Problems, Adventure Games and Trust Activities.* Dubuque, IA: Kendall/Hunt, 1984.

Wechsler, Howell, Mary L. McKenna, Sarah M. Lee, and William H. Dietz. "The Role of Schools in Preventing Childhood Obesity." *The State Education Standard* 5 (2004): 4-12.

About the Author

David Oatman, EdD, is a professor in the department of health, physical education, and recreation at Missouri State University. He has taught elementary, junior high, and high school physical education for 10 years and has taught physical education pedagogy at the university level for 20 years. These experiences have encouraged him to bring together thoughts, ideas, and practical solutions for creating a positive classroom environment full of physical activity. He believes that through such an environment—which is at the heart of this book—children are encouraged to be physically active throughout their lives.

Oatman is a member of the Missouri Association for Health, Physical Education, Recreation and Dance, from which he earned a Faculty Achievement Award in 1995. He has twice been nominated for Who's Who Among Professors in America's Colleges and Universities. In his leisure time, he enjoys playing golf, kayaking, biking, and jogging.